CP/M* — The Software Bus:
a programmer's companion

A. Clarke
J.M. Eaton
D. Powys Lybbe

*CP/M is a trademark of Digital Research, Inc.

ΣSigma Technical Press

ISBN 0-905104-18-8

Published by:
SIGMA TECHNICAL PRESS
5 Alton Road
Wilmslow
Cheshire
UK

Distributors:

Europe, Africa:
JOHN WILEY & SONS LIMITED
Baffins Lane
Chichester
West Sussex
England

Australia, New Zealand, South-East Asia:
Jacaranda-Wiley Ltd., Jacaranda Press,
JOHN WILEY & SONS INC.
PO Box 859,
Brisbane,
Queensland 40001,
Australia

Acknowledgement:

CP/M and MP/M are registered trade marks of Digital Research Inc. The contents of Chapter 18 are proprietary to Digital Research.

Printed in Great Britain by J. W. Arrowsmith Ltd., Bristol BS3 2NT

PREFACE

If you are new to CPM™ you may find that some of this book is way over your head at first reading - and if you are also new to programming, even more of it will be. Take heart, we've allowed for all levels of understanding.

Each relevant chapter starts with a few paragraphs of 'fundamentals' - sufficient outline to get you started. Then the detailed content of the chapter follows, and finally there is a reference summary of the points made in that chapter.

Newcomers to CP/M will find all they need in the opening paragraphs, and will also be able to dip into the summaries to extent their useful knowledge. After a little practice, the remainder of the material will begin to make sense - and by the time you've read and understood the whole book, you will be making CP/M dance to your tune.

You should be aware that there is a key called the 'Control' key (often marked CTRL) on your keyboard, which is used in a similar way to a shift key. A key pressed on its own has a meaning - usually a small letter or 'lower case'. A key pressed while the 'Shift' key is held down has a different meaning - usually the capital or 'upper case' letter. A key pressed while the **CTRL** key is held down has a third meaning - often an instruction to CP/M. These instructions or commands are usually written as ∧ C which means hold down the CTRL key while you press and release the C key. Holding down the CTRL key has no effect, however long you hold it, but some keyboards have letters which repeat, so apart from the 'shift' and 'control' keys, get into the habit of pressing any key firmly but briefly.

CP/M is a registered trademark of Digital Research Incorporated.

iii

A final point, some keyboards have both a CAPS LOCK and a SHIFT LOCK. The CAPS LOCK, when pressed, is engaged, and stays engaged until it is pressed again to release it. This only affects the **letter** keys, not the number or punctuation keys. When it is engaged, all letters are upper case - capital letters - but all the other keys work normally. For instance, the keyboard on which this was first typed has a key with a / on the lower half and a ? above. Whether the caps lock is pressed or not, touching that key produced a / but touching it while holding down the 'shift' key produced ?. If your keyboard has a shift lock it is suggested that you avoid it - leave it unlatched - off - not pressed. On some hardware implementations of CP/M the CTRL key won't work if the shift lock is 'on'. On the other hand, it is suggested that you **do** work with CAPS LOCK engaged, unless you are keying in text which requires upper and lower case. Where there is no apparent SHIFT, the hardware system may require (say) a ⌃ A to change from upper to lower case, and vice versa.

CONTENTS

CHAPTER ONE

A HISTORICAL SKETCH

1.1 Fundamentals.

An **operating** system breathes life into hardware. With an operating system, you can press a key on the keyboard and get a response. Press the right keys, and you can talk to the computer, and get its replies. Without a program, the hardware is lifeless - a sculpture in metal and plastics. Without an operating system, all the detailed activities of timing the movements of data bits betwen the main internal memory and the peripherals - keyboard, screen, disc drives, printer - would have to be written into every single program you write. Also, you would have to write your own special programs to do all the routine 'housekeeping' tasks, like keeping lists of files, copying files from here to there, naming and renaming them, and keeping the activities of one program from damaging another.

CP/M, which is what the Digital Research Inc 'Control Program and Monitor' is usually called, is an operating system. It is in several parts, one of which is held in the internal memory of your machine all the time the machine is active. This part is called the **'resident'** operating system. All the other parts (the **'transient** commands') are held on flexible disc and are called into the internal memory when they are wanted, and the space they occupy is then released as soon as they have done their task. The resident part of CP/M handles all the input and output, the communication with you, the operator, and some of the 'housekeeping' as we will see. This part of CP/M is also held on flexible disc, usually on the first one or two tracks of a disc and is not directly accessible by the programmer.

To load the resident part of CP/M from the disc into the internal store requires a program. But, as we said, until CP/M is in the store, the machine is lifeless - apparently a paradox. If you have ever worn or seen old-fashioned boots with

1

a loop at the back to help you to pull them on, you may have heard the expression 'to pull yourself up with your own bootstraps'. Of course, you cannot lift yourself off the ground that way - but that is why the tiny program which loads CP/M into the main store is called a '**bootstrap**'. All hardware has some kind of a bootstrap built in, or some way to get one in. Loading CP/M is called 'booting' - or 're-booting' - the system.

When you have CP/M loaded into the machine, waiting for your command, it will show the 'prompt' on the left edge of the console - thus -

   A>

This tells you that you are 'logged on' and that the first disc drive (drive A) is directly available to you. Other drives (as we will see) are indirectly available, if you include the other drive name in your instruction.

How your particular machine 'boots' CP/M depends on what machine it is - so look at the manual. Perhaps you just switch on, put a CP/M disc into the first drive and close the door on it. Some machines require you to press a key - B perhaps, or the RETURN or ENTER key. This 'loading from cold' is known as a 'cold start' or a 'cold boot'. If you already have CP/M loaded, perhaps with some other program as well, you can reload CP/M and clear the memory without losing what is on the screen - this is called a 'warm start' or a 'warm boot'. You 'reboot' ('warm boot') by using ^ C, or CONTROL and C, as we said earlier.

The CP/M operating system is an industry standard simply because it is used so widely - on computers from over 80 different manufacturers - by so many people. It is well understood, reliable, and although purists and academics criticise it, it is popular with users who understand it. The remainder of this chapter is concerned with the background to the development of CP/M. Skip to chapter 2 if you do not need the detail at this stage, and come back to this chapter when you need to understand more of the make-up and background to CP/M.

1.2 The history up to version 1.3

CP/M is a control program and monitor for computers running one or more floppy discs. It is by no means the most sophisticated disc operating system, and for all its merits, it has been compared unfavourably with other systems. One fact remains: it is by far the most popular system for 8080, Z80, 8085 and

2

possibly 8086 chips. Its strengths lie in its robustness, versatility, portability and flexibility. It has won almost universal acceptance as a general purpose operating system for small machines, and has been selected and supported by numerous microcomputer manufacturers and software suppliers, but above all by users.

CP/M's most important function has been to link standard user procedures and applications to a wide variety of computers. In this respect, it has come to resemble a 'software bus'.

The development of the cheap microprocessor meant that, for the first time, hobbyists could construct their own computers Suddenly in the United States, people who were involved in the computer industry in some way could have their own computer at home. The arrival of the floppy disc - and particularly the mini-floppy - meant that computers could be made that would rival the power of the commercially made micro-computers; but such complex devices and all that power are useless without software that can control and monitor the internal, interacting operations within the micro. As in the past, it proved to be much easier to make the physical hardware of a computer than to make the controlling program to run it. In programming terms even now we are still far from exploiting the full power of the obsolescent 8080 central processing unit. The floppy disc demanded control at the leading edge of the science of control software. In effect, there were suddenly a great number of 8080- based computers with floppy disc drives, looking for adequate software to drive and run them. CP/M fell almost by luck into this sudden market vacuum, and and established an ubiquitous position, which it retains and consolidates to this day, despite the regular gossip and product launches which predict its imminent demise and replacement with a 'better product'.

CP/M was the right software in the right place at the right time. It was created by one man, Gary Kildall, not as an end in itself but simply as a means of implementing PL/M on the 8080 chip. Gary Kildall - Doctor Kildall - was an experienced computer consultant, who had played a major part in the software development work for the 8080, and had developed PL/M as a software tool to facilitate this development work.

Many of the projects like Interp/80, which simulated the 8080 before the chip became a reality, were written in PL/M. The next stage was to be PL/M implemented on the 8080 by cross compilation, and by the construction of an operating system to support the compiler. It was at about this time that the floppy disc appeared, and Gary decided that the operating system should be based on this revolutionary mass storage device. CP/M was the result of the struggle to make the floppy disc work with the 8080 chip. Previous systems, before the floppy disc, depended on paper tape for storage of programs and data - and the Teletype 33 for input and output (some colleges and schools still use the type 33 - it can be a nerve-shattering experience !).

If fate had not intervened, CP/M might have become Intel's operating system. For most of us, it was fortunate that the firm was suffering growing pains due to the enormous success of their 8080. No-one, up to that moment, had succeeded in packing so many transistors onto a small piece of silicon, and Intel was, in consequence, swamped by the demand for it. Rapid growth meant re-organising management structures and the decision was taken - incredible in hindsight - to jettison the software projects and disband the brilliant team. CP/M went with Gary, and CP/M was gradually developed in his spare time, and as part of his work as lecturer at the Monterey Naval Postgraduate school.

John Torode, an electronics engineer, became interested in the development of CP/M from its early stages, and was responsible for the design of the disc controller. His company, Digital Systems, exhibited the 'wire wrapped' prototype of the controller board for the Altair computer at a local computer club meeting. To the considerable surprise of the spectators, and the relief of John and Gary, it worked perfectly !

CP/M is, in fact, a very simple and robust operating system that supports expansion and elaboration with great ease. It is a skilled and calculated compromise between size and versatility. It is possible to devise a a system which stores files more economically, or which accesses the information more speedily. One can certainly construct an operating system that is more helpful to the user. Whether one can do these things in as little memory space - or in such an adaptable way - is another matter.

Several qualities contribute to CP/M's popularity. It re- allocates disc space dynamically, it uses command files in preference to inbuilt functions, and it allows programs to access its primitive functions. It is not unique in these qualities, only in their combination within a simple and robust operating system. The fanciest system is useless if it occasionally malfunctions, or uses up an excessive proportion of the often rather cramped addressing space of an 8-bit micro. And there is one more very significant feature of current CP/M as we know it.

4

1.2.1 The structure of CP/M 1.3.

The qualities described above are insufficient to explain the success of CP/M. In common with most operating systems, the original versions of CP/M were designed for specific ranges of microcomputers. Probably more by accident than design, CP/M diverted from this rigid hardware dependence.

It was in 1976 that the profound change took place in the philosophy of CP/M and its structure. Imsai had suplied a large number of floppy disc units and approached Dr Gary Kildall for an operating system for them. He was reluctant to adapt CP/M to yet another controller, and thought to save duplicating effort by introducing a separated 'Basic input and output system' or 'BIOS'. In principle, now that this step was taken, the hardware dependent parts of CP/M were concentrated in the BIOS. Anyone could thus adapt CP/M to his own peculiar hardware while leaving a common standardised user interface. This led to the release of CP/M Version 1.3, the first system to be offered to the public.

Also in 1976, Dr. Kildall founded Digital Research to market the new product. Since then CP/M has been chosen by over 80 manufacturers, and there are estimated to be over 200,000 users worldwide, establishing CP/M as the 'de-facto' standard operating system. This was acknowledged when in 1979, CP/M was named to the Datapro Software Honor Roll.

We will now consider the developments of CP/M, and the general trends up to the present. We will look at the future in later chapters. However, it is important to realise that the whole concept of CP/M is to produce an appearance to the user which is the same for all implementations, and that this is achieved by inserting interfaces between what the user does (or receives) and what the computer itself receives (or sends).

1.3 CP/M version 1.4

All products which are widely used are subject to pressure for change. CP/M is no exception. The version of CP/M for 8 inch IBM standard floppy discs, which is still widely used, is the one immediately after 1.3 - so version 1.4 is the one which took CP/M into world-wide acceptance. However, the drives to handle 8 inch discs are quite large, and before long the 'mini-floppy' - the five and a quarter inch disc was launched. Fine - but this had a new recording standard, new numbers of tracks and sectors, new packing densities and so on. And there was not just one new standard, there were several. Density of recording on the track varied, mechanisms were developed for using both sides of discs as an alternative to the original 'single sided' standard. There are even different recording codes. Version 1.4 could not cope.

1.4 CP/M version 2.x

Just as CP/M came into existence as the operating system for microcomputers with IBM standard discs, so versions 2.x were developed to allow the impementors to cope with the vagaries of the multiplicity of new formats, particularly on the smaller 'mini-floppies'. There are undoubtedly enhancements in 2.2 which were not available in 1.4, but to the user - perhaps an individual running a business package - the differences are relatively small. To the programmer, the differences are more significant. In this book, we will be concentrating mainly on 2.2, with notes about differences which arise with 1.4, and with as much detail as we can give on later versions still. Essentially in CP/M 2.x, the BIOS passes to the BDOS a table of the parameters of the disc drive being used, rather than the BDOS assuming the 8 inch IBM standard as in previous releases.

1.5 CP/M PLUS - or CP/M version 3.1

Now that memory is becoming available relatively cheaply, memory 'banking' - the use of more memory than can be addressed directly in a two-byte address - has become of much greater significance. The old address limitation of CP/M version 2.2 was 64k. So subterfuges were resorted to such as making CP/M think that parts of memory were peripherals. Alternatively, more extensive modifications of the system were required. So just as 1.4 was 'disc', 2.2 was 'different discs', version 3.1 is 'memory banking'. There is more difference between 2.2 and 3.1 than there is between 1.4 and 2.2. The commands are more powerful, there is a 'help' system, and there are many different commands. We will try to cover them without confusing the users of earlier versions. CP/M 3 really is a version of CP/M that contains extended features allowed by the greater availability of banked memory, and this updates the product to make it more compatible with MP/M 2 and Concurrent CP/M86 v 2.

1.6 Concurrent CP/M

The availability of low cost memory, fast 16 bit micros - and the increased availability of a wide range of peripherals - also opened an opportunity for Digital Research in another direction. A single user, at a single keyboard, with one microcomputer, can only do one job at once, with CP/M 1.4 up to 3.1. However, the processor is almost always under-used in those circumstances, and there are often times when the computer could be set running on some task that does not need input from the keyboard, so the user just has to wait. Concurrent CP/M allows the user to switch the job that does not need keyboard input to the 'background'. The keyboard (and screen) are then free to initiate another task, so that the foreground and background tasks keep running together. Up to eight different jobs can be started in this way, and the screen display can be switched from one to another by the user. If you were familiar with the big computers of ten and more years ago, you would recognise this as the old 'multi-programming' approach. Now, with the advent of so much direct input by keyboards attached to the computer, there is another different approach.

1.7 MP/M

With the MP/M system - which is yet another version of CP/M - several users at separate terminals (keyboards and screens or printers) can use the same microprocessor to run different jobs simultaneously. This used to be known as 'time-sharing', among other things. Such a system places considerable demands on MP/M and some of the earlier versions of it came in for a good deal of criticism - but current versions appear to have overcome the problems of delays and 'bugs' satisfactorily. MP/M 2 also serves as a master for CP/M based networking systems where several computers can share common resources, such as large capacity discs and printers.

1.8 Sixteen bits.

With the arrival of the 16 bit (instead of the 8 bit) chips, and the consequent increase in directly accessed memory and the larger instruction sets available - Digital Research have been beavering away to produce versions of CP/M 2.2 and 3.1 and MP/M which will run on those processors. CP/M-86 was the first, which runs on the Intel 8086 chip. There is also an MP/M-86, for the same processor and Concurrent CP/M86 v 2. A range of CP/M operating systems is now available for the Motorola 68000 chip and will soon be available for the Zilog Z8000.

1.9 Summary of Chapter 1

The 'fundamentals' explained the requirements of an operating system, and how CP/M satisfies them.

The principal feature of CP/M which led to its success is the existence of the BIOS - the interface which is provided in skeletal form by Digital Research, for computer manufacturers to complete with the necessary hardware handling instructions. All the rest of CP/M is standard, provides a standard 'face' to the operator, and also happens (!) to offer an extremely effective compromise between powerful commands and minimal memory occupancy. Some transient CP/M commands exist only on disc until they are invoked, others are built into the Console Command Processor, part of CP/M which is loaded or reloaded at every cold or warm 'boot'

CP/M 1.4 is the operating system of the 8 inch standard disc. CP/M 2.2 followed it by opening up the possibilities for all the different sizes and formats of discs now available - principally the five and a quarter inch. CP/M 3.1 is the system which also allows the use of 'banked' memory - as we will see in later chapters. All the other versions are developments to take account of 16 bit processors, and/or multi-user or multi-job environments. There are also the 32 bit processors to take into account!

CHAPTER TWO

THE CONSOLE COMMANDS.

2.1 Fundamentals.

The whole of this chapter, with the exception of the information about MP/M, is important for everyone who uses CP/M. Even someone who is brand new to computers and operating systems should read everything including the USER part.

The **console** is the keyboard and vdu screen (or teletype) of your microcomputer. The keyboard is the principal input device, and the screen may be simply a television set which is tuned to the vhf output of your computer, or is more likely to be a special vdu screen which is part of, or at least directly connected to the keyboard. Your console may, alternatively, be like a typewriter, with keyboard input and 'hard copy' output. Note that a tv set cannot clearly display a full 80 column screen, so micro-computers which have no true video connection may not have the standard 80 column by 24 line screen either.

There is one part of CP/M called the Console Command Processor - something we will be dealing with in detail later - but what we need now is the idea that it exists, and it contains within it the utilities (each is a small program) which are invoked by one of six CP/M commands. In all versions of CP/M these are

> **ERA**(erase)
> **DIR**(directory)
> **REN**(re-name)
> **TYPE**(display on screen)
> **USER**(protection of files)

and in 1.4 to 2.2

> **SAVE**(copy memory to file)

but in 3.1

> **DIRS**(display system files)

9

The SAVE command exists in 3.1, but is invoked in a way slightly different from the version we will describe first - though the action of the command is identical. We will describe DIRS in the section covering DIR.

These six **'resident'** commands are the ones we will cover in this chapter - the remainder (**transient**) follow later. There are separate chapters on the **'statistics'** command (**STAT**) the **'peripheral interchange program'** (**PIP**) and the SUBMIT program, used to enter a preset chain of commands. Version 3.1 does not use STAT, but has additional commands which we will cover when describing STAT.

The **CCP** (Console Command Processor) is 'booted' into memory with the **BIOS** and **BDOS** - in the later versions of CP/M you will see it in the disc directory as CCP.COM.

All the six 'resident' commands refer to *files.*

If a collection of characters which have been put in through the keyboard is going to be retained - stored on a mass storage medium - then it has to be handled as a group which CP/M calls a *file.* Everything on the mass storage which you put there, whether it is a *data* file or a *program* is a *file.*

The mass storage will take one of several forms. Originally, as we saw in Chapter One, it was the arrival of the 'flexible' disc which stimulated Gary Kildall into producing CP/M as we now know it. Since then, there have been many technical advances. There are 'hard' discs which can be used on micros, some of them using the sealed unit Winchester technology, and others with replaceable discs. There are tapes, in cassettes, in cartridges and in other handling systems. There is the 'M-disc' - actually mass memory, but organised so that it looks like a disc to CP/M, but gives phenomenal access speeds. For brevity, we will simply refer to 'disc' for the remainder of this section, but all the comments apply equally to other forms of file storage.

Files which are *programs* are generally read in from the disc into the memory, all at once. One program cannot be larger than the available memory space unless it, in turn, invokes overlays which replace some of the code originally loaded with the new code in the overlay.

Files which are *data* are read by program instructions, in small groups of characters. Data files can be as large as a complete disc, or more, because they are only read into the 'Transient program area' in small groups. When a program is running, and a 'read record' instruction is encountered, this translates into a call to CP/M for a record. CP/M actually reads a sector - part of a track - not just a record. The sector may contain several records, so the first 'read record' causes CP/M to read the sector containing that record, and pass to the program the memory location of the start of the desired record. The second 'read record', if the second record required is in the same sector as the first, which is already in the memory, does not cause a sector read, but CP/M simply passes the appropriate memory address to the program. Similarly when writing data records, CP/M **'buffers'** data into logical groups of characters, each of which is a sector in size. There may be several records to a sector, one record to a sector, or even several **sectors** to a record - but the actual physical read and write instructions are 'transparent' to the program, CP/M handles them.

Sector sizes vary according to the device used (flexible or hard disc, or whatever).

2.2 File Names.

CP/M allows for filenames of from one to 8 letters, and allows for an extra one to three letters to indicate the *type* of file. In CP/M 3.1, a **password** may also be added.

All letters and numbers, and most symbols, can be used in a file name. These are permitted -

A B C D E F G H I J K L M N O P Q R S T U V W X Y Z
1 2 3 4 5 6 7 8 9 0 + - ! @ $ % ^ & ( ) _ ~ ` | { } / " '

and these are not permitted -

< >   .   , . ;   :   =   ?   *   [ ]

Notice that the lower case letters do not appear. This is because the Console Command Processor automatically translates any lower case letters in a command or a file name into upper case. Fred and fred would both become FRED. Program names, in some languages, may include lower case letters and these will be preserved into the directory, but would not be available to the CP/M console commands which we are covering here. You would be unable to ERAse (say) a file which has the name Myprog.BAS.

11

A file name is up to eight letters, plus up to three letters of type.

XXXXXXXX.XXX

If the type is specified (and the file need not have a type, or the type may be omitted in some cases) there *must* be a 'period' or 'decimal point' between the name and the type.

In 3.1, if a password is added to the filespec, it must follow a semicolon, and contain 0 to 8 letters and/or numbers.

XXXXXXXX.XXX;XXXXXXXX

All files may be stored on one or other of at least two, and often more than two disc drives. The name of the file is used as the storage key on the disc, but CP/M needs to know on which disc to look for the file. Disc drives are lettered from A to P. (Version 1.4 of CP/M only allowed A to D). To tell CP/M which drive to look on for the file, the letter is put first, then a colon, and then the name.

In 1.4 - 2.2,   D:NNNNNNNN.TTT
In 3.1,   D:NNNNNNNN.TTT;PPPPPPPP

If you do not use or do not need the drive letter, then the colon must not be used either. As we will see, if you do not use a drive name (A: or B: etc) then CP/M assumes one. The rules follow later. At present we will assume that a missing drive name 'defaults' to A:

CP/M allows you to refer to a single file by giving it the correct name, as above, or allows you to refer to a 'class' of files (e.g. 'all files with type .BAK'). 'Wild card' characters are used for this.

CP/M recognises two 'wild card' characters in a name, the ? and *. The file name with a ? or * is called an *ambiguous* file name. The file name in which all characters are given is an *unambiguous* file name. We will be referring to these, shortly, as *afn* and *ufn*. Note that neither ? nor * may be used as the Drive letter.

If a ? is used, it means 'any letter in this position'. If a * is used instead of a name, or instead of a type, it means 'any name' or 'any type'.

These illustrations show how file names are used.

ufn examples

FRED is a valid name on the logged drive.
FRED.COM is also valid.
A:FRED.COM is the same file, stated to be on drive A
B:FREDA.COM is a different file on a different drive.
A:FREDA.COM is the full name of FREDA.COM if you had taken the
disc out of B, and put it into A.
FREDA.COM is different from FRED.COM, whether on the same disc or not.

File names must be unique within a disc. You can have several discs with the
same file name on each, and the contents may be the same or different - but
you have to keep track if they are different - CP/M only recognises a file by its
name, not its content. 'Backup' copies of files are almost always exact
duplicates of the files, with the same names, held on a disc which is labelled
on the outside 'security copy taken 15.9.83' or something similar. You have to
do the labelling. Some programs which run under CP/M have ways of
keeping security copies which we will refer to when we look at specific file
types.

afn examples

FRED.* refers to FRED and FRED.COM and any other type, but not to
FREDA.type.
FRED?.* refers to FRED and FRED.COM and FREDA and FREDA.COM.
FRED????.* refers to all those, and FREDERIK and FREDERIK.COM.
FRED*.* is exactly the same as the line above.
*.COM refers to all files ending in .COM on the logged drive.
. refers to all files on the logged drive.
A:*.* refers to all files on drive A.

We will give more illustrations as we define the commands.

If we use *afn*, then either an unambiguous name or an ambiguous name
(including the ? or *) may be used.

If we use *ufn*, then the filename must be unambiguous.

Certain 'type' entries are reserved and others are conventionally used for
specific purposes, to describe the type of a file in a standard way.

This list of reserved and commonly used 'types' may be incomplete for your purposes - so add your own conventions. The common ones are highlighted in bold face.

ASC ASCII text file, usually used for Basic source code (CBASIC)
ASM ASseMbly language file (source for a program to be assembled)
BAK BAcKup copy file, the editor renames your original file to this.
BAS BASic source program file (MBASIC).
CBL CoBoL source program file.
COM COMmand file (an executable program).
DAT DATa file.
DOC DOCument file.
FOR FORtran source program file.
INT INTermediate program file - needs 'run-time' software.
HEX HEXadecimal format file (LOADable programs).
LIB LIBrary file used by macro assembler (see later).
LST LiSTing file - may be compiler output - for printing.
OVR OVeRlay file used by some packages (eg WordStar).
PAS PAScal program source file.
PLI PL/I source file.
PRN PRiNt file (source and object files produced by ASM).
REL RELocatable module of program.
SAV System file (Versions 2.x).
SRC Pascal intermediate file in assembler mnemonic form.
SUB SUBmit text file executed by the SUBMIT command (see later).
SYM SYMbol file.
TEX TEXt formatter source file.
TXT TeXT file produced by WordStar.
XRF Cross reference file.
$$$ Temporary file produced by ED, PIP and WordStar etc.

2.3 Command summary.

ERA afn   This command removes the named file(s) from the
                  directory. The space the file(s) occupy on the disc is
                  made available for re-use. In 3.1 ERASE may be used in
                  full, and the afn may be followed by [C] or
                  [CONFIRM], in which case each filename will be
                  displayed for confirmation before erasure. In all ver-

sions, ERA *.* (erase all files) will cause the ALL (Y/N)
? question to be displayed before erasure.

DIR afn   The directory command causes the names of all specified files to be listed on the console. If no afn is given,
all files are listed. In 3.1 DIRS lists all 'system' files.
Those are files which have been given the SYS
attribute, and are not displayed by DIR. In 3.1 also, DIR
can be followed by one or more 'options', which are
listed and explained after this summary and the examples following.

REN ufn1 = ufn2   The re-name command gives the file called ufn2 the
new name ufn1. ufn2 may specify a drive, but ufn1
may not. The file itself is unchanged, the directory
entry is altered to the new name (Think of 'Revised-
name Equals Name'. The syntax is the same as the
'LET' assignment conventions of programming languages.) RENAME can be used in full with 3.1.

SAVE n ufn   Versions 1.4 - 2.2. The 'n' is a number. It means a
number of 'pages' each of which is 256 bytes. The
command takes the specified number of pages from
the memory, starting at the bottom of the users program area, and puts then onto disc with the specified
name. This is a 'copy' function - the pages in memory
are unchanged. In version 3.1 SAVE works differently.
You enter SAVE< Rt> before loading the memory.
When you exit from the program, you are prompted for
the filename and size. See example later in this
chapter.

TYPE ufn   This displays the contents of the specified file on the
console. It assumes the file is held in ASCII and will
display it as such, expanding any Tab characters into
screen tabs as it does so If it is not an ASCII file, you
will get gibberish. In 3.1 you can add [PAGE] or
[NOPAGE] and if you added [PAGE], 24 lines would
be displayed, and the display would be suspended until
you press any key to see the next page, and so on. The
default is [NOPAGE]. Version 3.1 also has a DUMP
command, which is described at the end of this
chapter, because it is similar in action to TYPE.

15

USER n   This allows a user to move to the designated 'user
                         area'. n is a number between 0 and 15. User areas are a
                         simple protection device, allowing compatibility bet-
                         ween CP/M file directories and MP/M directories. In
                         3.1, the command USER< Rt> will prompt for the user
                         no.

To change from the currently logged drive to another, after the prompt, key in
the new drive letter and the colon. Then press return. We illustrate pressing
the return key like this - < Rt> . Nothing actually appears on the console when
you press return, but the command is not obeyed until you do. All commands
to CP/M require the return key at the end, to signify that you have completed
your entry. The single letter commands which use the 'control' key are the
exception to this.

This sequence shows 're-booting' and changing the logged drive.

```
A>^C
A> B:< Rt>
B>
```

The console actually shows this

```
A>^C
A> B:
B>
```

Whatever letter is shown before the prompt is the logged drive, and is taken
as the 'default' in a command. DIR < Rt> will display the directory of the
logged drive.

When the directory is displayed by CP/M, it does not show the 'decimal
point' between name and type, and it puts spaces where there are no specified characters. A sample directory looks like this

```
A> DIR
A: PIP        COM : STAT      COM : WS   COM : WSU       COM
A: WSMSGS   OVR : WSOVLY1   OVR : CPMBOOK : CPMBOOK   BAK
A: FULLNAME TYP : Z
A>
```

There are examples of files with a name but no type (Z and CPMBOOK) and
files with .COM types (the top row) and you can see that to the system,

16

CPMBOOK is different from CPMBOOK.BAK

The directory is displayed as above, but when you *enter* a file name, it must be entered as CPMBOOK.BAK *not* CPMBOOK BAK

Examples of the Resident commands, with the explanations, are:

DIR	Display file directory on logged (current) drive
DIR d:	Display file directory on the designated drive
DIR filename.typ	Search for stated file, current drive (replies NO FILE if not found, repeats name if found)
DIR *.typ	Displays all files of stated type, current drive
DIR filename.*	Displays all types of designated filename
DIR X*.*	Display all filenames beginning with letter X
DIR X????.*	Display all file names beginning with X which are five characters long, or less, any type.
DIRS	Display all files with the $SYS attribute on the logged drive (version 3.1 only).

(NOTE. There are options which considerably extend the DIR command which are only available under 3.1. These are described later in this chapter.)

TYPE filename.typ	Display at the console the file named on the current drive, treating it as ASCII
TYPE d:filename.typ	Display as above, but on the stated drive
ERA filename.type	Erase the named file from the current drive (but not a file of the same name on any other drive)
ERA *.*	Erase all files on the current drive. (In version 2.x, only erases in the current user area) Asks for confirmation ALL(Y/N) before continuing
ERA d:*.typ	Erase all files of the stated type on the named drive
ERA filename.*	Erase all types of named file on current drive

(**WARNING** - ERA only erases the directory entry - it actually sets the first (00) byte of each extent of a directory entry for the file to the value (in hex) E5. The space which the file itself occupies is untouched, until it is re-allocated, and until new characters are written into the space. If you use direct access data files (eg, BASIC 'random' files) then ERA will not empty the file space. (Nor will KILL.) Reading from a record in a random file to which you have **not** previously written will return the characters which happen to be left there from the previous use of the disc space.)

REN newname.typ = oldname.typ	Rename the file on the current drive.
REN newname.typ = d:oldname.typ	Rename the file on the designated drive.
SAVE n filename.typ	Save the first n pages from memory as named file.
SAVE n d:filename.typ	Save the first n pages from memory (a page is 1/4K or 256 bytes) as the named file on the designated drive. This is the 1.4 - 2.2 version of SAVE.
SAVE	In version 3.1, the SAVE command must be given before you load the memory image which you want to save. Then, when you have loaded the memory, and you exit, instead of returning directly to CP/M, the SAVE routine displays on the screen three prompts, asking first for the filespec of the new file, then for the hex address of the start (probably 100) and the hex address of the end. That end address is the first byte which is not to be copied to the new file. If you give a filespec of an existing file, you will be asked if you want to delete the existing version. If you enter < Rt> for the filespec, you will exit from SAVE without performing the SAVE.
d:	Change the logged drive to the stated one
USER n	Change user area (version 2.x) to the numbered one. (The system always 'boots' to user 0.)
USER	In 3.1 the CCP gives the prompt 'Enter user #'.

The purpose of USER areas is to allocate storage (disc) space to which other users cannot write. If you put a file onto disc while USER 1 is set - that is, you are at that time, user 1 - then no-one in USER 0 or USER 2 to 15 can erase that file, show it in a DIR or STAT command, or overwrite it. That presents you with a 'Catch 22' situation, initially, because you cannot load or run a program (a file) in another USER either. When you first enter USER 1 (or any other than 0), you are alone in there, and cannot PIP any file into your area. We will return to this in Chapter 7, when we look at DDT, but for the moment it is sufficient to follow the following sequence the first time you enter a USER other than 0:

2.3.1 How to start up a new USER area.

Enter PIP, and wait for the * prompt. Hit Return to get the A> back. Now enter the user area, say USER 1. Type SAVE 30 PIP.COM and hit Return. (Version 3.1 needs addresses 100 and 1E00). Note that earlier versions of PIP were only 28 pages (100 to 1C00) - you can check yours using DDT, as shown in chapter 7. Saving 30 pages is safe with either version.

That will give you the PIP program (Chapter 4) in your user area. Now you can coy any file into your area from area 0 by typing PIP A: = ufn[G0] and Return. The Gn in brackets (square brackets, no space before the first) allows PIP to read a file in another area and copy it into your USER 1 area. We will study this in more detail, but for the moment, it works.

DIR options in version 3.1.

An option is specified by adding the first two or more letters of the option name, after a square bracket. We show the option name in full, and the examples show the right hand square bracket as well, though it is not necessary. [DA is equivalent to [DATE].

The options allow you to search for files on any or all drives, and in any user number or numbers. They also allow display of the 'date stamps' which files may have in 3.1.

Two or more options require only one set of square brackets, and are separated by commas. The options do not apply to DIRS, because, as we will see, there is a [SYS] option for DIR which fulfils the same purpose.

ATT	Displays the file attributes (R/O, R/W, DIR, and SYS if the SYS option is also used.)
DATE	Displays the date and time stamps of files.
DRIVE = ALL	Displays the files on all on-line drives.

DRIVE = d	Displays the files on drive 'd'.
DRIVE = (A,B,C)	Displays the files on the listed drives.
EXCLUDE	Displays only those files which do **not** match the specification in the command line.
FF	Sends a 'form feed' (seek head of form) to the printer if it has been engaged with ∧ P, before displaying and printing the result of the command
FULL	Shows the name, size, number of 128-byte records and attributes of all files listed. If there is a directory label, FULL also shows the password protection mode and the time stamps. If there is no directory label, the display omits the password and time stamp columns, and shows two entries to a line. The display is sorted into ascending sequence of filename/type. (See the SET command in Chapter 6 for a description of file attributes, directory labels passwords and protection modes.)
LENGTH = n	If∧P has engaged the printer, n lines of output are printed and then a table heading is repeated. n is an integer with values from 5 to 65536.
MESSAGE	Displays the drive names and user numbers being searched as the search takes place.
NOSORT	Displays filenames in the order in which they are found in the directory.
RO	Displays only R/O files (but see 'EXCLUDE')
RW	Displays only R/W files.
SIZE	Displays the filename and size in kilobytes (1024 bytes). Not used with FULL.
SYS	Displays only files with the SYS attribute (which are 'hidden' from a normal DIR command).
USER = n	Displays files in the user number stated.
USER = (0,1,6)	Displays files in the user areas listed. Any number of user numbers may be included.
USER = ALL	Displays all files for all users on the default or specified drive(s).

The following examples will show the types of command which you may find useful. We show them in full, but any option may be specified in two letters, and the closing square bracket is optional.

20

A> DIR C: [FULL]< Rt>
This shows all the characteristics of all the files in user 0 on drive C.

A> DIR C: [DATE]< Rt>
This lists all the files in user 0 on drive C and their dates. (see Chapter 6 for SETting date stamps etc.)

A> DIR D: [RW,SYS]< Rt>
This displays all the files which have the SYS attribute, and are 'Read or Write', in user 0 on drive D.

A> DIR [USER = ALL,DRIVE = ALL]< Rt>
All files (except ones with SYS attribute) on all drives, in all user areas.

6B> DIR [EXCLUDE] *.COM< Rt>
This shows all files which are not command (.COM) files on drive B, in user 6.

3C> DIR [SIZE] *.PLI *.COM *.ASM< Rt>
This shows that more than one filespec can be included in a command line. The effect is that all files on drive C, in user 3, which have one of the three type specified will be displayed, and the name and size of each will be shown.

A> DIR [DRIVE= ALL,USER = ALL,MESSAGE] LOSTFILE.DAT< Rt>
This will show which drives and users are being searched while the whole of the on-line disc storage is being searched for the file. If found, LOSTFILE.DAT will be displayed. If not - NO FILE will be displayed.

A> dir [size,rw] d:< Rt>
If you enter a command to CP/M in lower case, it will be translated to upper case before being obeyed. In this case all R/W files on drive D will be displayed, with their name and size in kilobytes. Note that D: is the same, in a DIR command, as D:*.*

2.3.2 Console Editing Commands

During the entry of a command - or any other entry - you will occasionally mis-key, or perhaps get halfway through a command and realise that you should do something else first. If the command, as you have typed it, is invalid, you could just press Return or Enter, the console would repeat your 'part command' with a question mark after it, and re-prompt, like this -

    A> GOOD MORNING< Rt>
    GOOD?
    A>

However, this is dangerous, because your incomplete command may be valid, and may do something disastrous. (Murphy's Law !) Therefore you need to be able to 'edit' the line you are typing, and CP/M has reserved certain keys for this.

Hardware systems vary in the way they show deletion on the screen, but all have a key named RUBOUT or DELETE (on a few systems other names are used, or even a 'left arrow'). Pressing this key will delete the last character keyed, and may also 'echo' it. If you typed DIR FRED and then pressed RUBOUT four times, the console may show DIR FREDDERF

If you then pressed Return, the response would be a normal DIR output.

Since a line with 'echo' deletes in it can be confusing, CP/M has a way of re-typing the line without them. Simply press ∧ R - (Control and R together) and the console will show this -

A> DIR FREDDERF (now press ∧ R)
    DIR ■ (and you can now see what is in the command)

In versions 2.x onwards, there is a backspace and delete comand, which is ∧ H. Your keyboard may be marked to show this. If you have a screen (vdu or tv) there may also be a single key (perhaps BACKSPACE) which will backspace and delete a character. That is hardware dependent. The CP/M CONFIGUR program will, particularly with 2.2 onwards, allow you to make the DELETE key equal to BACKSPACE if you prefer that. See Chapter Fifteen.

With CP/M you can also delete the entire line typed so far. If you are keying something in - and you want to start all over again with that line, use ∧ U. Usually some special character will terminate the cancelled line, and you will be positioned ready to restart.

A> DISINFECTANTTTTTTTTTTTTT #
■

The same effect exactly is produced by ∧ X instead of ∧ U.

There is a convenient 'line feed' command - ∧ E - which returns the cursor or carriage to the start of a new line, but which does not 'transmit' the entry until you press Return. This is more used when you have a hard copy printer than when you have a screen, but it can be useful. A single command can be up to

255 characters long, and the ability to use ⌃ E to lay it out readably may be helpful.

If you have a small screen or a long directory, you may want to stop the display before it 'scrolls' the top lines off the screen. The command to interrupt console output **temporarily** is the ⌃ S. Use ⌃ Q to restart the output. (Versions 2.2 and earlier accept any key to restart.) In a language such as Micro-Soft BASIC, (MBASIC), this allows you to stop the display of a listing on the screen while you inspect a particular part of it. ⌃ S - Stop ! ⌃ Q - Continue !

CP/M does not contain any built-in commands to allow you to print out on a listing device the existing contents of the screen, but it does allow you to echo to the list device (LST:) anything which is next displayed, by typing ⌃ P first. So if you want a hard copy of your Directory, and you have a printer attached and powered up, type DIR, then before you hit Return, press ⌃ P. The ⌃ P is not echoed to the screen, but now, when you hit Return, the output will appear on printer and screen. ⌃ P is a 'toggle', so to disable the 'echo to printer', press ⌃ P again, or re-boot. ⌃ P is always 'off' when the system is booted. (See also the DEVICE command in version 3.1, covered in Chapter 3.)

There is one more command, ⌃ Z, which we will look at later. It is a type of interrupt which you will need with the CP/M editor (ED) and which is also used with PIP.

SUMMARY.

Console editing and control commands:

RUBOUT/DELETE	Delete last charater and echo
⌃ H	Backspace and delete (Version 2.x)
⌃ U	(also ⌃ X) Delete the entire line
⌃ R	Repeat the entire line on the console, no echos
⌃ E	Line feed and carriage return but not 'send'
⌃ C	CP/M 'warm boot'
⌃ Z	End console input (end of string) in ED and PIP
⌃ S	Pause console output. Any key to restart.
⌃ P	Echo all subsequent console output (including keyboard input) to list device until next ⌃ P or 'boot'.

Version 3.1 Console Editing

There are actually 18 commands plus Delete/Rubout available under 3.1, though not all of them are implemented on all systems. Some of them work under 2.2 as well, so try them for your system. There are hardware restrictions which affect the implementation of these commands - Apples don't allow ^ A through, and some SuperBrains don't allow ^ W, for example. This is the full set, with the corresponding ASCII codes for the commands.

Command	Meaning	ASCII code
^ A	Move the cursor one char left	01H
^ B	Move cursor within command line	02H
^ C	'Warm' boot	03H
^ E	Start a new line	05H
^ F	Move the cursor one char right	06H
^ G	Delete the char under the cursor	07H
^ H	Backspace and delete	08H
^ I	Tab 8 columns	09H
^ J	Line feed	0AH
^ K	Delete to end of line	0BH
^ M	Carriage Return (as < Rt>)	0DH
^ P	Echo to printer on/off toggle	10H
^ Q	Restart display after ^ S	11H
^ R	Retype current line	12H
^ S	Stop display - ^ Q restarts it	13H
^ U	Delete line, update buffer with the characters to the left of the cursor	15H
^ W	Recall previous command line if buffer is empty	17H
^ X	Delete from cursor to beginning of line	18H

The ASCII code for Delete is 7FH
The ASCII code for Backspace is the same as ^ H 08H

File Names.

Versions 1.4 - 2.2	X:XXXXXXXX.XXX
Version 3.1	X:XXXXXXXX.XXX;XXXXXXXX

The first X: is the drive and is always optional, the default assumed will be the 'logged' drive (the one in the 'prompt'). If a drive letter is stated, the colon (:) must be present.

The 'filename' XXXXXXXX may be from one to eight characters.

The 'type' .XXX may be from none to three letters. If it is included, the 'period' (.) must be included. When an unambiguous filename (ufn) is stated, the type must be included if it exists in the filename. The exception is when a 'transient command' - a '.COM' file is invoked. To load and run a .COM file, the name only may be entered.

The final group of characters ;XXXXXXXX is the password in version 3.1. Up to eight letters or numbers may be used, and the semicolon must be present if the password is present. Chapter 6 refers to the use of passwords, and the SET command.

Ambiguous filenames include one or more 'wild card' characters. The ? replaces any single character, and the * replaces a name or a type. (*.* is 'all files' and so is ????????.???)

2.3.3 Resident commands in the Console Command Processor.

d:	Change the logged drive to the stated drive
DIR afn or d:	Output directory to the console
DIRS afn or d:	In version 3.1, shows $SYS files (see chap. 3)
TYPE ufn	Output the content of ASCII file to console
ERA afn	Erase the directory entry for the file/s
REN ufn1 = ufn2	Rename existing file ufn2 as ufn1
USER n	Change to user area n (0 to 15)
USER	In version 3.1 prompts for number
SAVE n ufn	Put the n pages (each 256 bytes) in the transient program area into the named file. Version 3.1 requires SAVE< Rt> before loading memory, then prompts for ufn and start/end addresses in Hex.

Each of these commands needs RETURN/ENTER to 'send' it to the CCP for action. The editing commands (⌃ R etc) act immediately.

Version 3.1 accepts ERASE and RENAME in full, and allows [PAGE] as an option following the ufn in a TYPE command, displaying a page at a time. Note that some implementations of version 3.1 may only restart a display which has been stopped by ^ S when you press ^ Q. Earlier versions accepted any key to restart.

Transient commands are held as executable programs on disc. For example -

PIP ufn1 = ufn2	Make a copy of ufn2 and call it ufn1
SUBMIT filename	Enter a command sequence held in filename.SUB
DUMP ufn	Display the contents of the file ufn in both hexadecimal form and ASCII form.

There are more, as we will see later. Resident commands are obeyed immediately, and need no special files on the discs. Transient commands are first loaded from disc, then obeyed - so they must be present before they can be invoked.

CHAPTER THREE

The Information Transients - STAT,HELP,DEVICE and SHOW.

3.1 Fundamentals.

Transient commands are those which are held as a file on disc, and which are invoked by name as required. In CP/M version 3.1 there is an extensive HELP file, which allows you to display on the screen brief details of each topic and subtopic in the file. Previous versions do not have this facility.

HELP is intended to be self explanatory, and will be found very useful to jog your memory on the details of infrequently used commands. It works like this.

If you enter HELP, you get the new prompt

> HELP>

on the screen. Enter ?< Rt> and you will get a list of topics to choose from. If you enter HELP DEVICE (say), you get the subtopics in the DEVICE topic to choose from. You can enter a period (decimal point) "." to redisplay the last description you looked at, or as a topic name if you want to go straight to a subtopic.

> HELP> .< Rt>

will redisplay the last description.

> HELP> .PASSWORD (or just .PASS) < Rt>

will display the details of the subtopic PASSWORD

Pressing any key except < Rt> will take you back to the HELP> prompt. Pressing < Rt> only will take you back to the A>. There are two options which may be implemented, [NOPAGE] and [LIST].

By default, the HELP screens are displayed in 24 line units, but continuous display can be obtained by putting [NOPAGE] after the topic or subtopic you want. Similarly [LIST] echos the display to the LST: device (your printer) if that facility is implemented.

Since the HELP file is there for your use - use it, and you will find it a welcome addition to the otherwise rather uncommunicative displays which earlier versions of CP/M offered.

In the rest of this chapter, we will be describing the facilities available for you to obtain various statistics of the system and your files. In versions up to 2.2, these were available through the STAT command - a transient. In 3.1, the facilities have been extended, and they are available under a series of different commands. You have already seen the 'DIR with otions' (in Chapter 2), and there are DEVICE and SHOW commands as well in 3.1. However, we will ignore version 3.1, to begin with, while we cover the details of STAT, and then we will return to the 3.1 commands. You will see how the 3.1 commands parallel and extend the facilities available under STAT.

3.2 The STAT command.

The STAT command allows you to see how much space your files are occupying on disc, and how much free (not allocated in the directory) space there is. It also allows you to find out the physical characteristics of your discs, and to alter the assignments of logical devices to physical devices.

The simplest, most often used versions of the commands are these

        STAT
        STAT d:
        STAT d:*.*

where d is a drive letter.

If you type STAT (and < Rt>) alone, the screen will display a message like this -

d: R/W, Space: nnnK (if the disc is Read/Write)
d: R/O, Space: nnnK (if the disc is Read Only)

There will be as many lines as you have 'active' discs. If you have an active disc (from which you have read the directory, say) and you take it out and replace it with another, the CCP automatically sets that new disc to R/O (except version 3.1 which automatically logs onto a new medium.) In versions 2.2 and earlier, you cannot write to a replaced or new disc until you have done some form of 'reset' - such as a 'warm' boot.

STAT d: (and < Rt>) will result in a single line message

Bytes Remaining On d: nnnK

STAT d:*.* (and < Rt>) will scan all the files available on the specified drive (see notes about $SYS and USER, later) and will list them on the console in alphabetical order, will give the storage allocated to each, and will also give the amount of free space remaining. The format of the table will be like this:

```
Recs          Bytes      Ext      Acc
rrrr          nnnnK      ee       a/b  d:ufn (repeated for each file)
Bytes remaining on d:nnnnK
```

rrrr   =   the number of 128 byte records in each 'extent' of the file
nnnnK =   the number of bytes in K (= 1024) allocated to the file
ee   =   the number of 16K file extents
a/b   =   the access mode of the file (R/W or R/O or SYS)
d:ufn =   the drive and filename (in brackets if a SYS file)

A sample listing looks like this

A> STAT B:*.*

```
Recs          Bytes      Ext      Acc
285           36k        2        R/W B:CPM
277           36k        2        R/W B:CPM.BAK
48            6k         1        R/W B:CPM/CH11
Bytes remaining on B: 260k
```

A>

Now you can use these commands to check whether or not a disc is R/W(available for writing to) and find out how much spare space there is on a disc, and you can find out the size of any or all files on that disc.

29

3.2.1 STAT the multifaceted utility to show STATus.

You can add another column to the display above, by adding $S to the command -

stat d:*.* $S

That puts the 'Size' column in front of the 'Recs' column like this-

Size	Recs	Bytes	Ext	Acc
ssss	rrrr	nnnnk	ee	a/b d:ufn

where ssss is the number of 'virtual' records in the file. In a serial file, this will be the same as the Recs column, but in a random file which has space allocated but not yet occupied, the ssss will give the allocated size, and the rrrr the occupied size.

3.2.2 Setting file(s) or drive to R/O.

STAT d:R/O

Set drive d: to Read Only, so that an error will occur if an attempt is made to write to it, or to erase from it. The error message from CP/M (which can be 'trapped' in most programming languages) is -

BDOS ERR ON d: READ ONLY

This is a temporary 'read only' state. Whenever the system is re-booted, both/all discs are reset to R/W.

STAT d:ufn $R/O

This is not temporary. The command will set the *file* specified to Read Only. It stays in effect until you alter it with STAT. Even removing a disc, switching off the machine, and then re- starting from cold will not reset that file, nor can you erase it until you restore the R/W attribute.

The commands:
STAT d: ufn$R/W
STAT d: R/W
will set the file or the drive to Read/Write.

Note that the $ sign is omitted when a drive only is specified, but must be present when a filename is included in the command. (If you are using R/O or R/W.)

3.2.3 STAT to 'hide' a file from the DIR command.

As well as making a file R/O or R/W, there are two other indicators which you can use.

    STAT d:ufn $SYS

marks the file as a 'system' file, which will not appear when a DIR command is given. The file will appear when a STAT *.* listing is called up, but the filename will be in brackets (). Here is an illustration.

```
A> DIR A:
A: PIP           COM : STAT    COM : KARMA    DAT
A> STAT  A:KARMA.DAT $SYS
KARMA.DAT set to SYS      (this is a CP/M response)
A> DIR A:
A: PIP           COM : STAT    COM
A> STAT A:*.*
Recs        Bytes       Ext        Acc
18          4k          1          R/W A:(KARMA.DAT)
58          8K          1          R/W A:PIP.COM
42          6K          1          R/W A:STAT.COM
Bytes Remaining on A: 322k
A> STAT A:KARMA.DAT $DIR
KARMA.DAT set to DIR
A>
```

and there we are, back where we started. What we did, if you follow the sequence through was first to show the directory of the disc in A. Then we set the DAT file to SYS, and re-displayed the directory - no DAT file. Use STAT and the file is there, with the name in brackets. Finally, we used STAT $DIR to set the file back to directory status.

The purpose is to hide a file from a DIR or PIP (Chapter 4) command. It does not hide it from STAT, and if you know it is there, you can ERAse it, either individually or by using *.*.

Notice that $SYS is like $R/O for files, in that it is actually marked in the directory on disc, and is retained even when the disc is removed. Only a $DIR parameter will re-set it to allow DIRectory display. Re-boot does not re-set it. In fact, PIP *can find* it if you use a special parameter in the PIP command.

3.2.4 STAT to show the DEVICE assignments.

STAT DEV:

This gives the current 'mapping' of physical devices onto the logical devices which CP/M uses. Such a list could be -

CON: is CRT:
RDR: is UR1:
PUN: is PTP:
LTP: is TTY:

The four logical devices are all that CP/M handles (apart from discs !). They signify the following -

CON: is the system console for messages and inputs.
RDR: is the auxiliary serial input device, and in this case is set to a user defined device with a user routine.
PUN: is the auxiliary serial output device - in this case a paper tape punch.
LST: is the output list device, and in this case is set to 'teletype'.

The full list of possible physical devices is this -

TTY:	slow speed serial output device, eg teletype.
CRT:	high speed I/O device - eg cathode ray tube (vdu) and keyboard.
BAT:	batch processing (CON:input is RDR:, CON: output is LST:).
UC1:	user defined console.
PTR:	paper tape reader.
UR1:	user defined reader no. 1.
UR2:	user definer reader no. 2.
UP1:	user defined punch no. 1.
UP2:	user defined punch no. 2.
LPT:	line printer.
UL1:	user defined list device.

You can see a summary of the valid (VAL) STATus commands on your console at any time by entering the command STAT VAL:

This is the list -

Temp R/O disk:	d: = R/O
Set Indicator:	d:filename.typ $R/O $R/W $SYS $DIR
Disk Status :	DSK: d:DSK:

User Status : USR:
Iobyte Assign:
CON: = TTY: CRT: BAT: UC1:
RDR: = TTY: PTR: UR1: UR2:
PUN: = TTY: PTP: UP1: UP2:
LST: = TTY: CRT: LPT: UL1:

Note that a single STAT command can only set one of the indicators, and that the list of 'Input/Output Byte' assignments shows each of the four possible values for each logical device. You can alter the assignments as follows -

STAT ld1 = pd1, ld2 = pd2, ...

One or several logical devices (ld) can have physical devices (pd) allocated in a single command. Both the ld and pd must be complete with the terminating colon. (LST: not LST)

3.2.5 STAT used to find the characteristics of your drives.

You can specify a drive, or use the default to the logged drive. Valid commands are therefore -

STAT DSK:
STAT d:DSK:

A sample of the output for drive A of a particular system is -

A:	Drive Characteristics
2220:	128 Byte Record Capacity
340:	Kilobyte Drive Capacity
64:	32 Byte Directory Entries
64:	Checked Directory Entries
256:	Records/Extent
16:	Records/Block
40:	Sectors/Track
2:	Reserved Tracks

(That is the list for a particular 5 1/4" diskette, double sided, double density, soft sectored, with the the CP/M operating system on the first two tracks, 0 and 1, shown above as 'reserved'.)

The system checks directory entries when the device has a removable disc - so the number of 'checked' entries should equal the number on the line above. With non-removable media, the 'checked' counter is usually set to zero.

3.2.6 STAT and USERs.

To enable several users to have files and programs on the same discs - particularly important for fixed media, of course - without risk of accidental access or over-writing, CP/M allows up to 16 different users to 'log-in'. User 0 is always active when CP/M is loaded. In MP/M, the multi-user version of CP/M, it is clear which user is active, because the number precedes the logged drive letter in the prompt -

    0A>
    1A>
    etc

In CP/M versions up to 2.2, you have to ask for the active user by typing -

    STAT USR:

and the system will reply by telling you which user is active and which user numbers have files on the current logged disc - like this

    Active User : 0
    Active Files: 0 1 3

(There happened to be files for USER 1 and USER 3 as well as USER 0 on that drive. Note that although the line says 'Active Files', it means 'User Numbers which have Active Files'. It is not a file count !)

We covered the way of getting started in a new USER in the previous chapter, but we will repeat the sequence here, as it would appear on the screen

    A> USER 2
    A> DIR
    NO FILE
    A> USER 0
    A> DIR
    A: PIP   COM : STAT   COM : KARMA   DAT
    A> PIP
    *   (hit Return)

```
A> USER2
A> SAVE  30  PIP.COM                                  (or 28 PIP.COM)
A> DIR
A: PIP                    COM
A> PIP  A: = STAT.COM[G0]
A> DIR
A: PIP                    COM : STAT              COM
A>
```

and so on. The uses of SAVE and PIP will be covered in chapters 7 and 4, later.

3.2.7 SUMMARY of STAT commands.

We have covered the uses of STAT to:

- find free disc space (STAT or STAT *.*)
- set read only or read/write status (STAT B:R/O)
- list the characteristics of a drive (STAT DSK:)
- list the valid STAT commands (STAT VAL:)
- re-assign physical devices to the four logical devices
- find out what USER is active, and what files (STAT USR:)

Here is a summary of the commands, using d: for drive, afn and ufn as before.

STAT	Display STATus of active/logged drive(s) and free space.
STAT d:	As above, but for named drive.
STAT DEV:	Display current DEVice assignments.
STAT VAL:	Display VALid assignments.
STAT DSK:	Display the DiSK characteristics.
STAT USR:	Display current USeR and disc users.
STAT ufn	Display the record count etc of file.
STAT ufn $S	As above but with Size column.
STAT afn	Display the details of files which match the afn given, and the free space.
STAT d:R/O	Set the drive to Read Only.
STAT d:R/W	Set the drive to Read/Write.
STAT ufn $R/O	Temporarily set file to R/O.

STAT ufn $R/W   Reset to R/W.
STAT ufn $SYS   Set to SYStem status (not on DIR, not found by
                         PIP, in braces on STAT listing).
STAT ufn $DIR   Reset to DIRectory status.
STAT lll: = ppp: Assign physical device ppp to logical device lll.

3.3 The Version 3.1 commands.

If you are a user of version 3.1, and have skipped forward to this point, it is suggested that you may find it useful to read the details of STAT, not only to see the plethora of facilities which it includes, but also because in the next pages we will cover the 3.1 facilities in rather less detail, and the detail already covered may help you to understand. If you are a user of 2.2 or an earlier version, the following pages will not apply to you.

3.4 DEVICE

This command allows you to see what the current device assignments are, to change the assignments, and to set or change the communication protocol and speed. It also shows or alters the size of the console display. Device assignment is the process of telling CP/M which physical devices are to be handled by the routines within CP/M for its set of logical devices. There are several aspects to DEVICE, so we will take the simplest ones first, then progress to the more complex and powerful ones.

3.4.1 Display the assignments.

If you give the command on its own like this -

    A> DEVICE< Rt>

you will see a display of the physical devices, and a list of the current assignments of the logical devices in the system. It also prompts you for new assignments, should you want to make any. We will look at the assignment commands shortly.

If you only want to see the assignments, then enter -

    A> DEVICE VALUES< Rt>

and this will display the current logical device assignments.

3.4.2 Protocol and baud rate.

Some peripherals expect the processor to send a message enquiring if the device is ready to receive data. The message is answered if the peripheral is ready, and the processor initiates the transmission. If the device is not ready, no acknowledgement is sent, and the processor does not transmit. The 'not ready' state could arise because the buffer in the peripheral is full, because the peripheral is not powered up or connected - or for any similar reason. The protocol which CP/M uses is called XON/XOFF. You can choose, according to the peripheral you are using, whether to tell CP/M to wait for an acknowledgement before transmitting data, or to just send it whether the peripheral is ready or not. You do this by telling CP/M, for the device chosen, either XON or NOXON - 'use the protocol' or 'do not'.

Baud rate is the transmission speed between the processor and the peripheral. Some peripherals 'sense' the baud rate, and automatically adjust to it, or may work at a fixed rate, but much more often, the baud rate at which a peripheral can work can be set at one of a number of different values, with internal or external switches. You can set the CP/M baud rate for a particular peripheral at any one of the following values -

50	75	110	134	150	300
600	1200	1800	2400	3600	4800
7200	9600	19200			

In versions 2.2 and earlier, setting the baud rates was usually done by running a 'transient' called CONFIGUR or CONFIG. In 3.1, the DEVICE command achieves these settings. We will use examples. First, you can set a physical device directly, without affecting the logical device to which it is linked. Examples of this command are -

    A> DEVICE CRT [XON,9600]< Rt>
    A> DEVICE LPT [NOXON,1200]< Rt>

37

These set the physical devices as shown, with the CRT using protocol, but the LPT not, and the different baud rates as shown. Note the use of the square brackets [], they are part of the syntax of the command.

3.4.3 Displaying the device names and characteristics.

If you want to see the physical device names, and a summary of the characteristics of each of those devices, then type in -

    A> DEVICE NAMES< Rt>

If you know the name, and just want to see the characteristics, then type the name after DEVICE. For example, if you want to see the characteristics of the physical device CRT, you would type -

    A> DEVICE CRT< Rt>

If you put a *logical* device name instead of the physical one, you will be shown the current assignment of that logical device. For instance, to see the assignment of the CON device, you type -

    A> DEVICE CON< Rt>

You can also ask DEVICE to display or set the number of columns and rows used on the console display. To see what the current page size is, you enter -

    A> DEVICE CONSOLE [PAGE]< Rt>

and the width in columns and length in lines will be displayed. To alter them, you would enter, say,

    A> DEVICE CONSOLE [COLUMNS = 60 LINES = 20]< Rt>

or

    A> DEVICE CONSOLE [COLUMNS = 80 LINES = 24]< Rt>

3.4.4 Making assignments.

You will have noticed already that we have not needed the colon (:) after the logical or physical device name so far. However, you do need it if the name is followed by a equals sign (=). So when we use DEVICE to make an assignment, we use it like this -

38

A> DEVICE CONOUT: = CRT< Rt>

The logical device CONOUT is now assigned to the physical device CRT. We can also assign a logical device to *more than one* physical device - like this -

A> DEVICE CONOUT: = CRT,LPT< Rt>

and now everything we get on the screen of the CRT will be echoed on the LPT (printer).

Earlier, we looked at the protocol and baud rate settings of physical devices. Now we can see that we may assign a logical to one or more physical devices, and set the comms. at the same time, like this-

A> DEVICE LST: = LPT [XON,1200]< Rt>

or

A> DEVICE LST: = LPT [XON,1200],CRT [XON,9600]< Rt>

With earlier versions of CP/M, switching between two printers which were used at different baud rates - say a 'daisy wheel' which could not be set higher than 1200 baud, and a fast 'dot matrix' which needed to be set at 9600 baud to achieve satisfactory performance - was a little troublesome - and often meant two sets of discs, one configured for each. Now, with CP/M 3.1, it is simple to modify the protocol and/or speed at the keyboard, using the DEVICE command.

There is one more assignment which we have not mentioned, and that is actually a disconnention. If you want to suppress output, perhaps from the LST device, you can disconnect it by using the command -

A> DEVICE LST: = NULL< Rt>

Notice that this disconnects *logical* devices, and that the colon is used because the equals sign follows the device name. You would have to re-assign an appropriate physical device to start using the logical device again.

3.5 SHOW in version 3.1.

The functions performed by STAT in earlier versions of CP/M, which relate to the characteristics of a drive and the usage of a disc, are performed by SHOW in version 3.1. You can use SHOW to obtain a display of information about the drive characteristics by entering -

> A> SHOW [DRIVE]< Rt>

To get the display of the access mode (R/W or R/O) and free space on all the logged in discs, you type in -

> A> SHOW [SPACE]< Rt>

To get the same information about the logged drive, SHOW alone will suffice - and to get that information about another drive, say drive B, type in -

> A> SHOW B:< Rt>

Since version 3.1 allows for disc labelling, you can display the label information by entering (for drive D, in this case) -

> A> SHOW D:[LABEL]< Rt>

Omitting the drive letter gives you the label information on the logged drive, as you would expect.

The USER command is somewhat different in version 3.1, as we indicated in Chapter 2, and to obtain details of current users and files, you enter -

> A> SHOW B:[USERS]< Rt>

This will give you the current user number (which is not displayed in CP/M, only in MP/M) and all the user numbers which are 'active' on drive B, together with the number of files assigned to each user. Omit the drive letter (and colon) and the default drive will be the logged drive.

The same display would be obtained with -

> A> B:
> B> SHOW [USERS]< Rt>

A final useful facility in SHOW is the ability to show the number of unused directory entries on a disc. This is -

> A> SHOW [DIR]< Rt>

and simply shows how many free directory entries there are on the logged drive. The drive letter (and colon) may precede [DIR], if you want a drive other than the logged drive.

In case you may have missed it in Chapter 2, the STAT command which versions 2.2 and earlier used to display file sizes has been replaced with the extended DIR command (eg DIR [FULL]).

Setting files to Read Only or Read/Write is done with the SET command, which we will cover in Chapter 6.

3.6 Summary of DEVICE and SHOW commands inversion 3.1.

DEVICE	Displays the logical and physical assignments.
DEVICE NAMES	Displays the physical devices and characteristics.
DEVICE VALUES	Displays the logical device assignments.
DEVICE physical-dev	Displays the attributes of the device.
DEVICE logical-dev	Displays the assignment.
DEVICE log-dev: = phy-dev	Assigns as stated.
DEVICE phy-dev[protocol,baud-rate]	Sets XON or NOXON and speed.
DEVICE log-dev: = NULL	Disconnects the assignment.
DEVICE CONSOLE [PAGE]	Displays the columns and lines set.
DEVICE CONSOLE[COLUMNS = nn ,LINES = mm]	Sets as stated.
SHOW	Displays the space on the logged drive.
SHOW [SPACE]	Displays the space on all drives.
SHOW d:	Displays the space left on the specified drive.
SHOW [USERS]	Displays the users on the default drive and how many files each has.

SHOW [LABEL]   Displays label
                                    information for the
                                    default drive.
SHOW [DIR]   Displays the number of
                                    unused directory
                                    entries on the default
                                    (logged) drive.
SHOW [DRIVE]   Displays the drive
                                    characteristics.

These apply only to CP/M version 3.1. For earlier versions, see the STAT
command earlier in this chapter.

CHAPTER FOUR

PIP

4.1 Fundamentals

PIP is the Peripheral Interchange Program - it is principally used to move files about between peripherals. You can use it to copy the whole of a disc to another, for 'back-up', and to copy a particular program or file from one disc to another, and you will find it a quick way of 'dumping' the contents of a file to the printer. The basic format of PIP is this -

PIP d:ufn = d:ufn

The command requires the DESTINATION first, then the SOURCE. If you find it difficult to remember which comes where, then think of LET instead of PIP. The command then becomes 'Let x equal y' and you can see that x is where the file goes to, and y is where it comes from.

PIP leaves the original file where it is at the start - so it is a *copy* program. Also, the original file has the same *name* as it had at the start - it is *completely* unchanged. However, when you copy the file, you can re-name it if you want to. There are plenty of defaults and options, and ways of using the ? and * characters as well.

To copy everything on the disc in A: to a disc in B:, keeping the same names for all the files, you can type

    PIP B: = A:*.*

The screen will show

    COPYING -

and then there will be the name of the first file being copied, followed by the next and so on, like this -

A> PIP B: = A:*.*

COPYING -
PIP.COM
STAT.COM
KARMA.DAT

A>

Now, on drive B:, you have an exact copy of all the files which are $DIR files on drive A: To make sure that it really is an exact copy, you can tell PIP to do a 'read after write' check. If you do that, then a block is read from the original file, and that block is written to the destination file. Then, immediately, the destination file is read, and the block is compared with the block in the memory. If they are the same, then the write was successful. This is called 'verification' and is invoked by putting a V in square brackets after the PIP command, thus -

PIP B: = A:*.*[V]

That command, as it stands, is the ideal 'back-up copy' command for creating a new program disc.

However, you do not have to copy a whole set of files, you can copy just one file, like this -

PIP B: = A:FRED.COM

and you can have the copy file with another name, like this -

PIP B:BILL.COM = A:FRED.COM

That last command takes an exact copy of the file FRED.COM, puts it onto drive B:, and names it, in the drive B: directory, BILL.COM as you require.

And finally, for the fundamental uses of PIP, you can invoke PIP without any file names, which loads PIP into the memory, and gives you a 'prompt' to ask you for a destination and source. This is the interactive mode of using PIP. The prompt is an *. This is how it looks -

A> PIP
*

44

and you enter the appropriate details after the *. Let us say that you have PIP on a disc in drive B:, and you are logged onto drive A. You want a copy of KARMA.DAT taken from drive A: and put onto drive B:, and a copy of PIP.COM itself, taken from B: put on A: and called LET.COM This is the sequence -

    A> B:PIP
    *B: = A:KARMA.DAT
    *A:LET.COM = B:PIP.COM
    * (just press return to 're-boot')

    A>

You can even, if you wish, make a copy of a file on the same disc as the original, provided that you give it a different name. The command could be (assuming that PIP had already been activated) -

    *B:BILL.DAT = B:FRED.DAT

4.2 PIP - The Peripheral Interchange Program

The 'fundamentals' paragraphs above show one use of PIP for simply copying files. However, as the name shows, it can do far more than that. The 'destination' can be a file, or an output peripheral, such as one of the logical devices for output (CON: PUN: LST:) or one of the physical devices. If a logical device is specified, then the output will appear on the currently assigned physical device.

Also, the source can be a file or a device, or can be a list of files, which are output to the destination as one concatenated file.

Last, there are numerous parameters which can be supplied to any PIP command, which edit the files before output, or which (as the [V] mentioned above) invoke some extra facility. These are often called the 'options'.

In all these uses of PIP, the original (the source) is not affected by the use of PIP, but the copy (the destination) is controlled by the command and any parameters added.

4.2.1 PIP with and without a command line.

If PIP (and Return) is typed, then this is an empty command line, and the PIP program is loaded, displays the * prompt, and waits for a command. When a command is completed, the * prompt is re- displayed. To exit from PIP and re-boot, another empty command line is entered (i.e. the Return is pressed, or ^ C typed as the first character of the command).

If PIP dest = source[parameter list] is typed, then PIP is invoked, the command is obeyed, and on completion, the CP/M system is re-booted automatically.

4.2.2 General forms of PIP command lines.

(After PIP is invoked, and the * prompt is on the screen)

x: = y:afn	Copy all files satisfying the afn from drive y to drive x, keeping the same names. If y is omitted, then the currently logged drive is assumed.
x:ufn = y:	Copy the file given by ufn from y to x. If x is omitted, the currently logged drive is assumed.
x:afn = y:afn	Like the above, but x and/or y may be omitted, and the logged drive is assumed for the drive(s) omitted.
ld = pd	Copy from the specified physical device to the specified logical device. Valid physical devices are TTY: CRT: UC1: PTR: PTP: UR1: UR2: UP1: UP2: LPT: UL1: Valid logical devices are CON: RDR: PUN: LST:

4.2.3 PIP destinations.

A valid destination is any filename, or a logical or physical device which can accept the file (a paper tape reader, for instance, cannot be a destination). An invalid destination will be rejected, without any 'PIP' action taking place.

x:	The drive is the destination.
x:ufn	The file stated is the destination.
x:afn	The ? or * characters are replaced with their equivalents in the source.

46

OUT: This is the user patched output device (requires modification to PIP).
CON: Currently assigned console - usually VDU.
CRT: The VDU.
UC1:   Alternative console.
LST: The currently assigned printer.
LPT: Alternative printer (line printer).
UL1:   User defined list device.
TTY: Teletype.
PRN: This is the list device, but tab characters are expanded, form feeds are obeyed, and line numbers are printed.
PTP: Paper tape punch.
UP1:   User defined punch no.1.
UP2:   User defined punch no.2.

4.2.4 PIP sources.

A valid source is a filename, a list of filenames separated by commas, or a logical or physical device. There are also two special 'pseudo-sources' (see below).

x: The drive is the source.
x:ufn   The specified file is the source.
x:afn   The set of files, each treated separately.
ufn,ufn,ufn...   The files listed, in the sequence shown, concatenated to the single destination.
INP: The user patched input device.
CON: The console.
TTY: Teletype.
CRT: The VDU console.
UC1:   Alternative console.
PTR: Paper tape reader.
UR1:   User defined reader no.1.
UR2:   User defined reader no.2.
NUL: Pseudo-source which sends 40 null characters.
EOF: Pseudo-source which sends an 'end-of-file' marker.

Any of the above devices can only be used, of course, if they exist. OUT: and INP: require patches to PIP, and the physical devices can only be referenced if the 'IOBYTE' is implemented (see section 14.5 for details of the IOBYTE). In version 3.1, the DEVICE command can switch a physical device to a desired logical device before the PIP command, and then DEVICE will switch back to the original physical device. See Chapter 3.

Note that an afn can be a *source*. All files which match the afn given will be copied, but not concatenated. They will be copied as separate files, with the same names.

4.2.5 Sample PIP commands.

PIP	Load PIP into memory and display the * command prompt.
*d: = s:filename.typ	Copy the named file from s to d.
d:newname. = s:old name.typ	Copy and rename, same type.
PIP filename.typ = s:	Copy the file from s to current drive.
PIP d:filename.typ = s:	Copy the file from s to d.
PIP d: = s:*.*	Copy all directory files from s to d.
PIP d: = s:filename.*	Copy all files of that name (s to d).
PIP d: = s:*.typ	Copy all files of that type (s to d).
PIP LST: = filename.typ	Print the named file on the current list device.
PIP PUN: = filename.typ	Send the file to the punch device.
PIP CON: = filename.typ	Display the named file on the console.
PIP filename.typ = RDR:	Copy data from reader device to file.
*newname.typ = aname.typ,bname.typ,cname.type	Copy and join together ASCII files.
*d:newname.type = s:aname.type,s:bname.typ	
*newname.typ = aname.typ[X],bname.typ[X]	Copy and join non-ASCII files) see parameters).
PIP LST: = aname.typ,bname.typ	Print files in sequence.
PIP PRN: = aname.typ,bname.typ	Print files in sequence.
PIP filename.typ = CON:	Write whatever is typed on the screen to the named file.

PIP LPT: = CON: Write whatever is typed on the
                                    screen to the line printer. This and
                                    the command above are terminated
                                    by ⌃ Z.

4.2.6 Using the PIP parameters.

We have used two parameters already, the V and the X. There are several
more, allowing you to start and/or stop at specified strings of characters, to
check the validity of the characters in the file(s), and to perform some layout
editing.

Any parameters can be used in combination - as long as the combination
makes sense - and the parameters may be separated by one or more spaces,
or may be entered one after the other with no spaces and no other separators.
The parameter or the group of parameters must be enclosed in a pair of
square brackets [], and the parameters apply only to the file which they
follow. The example of [X] above shows the parameter repeated for each file.

We will list all the parameters, including the ones which only apply to version
3.1. These are indicated with (3.1 only) after the parameter (or option) name.

[A] *Archive. (3.1 only)*. This option is used to copy only those files which have
been changed since the last copy.

[B] *Block read. (2.2 and earlier version only*.) This reads blocks from the file
(see STAT DSK: for the blocking on your hardware) and fills the memory
buffer until the ASCII 'x-off' character is detected. This is the end of block
character, put in by the system, and is the same character as the⌃ S generated
at the keyboard. As soon as a ⌃ S is detected, the memory buffer is emptied
into the destination and the next block read is initiated. This is useful, among
other things, for continuous read/write devices, with no start/stop
controlled by the system, such as a cassette player.

[C] *Confirm. (3.1 only*.) PIP displays a prompt asking for confirmation before
carrying out the copy. This is normally only used when the source filename is
ambiguous. It considerably eases the copying of a selection of files for which
no suitable afn exists, since an afn of wider scope can be specified in the
command line, and at the prompts, the final selection can be made.

[Dn] Delete characters after the 'nth'. This is used for records with a known length greater than n characters - and is effectively a 'delete all after column n'.

[E] *Echo all transfers to the console.* You can see the 'write to destination' operation being performed by adding the E to the source filename.typ

[F] *Formfeeds removed.* Whenever the formfeed character is encountered, omit it from the output to destination. This is the ASCII decimal code 12, usually listed as 'FF' (note, that is **not** the hexadecimal FF). See also the P parameter below.

[Gn] *Get the file from user n's area.* This allows you to operate in user 3, say, and copy into your user area a file from another user, say 0. That would require [G0]. (We mentioned this in connection with USER, in Chapter 2.) In CP/M version 3, this option can be used to put a file into a different users area.

[H] *Hexadecimal characters are assumed*, and PIP checks that valid hex characters only are in the file. Errors are reported on the console.

[I] *Ignore any ":00" characters in the source file*, omitting them from the output. This also checks for hex as H above.

[L] *Lower case only required.* Converts any upper case characters to lower case before output. See also U below.

[N] *Number all lines.* This adds line numbers to the output file, with leading zero suppression. See next parameter.

[N2] *Number all lines but* include leading zeros and put a 'tab' after each number, before the text.

[O] *Object files are being copied*, and the end-of-file or end- of-string character ($\wedge$ Z) is to be ignored. This is for non-ASCII files, and the $\wedge$ Z's to be ignored are those encountered when concatenating files.

[P] *Page.* This parameter inserts the formfeed character (ASCII 12) after every 60 lines of the text. This is the default form of the next parameter.

[Pn] *Page length n.* Inserts the formfeed character after every n lines of text. See the F parameter for removal.

[Qstring⌃ Z] Quit the copying process after the string (which must be terminated with the ⌃ Z character in the command) is encountered. An example could be [QChapter 4⌃ Z]. That would copy everything up to, but not including, 'Chapter 4'. A word of warning here. We said earlier that we always use upper case when giving commands to CP/M. If we used lower case, then CP/M would automatically convert them to upper case before obeying them. And there is the warning. If you want to specify a string which has lower case letters in it, as we just did, then you must have invoked PIP first, to get the * prompt, and **then** give your command with the lower case letters. PIP itself does not change lower case to upper - it is the CCP which does that. This also applies to the [S... parameter below. Notice that we have printed the⌃ and then the Z. In the command string you must put that in as a single character, by holding the control key while you hit Z. It will appear on the screen as ⌃ Z.

[R] *Read System (SYS) file(s).* This allows you to copy a SYS file (the copy will be a SYS file too) without first changing the attribute, and then changing it back after the copy. Without one or the other, the file would not be accessible to PIP.

[Sstring⌃ Z] Start the copying process with the specified string. This can be used to re-start a copying process which was interrupted for some reason (useful when copying to the LPT: or LST: device is interrupted), or to extract a section of a file, when used in combination with [Q... Notice that the string specified in a S (start) parameter **is** included in the output to the destination file/device, but the string specified in a Q (quit) parameter is **not**. Therefore the whole of Chapter 4, but none of Chapter 5, would be selected and copied with the parameters [SChapter 4⌃ ZQChapter 5⌃ Z].

[Tn] *Tabulate,* expanding the tabs from whatever are specified to every nth position (every n columns).

[U] *Upper case* is required at output to destination, all lower case characters are converted to upper case. See L above.

[V] *Verify* all copied data by comparing source and destination files. The comparison is done by reading after writing and comparing what is read with what is still in the output buffer.

[W] *Write-over* files of the specified name even if they are set to R/O. Note here that if you copy a file to a filename.typ on the destination drive which already exists and is R/W, the copy will take place, and whatever was there before will be deleted from the directory. Effectively, you will have over-written the original. In practice, you will have created a new version and the directory entry for the old on will have character 00 set to E5H. If you use the [W] parameter to over-write a protected (R/O) file, the same applies. The new file is not set to R/O if you do this. The new file actually occupies a different part of the disc than the original did, and the 'overwrite' is actually a 'write to filename.$$$ - then erase filename.typ from directory and rename .$$$ to .typ'. You may see this because the position of the file in the directory may change.

[*X*]*Copy* files which are not strings of ASCII characters. This negates the check for valid ASCII characters which is otherwise performed.

[*Z*] *Zero* the parity bit on all ASCII characters input. This may be used when you are using INP: as the input device.

And that is the full list. We mentioned in the previous chapter that there was something special about the PRN: device. Here is the explanation. If you had a text file called, say, FRED.TXT, then you could put it out onto the currently allocated list device (LST:) with line numbering, tabs every 8 columns, and page changes (formfeeds) every sixty lines, like this -

A> PIP LST: = FRED.TXT[N T8 P60]

(The parameters are separated by spaces to make them easier to read.)

The same result exactly would be achieved by using the pseudo device PRN:, like this -

A> PIP PRN: = FRED.TXT

Different page lengths, leading zeros and so on do require you to specify the full parameter list, but PRN: is very useful as a standard listing format.

4.3 Summary of PIP.

We started by looking at PIP as a simple file coying program. PIP can also be used to concatenate files, and produce a single output at the destination. ASCII files can be split, and parts of a file can be copied, together with parts of other files, if you wish. There is a powerful list of parameters which allow PIP to perform fairly complex selection and editing work. The PRN: device assumes a standard set of parameters.

PIP can be invoked without a command line, in which case the * prompt is displayed ready for a command, or the single command can follow PIP on the console, and you will be returned to CP/M after the command is obeyed. To return to CP/M when the * is on the screen, press Return, or use ^ C.

The basic format after PIP or after the * prompt is -

destination = source or source list

Files specified with ambiguous file name (afn) are treated by PIP as 'the set of files which match the afn'.

Parameters must be enclosed in square brackets [], must follow immediately after the filename to which they refer, and must be repeated for each filename as necessary, if concatenation is specified.

CHAPTER 5.

The 'Batch Processing' transients, SUBMIT and XSUB, PROFILE and GET.

5.1 Fundamentals.

All the commands which we have so far given to CP/M have been given through the keyboard. SUBMIT is a routine which, when loaded into memory, tells CP/M to take its next command from a file which we have provided, and to go on taking commands from that file until it is empty.

This allows you to process a 'batch' of commands, one after the other, without any keyboard entry.

Also, SUBMIT allows you to store one or several long or complex commands in a file, and invoke them with just a two-word command.

In CP/M 2.2, with SUBMIT on its own, the batch of commands can only be CP/M commands, not keyboard entries required by the program which the command loads. With SUBMIT and XSUB, even those commands can be built into the file (or 'batch') of commands.

In CP/M 3.1, SUBMIT contains the XSUB facility, so it is not a separate, transient, and does not need to be invoked separately. 3.1 also has a GET facility and an auto-search for a file PROFILE.SUB. We will define these at the end of this chapter. Briefly, GET acts as a temporary re-direction of the CONIN: device, taking all input from a specified file, instead of the console. PROFILE.SUB is a special form of .SUB file which gives automatic command processing whenever the system is 'booted'. PROFILE.SUB can be simulated in 2.2, as we will see.

In version 2.2, XSUB was introduced, and allows you to put into the command file, entries which are passed directly to the program you are running, not held until CP/M is invoked after the run. However, that only applies to those programs which use the BIOS Function 10 - the buffered console input. MBASIC programs do not use Function 10 - so you cannot use XSUB to pass commands from a file in response to an INPUT statement in MBASIC. However, most fully compiled or assembled and linked (.COM) programs (COMmand files) do use Function 10.

You must have SUBMIT.COM on the discs in the machine, of course, and you must also be able to create your file of commands. You could do this by using PIP, but it is normally done using the CP/M editor (ED) or one of the Word Processing packages.

The PIP command to enter text into a .SUB file through the keyboard is this -

PIP filename.SUB = CON:< Rt>

which loads PIP and then leaves the cursor at the start of a blank line on the screen. Type in your command, or your list of commands, ending each one with 'LINE FEED' **and** < Rt> . After the last command, use ^Z (Control and Z) to indicate to PIP that you have finished. That will create the file filename.SUB.

We will be discussing ED and friends in Chapter 10, so for the moment, we will assume that you can create a file. The file can be called any name you like, of course, provided that you give it the extension .SUB

To take a simple example, if you are using MBASIC (see chapter 9) and you want to have six files open simultaneously, you need to start with the command MBASIC /F:6

If your first program is called, say, START.BAS - then the command to enter that program automatically becomes -

MBASIC START /F:6

If you forget the /F:6 and your program tries to open a file with a number greater than the initial allocation (usually 3), the program will halt and the only way to continue is to return to CP/M. Irritating. Use SUBMIT to avoid that problem.

Set up a file which has just the instruction we looked at in it -

    MBASIC START /F:6

and call it SPECIAL.SUB (or some other name of your choice.)

Now to run the program, you type in SUBMIT SPECIAL< Rt> and CP/M will load SUBMIT, then take the instruction from the .SUB file (and show it on the screen) and obey it.

The screen would look like this -

    A> SUBMIT SPECIAL

    A> MBASIC START /F:6

    BASIC Rev. 5.01
    [CP/M Version]
    Copyright 1977, 78, 79 (C) by Microsoft
    Created ..... etc.
    etc.
    - - and the program START.BAS is loaded and runs.

5.2 Using XSUB with SUBMIT.

If the XSUB program is also invoked, then the list of commands must start with XSUB. XSUB is seldom invoked alone, and if it is invoked, it is always the first of the commands in a .SUB file. It is loaded into memory, and stays there for the duration of that SUBMIT run. You can then mix commands as appropriate.

As we said earlier in the chapter, you cannot use XSUB with interpreted programs in MBASIC, so to illustrate XSUB, we will use a different illustration.

Let us say that you have formatted and 'sysgen'ed some new discs, and you want to copy onto them four of the CP/M transient commands. One way would be to invoke PIP, and then, in response to the * prompt, to enter each name in turn. However, it would really be quite convenient to enter the names once, and once only, and to let SUBMIT do the copying for you.

You could create a file, let us call it PIPSTATS.SUB, containing the following

```
XSUB
PIP
B: = A:PIP.COM
B: = A:STAT.COM
B: = A:SUBMIT.COM
B: = A:XSUB.COM
B: = A:PIPSTATS.SUB
```

Note here that although you actually want to finish the commands with an extra < Rt> , to re-boot from PIP, you cannot, because a file (.SUB) which ends in two < Rt> s exits back to CP/M without doing anything useful.

If you now use that file in a SUBMIT statement, you will copy all the five named files - including the .SUB file itself - from the disc in A: to the disc in B:, regardless of what else was on the A: disc.

This is what it will look like on the screen -

```
A> SUBMIT PIPSTATS

A> XSUB

A> PIP

*B: = A:PIP.COM

*B: = A:STAT.COM

*B: = A:SUBMIT.COM

*B: = A:XSUB.COM

*B: = A:PIPSTATS.SUB

* - and at this point you press < Rt> to re-boot CP/M

A>
```

If you were copying the five files to several discs, you would change the disc in B: before pressing < Rt> , otherwise changing the disc would set the new one to R/O. (But version 3.1 would not set the disc to R/O.) Then you would simply repeat the SUBMIT PIPSTATS command.

5.3 Putting a run-time PARAMETER in SUBMIT.

Any of the commands or part commands in the .SUB file can take the form $1 $2 $3 and so on. These are variables, meaningless as they stand, but given a value at the time SUBMIT is run. To give the values, you follow the SUBMIT command with the actual value to be inserted instead of the $1 $2 etc. Logically, the first value entered in the command is put into $1, the second into $2 and so on.

The way it is done is that SUBMIT creates a temporary file called $$$.SUB, with the actual values in, and CP/M (etc) uses that as its source of commands. SUBMIT also deletes the $$$.SUB file after the last command is obeyed, but does not delete the original .SUB file. That is preserved. We will mention that $$$.SUB file again towards the end of the chapter.

To continue with our example, we might want to put in the name of another file, perhaps an MBASIC program, at the time we enter the SUBMIT command. Our file called PIPSTATS.SUB now looks like this

```
XSUB
PIP
B: = A:PIP.COM
B: = A:STAT.COM
B: = A:SUBMIT.COM
B: = A:XSUB.COM
B: = A:PIPSTATS.SUB
B: = A:$1.BAS
```

To include the program JOBCOST.BAS in the copying, the command becomes SUBMIT PIPSTATS JOBCOST< RT>

The $$$.SUB file is created, with the commands in reverse order, and with other significant characters, as we will see. It is that $$$.SUB file which is actually used. The .SUB file contains JOBCOST.BAS instead of $1.BAS.

The parameter does not have to 'stand alone', it can be just part of a command line, as you see. If the whole of the identity of the extra file to be copied was unknown until the time of copying, the last line of the file would be B: = A:$1 instead of B: = A:$1.BAS - and then the full filename.typ (the ufn) would be used in the SUBMIT command.

To stop a sequence of commands, type RUBOUT (DELETE) as soon as the next command is echoed onto the screen.

The CCP itself will terminate a sequence if it finds an error, or a missing parameter.

For a continuous operation sequence, make the last command in the file (.SUB) a repeat of the SUBMIT command ! That will simply re-start the sequence from the top of the list. (Gets complicated if you also have parameters in the list !)

5.4 Making a 2.2 program disc into an 'auto-start' system.

If you create a file $$$.SUB, in the right format, then as soon as you re-boot that disc, (must be in A drive), the command line contained will be obeyed immediately, as though SUBMIT had created it. You do not even need to have SUBMIT on the disc ! The format - and we will concentrate on a single command line because that is all you need for 'auto-start' - is that the first character of the file must contain a value equal to or greater than the number of characters (in hex) in the command. For simplicity, put a 'space' character there. That give you up to 32 characters in your command. Then the command follows, and finally there must be at least one 'null' - 00H - to stop the CCP from reading beyond your command.

A $$$.SUB file is normally a maximum of 128 characters long, so a small MBASIC program to create a $$$.SUB file on drive B: would be like this -

```
10 PRINT"ENTER THE COMMAND FOR THE 'AUTO-START' FILE -";
20 LINE INPUT B$:IF LEN(B$)>32 THEN 10
30 A$ = " "
40 C$ = STRING$(95,CHR$(0))
50 OEN"O",#1,"B:$$$.SUB"
60 PRINT#1,A$;B$;C$
70 PRINT"THE DISC IN B: NOW HAS YOUR $$$.SUB FILE ON IT,"
80 PRINT"CONTAINING THE COMMAND - ";B$
90 CLOSE:END
```

This will allow you to put in a command such as -

BASIC START /F:6/S:256

or just -

BASIC

or the name of a .COM file, without the .COM, say -

PIP

When you have run that program, take the disc out of B: and put it into A: and reboot. The A> will appear, and then your command, and it will be obeyed. The one thing that you **must not** do, is to exit to CP/M. If you do, the CCP knows that it has used your $$$.SUB file and it will be deleted. However, if you do not exit to CP/M (if SYSTEM does not appear in your programs) the $$$.SUB file will remain, ready to auto-start the next time you boot to that disc. Even without SUBMIT !

5.5 Making a 3.1 disc into an 'auto-start' system.

Easy. Create a file called PROFILE.SUB, with an editor, or with PIP as we showed earlier. No complicated 'first character' or 'null' characters. The CCP will automatically treat a PROFILE.SUB file as though you had typed SUBMIT PROFILE at the keyboard. And it will not be deleted when you re-boot. But it will be re-entered if you re-boot, so unless you have a series of commands in your PROFILE.SUB, you might as well not bother to re- boot.

5.6 SUMMARY

SUBMIT allows use of a file of commands (one or several) which are contained in a .SUB file, and are extracted from the file and used instead of keyboard entered commands until the list is exhausted. XSUB entered in the file as the first of such a list of commands also allows you to incorporate keyboard commands or inputs which are required by the program which the command invoked (ie not CP/M commands). XSUB stays in memory for the whole of a SUBMIT sequence, so it does not need to be re-invoked if CP/M and program inputs are mixed. XSUB is part of SUBMIT in version 3.1, so must not be invoked.

Parameters may be entered in a .SUB file using $1 $2 etc, and these are replaced by the values which you enter at the keyboard after the .SUB filename, separated from the filename and each other by spaces.

You can use a parameter in any position, and the use or not of parameters is entirely independent of the use of XSUB.

Clearly, if your file contains $1, $2, $3 etc, then you must supply the values which are to replace these when you SUBMIT the file. If you do not supply them, the CCP will terminate the SUBMIT run.

You may use as many parameters as you need, and you are not even prevented from using an actual $ sign as part of a command, not as a parameter. To do that, simply put two $ symbols, i.e. $$, and they will be interpreted as a single $. (eg If one of your filenames happened to be TEMP.$$$ then you could include it in a SUB file by entering TEMP.$$$$$$)

To escape from a .SUB sequence, type RUBOUT or DELETE as soon as the next command appears on the screen.

Alternatively, if one program in a sequence detects an error from which it cannot recover, the sequence can be terminated by the program ERASing (or KILLing etc) the $$$.SUB file. It is unwise to allow the program to ERAse a filename.SUB file, unless you have a back-up copy (filename.BAK, perhaps). Make sure that you indicate clearly on the screen when there has been an early termination due to a fault !

We submit (!) that this command is probably one of the most powerful available under CP/M - because it contains the potential for fully automatic processing.

PROFILE.SUB is the CP/M 3.1 'auto-start' file, and you can simulate it by creating a $$$.SUB file.

CHAPTER SIX

Creating and controlling CP/M's operation.

6.1 Fundamentals.

For the user of CP/M 2.2 and earlier, the sections on SYSGEN and MOVCPM are fundamental, but the following sections do not apply at all.

For the user of 3.1, the sections on COPYSYS, INITDIR and SET, GET and PUT, SETDEF and GENCOM are equally fundamental.

Users of 3.1 and users of some implementations of version 2.2 will have the DATE command, which will be found at the end of this chapter.

Since CP/M 2.2 and earlier versions work with a maximum memory size of 64k, but can work with smaller memories, the MOVCPM command allows you to create a CP/M system to fit your memory exactly. Having created it, you can then use SYSGEN to copy it onto the system track(s) of any disc.

CP/M 3.1 works with 'banked' memory, as we will see later in Chapter 11, so there is no direct equivalent to the MOVCPM command. However, COPYSYS is similar to SYSGEN, allowing you to copy the system track(s).

INITDIR and SET are the commands which prepare for, and then initiate, the date stamping and password protection available only under 3.1.

GET and PUT re-direct console input and console or printer output to specified files, as needed. Again, this is applies only to version 3.1.

SETDEF allows you to tell CP/M to search on more than one disc for a program or command - and to indicate the search order.

GENCOM allows you to add special system extensions - such as a graphics extension - to your command files, so that they will be loaded when your command is obeyed, and then act as part of the BIOS, but do not have to be resident when you do not require them. This is yet another way of reducing the resident portion of CP/M without sacrificing any facilities which a program may need. SETDEF and GENCOM are commands in version 3.1 only.

The command descriptions now follow in the sequence in which we have listed them above.

SYSGEN (versions up to 2.2)

Before a disc can be used to load the operating system (to 'boot' or to 're-boot'), the operating system must be in position on the first track (0) or the first two tracks (0 and 1), depending on your discs. You have a disc with your system which is the CP/M master disc. Put it into drive A, and type

SYSGEN< Rt>

The program (a transient command) is loaded, and announces itself with SYSGEN VERSION 2.0 (or whatever version you have).

Then it asks where it is to take the 'system' from with the question

SOURCE DRIVE NAME (OR RETURN TO SKIP)

(This question will be suppressed if you supply SYSGEN with a filename from which the system is to be loaded - the command is SYSGEN CPMxx.COM< Rt> - and xx is the CP/M version.)

Your operating system is in the memory and is on the disc in A (but see the MOVCPM command below). Answer with the single letter A to tell SYSGEN to take the system from the disc. (Or if the actual system which you want is on a disc in another drive, then give the letter of that drive.)

Now the program allows you to change disc if you want to by asking you to put the required disc in A (or wherever you said) and the screen shows

SOURCE ON x THEN TYPE RETURN

where x is the letter you entered. If you did not enter a drive name, but pressed RETURN in answer to the first question, this instruction (SOURCE ON etc.) is skipped.

When you have pressed return, the next message shown is

FUNCTION COMPLETE

This tells you that CP/M has been loaded into memory from the disc, and immediately the next prompt appears

DESTINATION DRIVE NAME (RETURN TO REBOOT)

You can abandon the operation at this point by pressing < Rt> , but usually you want SYSGEN to create the operating system on a new disc. The new disc can be in any drive - you can take the master disc out of A at this stage, if you want to, and use drive A to create new initialised discs. However, let us assume that you want to initialise new discs in drive B. You press B, and the prompt invites you to put the new disc in B (it is probably there already !) by displaying

DESTINATION IN B THEN PRESS RETURN

(or if you pressed some other letter - that will be shown).

Put the disc in B, press < Rt> and the program will write the operating system (CP/M) onto the first track(s) of the disc in B. When that is completed, the screen displays

FUNCTION COMPLETE

and immediately offers you the opportunity to SYSGEN another disc, with the prompt

DESTINATION DRIVE NAME (OR RETURN TO REBOOT)

At this point the disc in B has the system on it. If you want to SYSGEN a box full of discs, then press B again, change the newly initialised disc in B for a blank one, and reply with < Rt> to the repeated prompt

DESTINATION IN B THEN PRESS RETURN

Continue like this for as many discs as you want to initialise. When you have no more to do, press < Rt> in answer to the DRIVE NAME question, and the system will re-boot from drive A. To SYSGEN a number of discs quickly, take the source disc out of A after the first 'FUNCTION COMPLETE', and then flip-flop between B and A as the Destination drive names. You will be able to change a disc in the drive which is **not** the destination in the time it takes to carry out the SYSGEN.

6.2.1 What SYSGEN does (and doesn't do).

The sequence of operations which you have just completed has taken a copy of the operating system from a disc, loaded it into memory, and then written it onto the first track(s) of the discs which you put in drive B (in our example). All other tracks are completely untouched by SYSGEN. If the disc had files on it, they are still there, unaffected.

CP/M can be constructed in a form which will use a limited amount of memory - or the whole of your available memory (random access memory, or 'ram'). Also, CP/M can have various different options, like the speed at which data is transferred through the 'ports' (the connection sockets used for printers etc.).

You can quite easily have one particular configuration of CP/M which you are **using**, and a different configuration that you are **copying**. SYSGEN only uses the source which you tell it to use, and puts that system configuration onto the destination discs which you nominate, and does not affect anything else.

You do not need to have CP/M on a disc, provided you will not want to 'boot' from it. If discs have not been 'SYSGENned', then they obviously cannot be the source of a 'boot' or 'reboot' command. In fact, of course, the track(s) used to record CP/M are not actually available to you for any other purpose. You cannot put your own files onto them. So you do not 'waste space' by having CP/M on all discs.

If you have several different 'current' versions of CP/M or different configurations to drive special peripherals - even different printers - you may prefer to keep your CP/M initialised discs separate, labelled appropriately, and leave the first track(s) of all your program and data discs blank, so that you only load the version/configuration of CP/M which you want, when you want it.

6.3 MOVCPM (versions up to 2.2)

Some of the 'resident' part of CP/M is at the 'bottom' of memory (the lowest numbered locations, starting at 0000H) and the rest, the majority, is at the 'top' of memory, in the highest numbered locations.

We mentioned above that CP/M can be tailored to fit the memory you have available. This is one of the jobs that MOVCPM does. The other job which MOVCPM does is to create an actual file called CPMxx.COM (where xx is the version number) within the data area of the disc, so that it can be modified to suit some special hardware requirement. Two jobs, two parameters.

When you invoke MOVCPM, you add two parameters, separated by spaces. The first is either a number (the memory size in 'kilobyes') or an *. If you have a 32k version of CP/M, and a 48k memory, then either of these commands

        MOVCPM *< Rt>
        MOVCPM 48< Rt>

will take the version you have, re-locate it in memory so as to use the whole of the available space, and then wait for your next command (which would probably be SYSGEN - to put that version from memory onto a disc, from where it can be 'booted').

The second parameter was omitted, in those two commands. That second parameter has only one permitted value - the *. So to use MOVCPM to take all available memory, and to take a copy on a file in the data area, you would enter

        MOVCPM * *< Rt>

That would result in the message

        "SAVE 32 CPMxx.COM"

which tells you how to create CP/M on the file CPMxx.COM - and xx is the version number. This is the file image which you would load with SYSGEN CPMxx.COM, as we noted earlier. You enter the SAVE command exactly as it is shown. CP/M (up to version 2.2, remember) occupies 32 pages of 256 bytes, or 8k bytes. Make sure that you have that much space available on the destination disc. If the disc on which you want to store the new version is not in the default drive, you can put the drive letter before the filename as usual.

6.3.1 Summary of MOVCPM.

MOVCPM< Rt> results in the loading of CP/M unchanged in size, and CP/M then 'executes'. That is, the A> appears. Your original CP/M is unaltered, and is the same as the one in memory.

MOVCPM *< Rt> results in the loading of CP/M, relocated to take advantage of the whole of the available memory, and again CP/M 'executes', giving the A>. Your original version is unchanged, and there is no copy of the new CP/M. To copy it into the 'operating system track(s)', you would use SYSGEN.

MOVCPM * *< Rt> is the same as the previous one, but you are invited to "SAVE" the new CP/M by creating a file.

You can use MOVCPM to (say) create a smaller version which can be used on your machine with less memory allocated. This might be useful to simulate the operation of some software which you have produced, on a smaller machine. What you can not do is to produce a 'brand new' CP/M with a different serial number in it. CP/M owes its existence to the fact that many people buy it !

6.4 Summary of SYSGEN and MOVCPM, the commands up to version 2.2.

SYSGEN takes either the version of CP/M currently in memory, the version in a specified file, or the version on the first track(s) of a disc in a drive which you nominate, and copies it onto the first track(s) of one or several discs in a nominated drive. It is then available on those discs for 'boot' or 'reboot' operations.

MOVCPM loads CP/M into memory, relocating it to suit the stated or available memory, and offers the opportunity to file it within the data area of a disc, ready for 'user patching' (see Chapter 15). The use of MOVCPM *< Rt> before SYSGEN makes sure that the CP/M which goes onto the 'operating system' tracks is relocated to utilise the whole of the memory available, if a smaller version (say) was provided initially. MOVCPM * *< Rt> is the command required to obtain the invitation to file CP/M. If the second parameter is to be used, the first must also be present. The first parameter only, or none, may be used.

6.5 COPYSYS. (version 3.1)

The command in version 3.1 to copy the system track(s) from one disc to another is COPYSYS. There are no 'options' - the command is entered as the single word. Your system will be provided with a 'master disc' – and after formatting a new disc if that is needed for your hardware, you will put use COPYSYS to put the system on the first track(s) of that new disc.

Since the system track(s) may not be used for any other purpose, there is no reason not to put the 'system' onto those tracks, unless you are using a 'package' which needs data discs that are never used in drive A, and therefore are never used to 'boot' the system.

6.6 INITDIR and SET. (version 3.1)

Since version 3.1 has a facility to carry two date and time stamps and a password for each file, you need to set up the directory on a disc in a form which can accept those extra items. Unless you have used INITDIR, you cannot use SET, and you cannot use the date stamps and password.

The command is either -

INITDIR< Rt>

which initialises the directory on the logged (default) drive, or

INITDIR d:< Rt>

which does the same thing on the disc in the specifed drive.

The response to the command (if you had specified drive B:, say) is -

INITDIR WILL ACTIVATE TIME-STAMPS FOR SPECIFIED DRIVE.
Do you want to reformat the directory on B: (Y/N)?

and you enter Y or N as appropriate. However - all that INITDIR does is to make space available. It does not actually start the 'stamping'. To do that you need to use SET and one of the options available.

SET itself can take several forms, depedent on what you want to do. As we said, it can initiate password protection and date stamping of **files**.

SET can also change the **drive or file** attributes to Read-Write, Read-Only, DIR and SYS.

SET allows you to label a disc and password protect the label.

We will start with the labelling and password protection of a **disc**.

A label has the same rules exactly as a filename, and may have a 'type' suffix. If you want to label the default drive, you omit the drive name and the colon - but note its position if you want to specify a particular drive. To put 'CPMBOOK2.TXT' as the label on a disc in drive B:, you would enter -

SET B: [NAME = CPMBOOK2.TXT]< Rt>

To apply password protection to that same disc, (a password is up to 8 characters, as we saw in Chapter 2), you choose your password - we will choose the password 'JME' for our illustration - you enter -

SET B: [PASSWORD = JME]< Rt>

If you are putting the password protection on the default drive, you omit the drive letter, of course. The closing square bracket can also be omitted, if you wish.

To **remove** password protection from a disc, you simply press 'Return' after the equals sign, like this -

SET B: [PASSWORD = < Rt>

Now we can look at password protection of **files**.

First, before you can assign passwords, you must switch password protection on. You do this with the command -

SET [PROTECT = ON]

To disable file password protection, the command is -

SET [PROTECT = OFF]

as you might expect !

To assign a password to a file, simply give the filespec, and specify the password as we showed it for use with a disc, like this -

SET filespec [PASSWORD = password]

To remove a password from a file, you cannot use the 'PASSWORD = < Rt> ' which we showed above for discs, instead you use this command -

SET filespec [PROTECT = NONE]

69

Now we come to the **levels** of password protection which are available. If you simply want to prevent deletion of a file unless the password is given, or to prevent re-naming of the file unless the password is given, use this command -

SET filespec [PROTECT = DELETE]

or combine the specification of the password with that same level of protection, like this -

SET filespec [PASSWORD = password, PROTECT = DELETE]

However, you can add another level of protection, to prevent the file from being altered in any way without use of the password. This is the 'WRITE' protection. If you set WRITE protection, then anyone who wants to write to the file, or to re-name or delete it, must give the correct password. The command is -

SET filespec [PROTECT = WRITE]

The highest level of protection also prevents anyone (any program, or any console user) from READING the file, unless the password is given. If you set READ protection, then all file manipulations, reading, copying, writing, re-naming or deletion will be blocked unless you include the password in the full filespec. The command to set this level of protection is -

SET filespec [PROTECT = READ]

The filespec can be an afn. If you are logged onto drive A, to protect all files of type TXT with the password KEEPIT, at the lowest protection level, on drive B, the command would be -

A> SET B:*.TXT [PASSWORD = KEEPIT, PROTECT = DELETE]

or you could log onto B: and get the same result exactly with -

B> SET *.TXT [PASSWORD = KEEPIT, PROTECT = DELETE]

So now you can set password protection for a disc or a file, and you can label a disc. We indicated, back in Chapter 2, how to include a password in a filespec, but it is worth repeating here, now that you know how to get the password onto the file. To include a password in a filespec, you put a semicolon after the name and type (if any) and then the password. These are all valid filespecs including passwords - in each case, the password follows the semicolon (;).

MYPROG.BAS;JME
JOBCOST;SECURE
C:CPMBOOK3.TXT;HIDDEN

For any of these, one of the levels of security will apply, dependent on which you have allocated, with 'PROTECT = '.

There are two more areas in which SET is used, one we mentioned briefly in Chapter 3, for setting 'attributes', and the other for defining what the date-stamping is to be. There is a range of available attributes, so we'll look at those first.

Each of the attributes listed is used in square brackets, after the 'SET filespec' part of the command. Several attributes may be set in one command, they are simply listed within the square brackets, with commas as separators. These are the attributes -

RO   Set the file to Read Only
RW   Set the file to Read/Write

(Note that password protection is applied in addition to these, so that it would be quite possible to have a file with RW attribute, but with password protection to prevent deletion without the correct password. Setting a file to RO will stop anyone from writing to the file, even if they have the right password.)

SYS   Set the file attribute to SYS
DIR   Set the file attribute back to DIR

(Those we referred to in Chapter 3)

ARCHIVE = OFF   means that the file has not been 'backed-up' (or archived).

ARCHIVE = ON   means that the file has been 'backed-up'. You can turn the ARCHIVE attribute on directly by SET, as we are showing it here, or by using the [A] option with PIP as we showed in Chapter 4. If you copy a file with PIP, using the [A] option, then the file you copy from will have the ARCHIVE attibute set ON.

There are four user-definable attributes which can also be switched on or off. The attributes are known to CP/M 3.1 as F1, F2, F3 and F4, and are set ON or OFF with ' = ON' or ' = OFF'. These are examples -

71

F1 = ON
F3 = OFF

Just as with all the rest of the attributes we are discussing here, you enclose the attribute in square brackets after the filespec. This is an example of a full command, setting several attributes -

A> SET INITIAL.BAS [RO SYS F1 = ON F4 = OFF]

Note that the attribute list is separated by spaces.

The last of the functions of the SET command is the initiation of date-stamping. (Sometimes called 'time-stamping'. The time **and** date are recorded.)

These are three possible time/date stamps which you can choose, but only two may be applied to one file. CREATE and ACCESS are mutually exclusive - turning one on, turns the other off. In each case, as you will see, the command is completed with the ' = ON', and that is necessary in the command.

Each of the three is specified for a **drive** - and therefore for the whole disc in that drive. You cannot set time/date stamping for a single file on a disc - all the files are handled in the same way on that disc. Therefore, the command does not and may not include a filespec - but it may include a drive letter and colon.

CREATE = ON   If this is set on, then when a new file is created, the time/date stamp is marked in the directory for the file. This is not updated, because it is inherently a 'one-off'. It cancels ACCESS if that was set previously.

ACCESS = ON   If this is set, it cancels CREATE, if that was set previously. Whenever the file is opened, whether for 'read' or 'write', the ACCESS time/date stamp is updated.

UPDATE = ON   This is independent of the previous two, and records the time/date on which the file was last altered. The alteration could be writing to any record in the file, or increasing or reducing the length of the file.

There is one final use of SET which we did mention in Chapter 3, but which we include here for completeness, and that is the use of SET to make a disc

Read-Only, or Read-Write. RO set this way is a temporary condition, reset to RW by re-booting. The command may have a drive letter, or the default drive is assumed. the command forms are -

SET [RO]
SET C: [RW]
SET B: [RO]

It is worth mentioning again here the fact that although versions 2.2 and earlier would detect a changed medium, and would set the disc RO attribute automatically, version 3.1 does not set the medium to RO - but does prevent any further access to files which were open on the first disc when the disc itself was removed and replaced.

6.7 GET and PUT.

GET tells the system to take console input from a file for the next system command, or user program enterd ar the console.

PUT tells the system to direct its console or printer output (you specify which) to a file until the next program terminates.

Both GET and PUT have ECHO/NO ECHO and SYSTEM options, and there is a FILTER/NO FILTER option on PUT, so we will cover the options first.

ECHO	means that console input or output are displayed at the console - this is the normal condition, the default. If it is used with a 'PUT to printer' command, then printer output is also echoed to the console.
NO ECHO	tells the system not to echo console or printer (as stated) input or output to the console. This is the default in a 'PUT to printer' command.
SYSTEM	in a GET command means that all system input is immediately taken from the file specified, and the system continues to take input from the file until the file is empty, or until another GET is encountered in the file itself.

73

SYSTEM	in a PUT command intercepts any system output to the console, and re-directs it to the same file as that specified in the command. The system output will continue to be directed to the file until another PUT CONSOLE command re-intates the usual condition.
FILTER	is used in a PUT command if you want control characters to be recorded in printable form. For instance, if FILTER is on, an 'ESCAPE' character will be translated into ◄[so that it can be recognised, but not acted on during the transfer to file.
NO FILTER	switches FILTER off, and is the default, and means that any control characters are passed into the file exactly as received.

The full GET command is -

GET CONSOLE INPUT FROM FILE filespec

or -

GET CONSOLE INPUT FROM CONSOLE

but the words 'CONSOLE INPUT FROM' may be, and usually are, omitted. The command is therefore

GET FILE ... or
GET CONSOLE

Examples will show more clearly the use of the command.

A> GET FILE DATAINP< Rt>
A> EXECPROG< Rt>

This shows that console input is to be taken from the file DATAINP, but not until the program which expects console input has been loaded and run. Any request for console input in the program EXECPROG will be answered with data from DATAINP. If DATAINP has no more data, EXECPROG is redirected to the console. When EXECPROG ends, the system reverts to console input, whether DATAINP is all 'used' or not.

A> GET FILE DATAINP [SYSTEM]< Rt>

It may reasonably be assumed that DATAINP in this case contains a valid command at the start of file - because the 'SYSTEM' option has told the system to go immediately to DATAINP for its next console input.

74

GET CONSOLE

This may be included in a file to re-direct the system back to the console for console input even though the file may not be empty, and/or the program may not have terminated.

Because the default is 'ECHO', you would expect to see the command echoed on the screen, like this -

```
A> GET FILE DATAINP [SYSTEM]
A> GET CONSOLE
A>
```

If you included 'NO ECHO', you would get this -

```
A> GET FILE DATAINP [NO ECHO,SYSTEM]
A>
```

And the system would wait for your input.

Now for the PUT command. There are the two types of command, one for the console, the other for the printer. In the PUT command, you can omit the words 'OUTPUT TO', but in fact you will probably find it easier to include them, so that the command is more understandable to you ! The commands, two for the console and two for the printer, allow you to redirect output to a file, like this -

```
PUT CONSOLE OUTPUT TO FILE filespec
PUT PRINTER OUTPUT TO FILE filespec
```

or to direct it back to the original device like this -

```
PUT CONSOLE OUTPUT TO CONSOLE
PUT PRINTER OUTPUT TO PRINTER
```

The ECHO option is the default for PUT CONSOLE... commands, and the NO ECHO option is the default for PUT PRINTER... commands.

The NO FILTER option is the default for PUT PRINTER commands, as we said when we listed the options above.

The SYSTEM option for the PUT commands means that system output as well as program output is written to the file. PUT CONSOLE CONSOLE cancels the SYSTEM option.

The examples below illustrate common commands.

A> PUT CONSOLE OUTPUT TO FILE PROGOUT [NO ECHO]

Note that you do not need to use [ECHO] in a PUT CONSOLE... command, because that is the automatic default. The above command would put anything which the program displays at the console onto a file called PROGOUT instead. The file could have a full filespec, such as B:PROGOUT.TXT;SECRET, if that was needed.

A> PUT PRINTER OUTPUT TO FILE PROGOUT.DAT
A> START

The output from program START would be filed instead of printed. Because this is a PRINTER command, there is no ECHO to the console, unless you specify it as an option. There is no FILTER in operation, either.

A> PUT PRINTED OUTPUT TO FILE PROGOUT2.DAT[ECHO,SYSTEM]
A> THISPROG

Here you have a command which directs the output of THISPROG to the file, and echos it to the console. All system output is also put on the file and echoed to the console. This stays in effect until you enter a system command PUT PRINTER TO PRINTER.

6.8 SETDEF. (version 3.1 only)

One of the minor restrictions with versions 2.2 and earlier is that the system requires a single drive to be specified for any file which is to be opened. This could be the default drive, or could be explicit. Version 3.1 allows you to define a list of up to four drives which will be searched for the filename specified. Also, version 3.1 allows you to specify two filetypes, so that a filename of the first type will be sought, and if it is not found, then a file of the same name, but with the second type will be sought and opened if found.

Also, in versions up to 2.2, the SUBMIT command always created its special $$$.SUB file on drive A, the 'boot' drive. This was almost always a 'floppy disc', and was therefore much slower than, say a Winchester disc or M-disc (see Chapter 11), which would have a different drive letter. Version 3.1 allows you to specify onto which drive the 'temporary' files (like $$$.SUB) are to be created.

To help you to keep track of what the system is doing, you can direct version 3.1 to display the identities of all programs loaded, and any 'submit' files executed.

When you have a reasonably fast console display, it can be mildly irritating to have information which is being displayed, and which you therefore presumably want to read, scrolled off the top of the screen, before you have chance to see it. Version 3.1 can set the console into 'PAGE' mode, which always fills a screen page (which you can define with the DEVICE command, Chapter 3) and then wait for you to release it, before accepting the next page, and so on.

All these facilities are available through the SETDEF command.

> A> SETDEF [PAGE] and
> A> SETDEF [NOPAGE]

turn the console 'page at a time' feature on and off.

> A> SETDEF [DISPLAY] and
> A> SETDEF [NO DISPLAY]

turn the 'trace program and submit files on the screen' feature on and off.

To set a particular drive (say drive M:) as the one to which temporary files (like $$$.SUB) are to be sent, you enter the command -

> A> SETDEF [TEMPORARY = M:]

For the type search order, the command (which must not have more than two 'types' in it) is like this -

> A> SETDEF [ORDER = (SUB,COM)]

This will look for a file of type SUB first (instead of type COM, which is what it would normally look for, and then, if it does not find one, look for a type COM. If your executable command files were all of type JME, for some reason, you would want the system to search for them, not for type COM files. So you would first enter -

> A> SETDEF [ORDER = (JME)]

and then, if your command file was called SPECIAL.JME, you could type in

> A> SPECIAL< Rt>

and SPECIAL.JME would be found, loaded and executed.

Finally, to define a search order for the system, you simply list the drives (up to 4) with commas between, after the SETDEF. You can even use * as 'the default drive'.

A> SETDEF C:,B:,A:

will tell the system to search for your command file (program name) on drives C, then if it is not there, B, and if it is not there either, try A.

Once you have set the search order, it stays in operation even though you may change logged drives, so you can enter -

A> SETDEF C:,*

to tell the system to search C first, then the default drive. If the default drive stays at A as shown, that drive will be searched. However, if you changed to B, and then gave this command -

B> FINDPROG< Rt>

the system would look first on C for FINDPROG.COM (or whatever ORDER you have set) and then on B: - because the SETDEF included the * for the default drive.

6.9 GENCOM. (version 3.1 only)

There are some RSX modules (Resident System eXtensions) which are needed as resident parts of the system when they are in use, but which occupy space in the memory which is best released, when the modules are not needed. There is a 'graphics' module, for example. They are handled by BDOS calls, from the resident BIOS, so they must be 'attached' to the BDOS up at the 'top' of memory, when they are needed.

Version 3.1 has a mechanism for creating special COM files which include not only the COM program itself, but also a 'header' to tell CP/M that there is an RSX attached, and the RSX itself.

The mechanism is the GENCOM command. Examples will show the use of the command and its options. We will call our COM program MAINPROG and the RSX modules PROG1 PROG2 etc.

A> GENCOM MAINPROG PROG1 PROG2

This command will create a new version of com-filespec, with the same name, but with the necessary header and with the two (in this case) RSX modules attached, in the same file. Now, when you give the command, you will automatically load the RSX modules with the program.

To re-instate the original version of MAINPROG, without the header and RSX's, we simply enter -

A> GENCOM MAINPROG

This strips off the additional items.

If we have a new version of PROG1, say, and perhaps another RSX, we could take the already 'GENCOMmed' version of MAINPROG and repeat the command, adding the third RSX, like this -

A> GENCOM MAINPROG PROG1 PROG2 PROG3

Even though MAINPROG already has the header etc, GENCOM will look at MAINPROG, rebuild the header to take the third RSX into account, and will replace the existing PROG1 and PROG2 with the ones on disc as separate modules, and will add the new PROG3.

You do not even have to have a MAINPROG. GENCOM will create a file with a header and an RSX (or more than one) if you indicate that there is no MAINPROG with the NULL option, like this -

A> GENCOM PROG1 PROG2 [NULL]

This creates the dummy COM file with the two RSX's in it, and calls it PROG1.

There are two further options, 'LOADER' and 'SCB = '. The first tells CP/M to keep the program loader active after completing the creation of the file with the RSX's specified. The second (SCB =) allows you to set the System Control Block from your program, by taking the values from the command line. The command would be, say, -

A> GENCOM MAINPROG PROG1 [SCB = (offset,value)]

The purpose and use of the SCB will be shown in Part Three, from Chapter 11 onwards.

Any of these options is enclosed in square brackets, as shown. The principal use of GENCOM is the one we started with - the creation or dismantling of a

79

file which allows RSX modules to be loaded with the program, without any special command at run time.

There is a command loosely related to the ones we have covered in this chapter, called PATCH, but we will be covering the CP/M assemblers in Chapter 8, so we will come back to that one in due course.

CHAPTER SEVEN

DUMP, LOAD, DDT and SID

7.1 DUMP

DUMP is a program (or a transient command if you prefer) which will take any
named file, and display the contents on the monitor. Versions 1.4 and 2.2
display the file content in 'hexadecimal' only, but Version 3.1 displays the
content in both 'hex' and ASCII. If 'Control P' (ˆP) is used first, you will also
get a printout. At the 'fundamental' level, you may not wish to get involved in
'hex', or in programs or files held in that way. If you do want to use it, the
commands are -

DUMP ufn (display the content of the file ufn in hex)
DUMP d:ufn (as above, but the file from drive d:)
DUMP d:*.typ (display the first file in the directory of .typ)

The display - or printout - can be stopped with any of the
Delete/Backspace/Rubout keys. That returns you to CP/M. A temporary
stop is achieved with ˄ S as for many other 'rolling screen' commands. (And
any other key - such as ˄ S again - to restart.)

So DUMP allows you to inspect any file/program on the screen. The layout of
the 'hex' display is illustrated below.

```
0000  21  00  00  39  22  15  02  31  57  02  CD  C1  01  FE  FF  C2
0010  1B  01  11  F3  01  CD  9C  01  C3  51  01  3E  80  32  13  02
0020  21  00  00  E5 etc.
```

The four digits on the left (our italics, not 'DUMP's) are a byte count - the
number of the first byte on that line, numbering from zero at the beginning of

81

the file. The counting is also done in 'hex', so the rows are numbered --- 0080 0090 00A0 00B0 etc.

Then the contents of the first sixteen bytes are shown in 'hex'. The next row has the next sixteen and so on.

7.2 LOAD and HEXCOM

Versions 1.4 and 2.2 of CP/M use the 'LOAD' transient, version 3.1 uses the HEXCOM transient. They fulfil exactly the same function. We will refer to LOAD, but you could substitute HEXCOM for LOAD in what follows, and it would be perfectly correct.

LOAD is a program which simply converts an assembled file - produced by ASM (see later) which will be in INTEL format HEX, to the COM file in binary which you can run on your machine. The command is -

LOAD ufn

The ufn may omit the '.typ' because it must be .HEX, and is assumed to be .HEX if you omit it. You use ASM (or MAC etc) first, to produce the HEX file, and then use LOAD to produce the COM file. ASM takes your file called, let us say, YOURFILE and produces YOURFILE.PRN (which is a source listing, with line numbers) and YOURFILE.HEX (which is in INTEL format). To create the 'runnable' program, you enter -

LOAD YOURFILE< Rt>

and YOURFILE.COM is produced. If a drive is specified, the .COM file is produced on the same drive as the .HEX version.

Now you can use the YOURFILE command to run that program, just as you do with PIP or MBASIC or whatever.

DDT and the developments of it (version 3.1 of CP/M has SID) are a little beyond the 'fundamental' level.

7.3 DDT

This is the 'assembler level' programmer's monitor in versions up to and including 2.2. It is absolutely essential, contains all kinds of useful facilities, and looks pretty incomprehensible in the manuals, until you realise what it is actually for.

We will cover SID (the version 3.1 de-bugger) after this section.

If you write a program in Assembler Language, (we will call it 'asm' from now on) then you have your source program - the asm code that you write - and you have to use ASM to "assemble" the object code which is in 'hex'. Fine - but it is a little confusing that you cannot run your asm program, and you may not find it easy to read your assembled program in hex, either.

So the DDT program sits in the memory of the machine, and allows you to load your hex program, and then run it, alter it in hex or asm, display it either in hex (like DUMP) or in dis-assembled form (back to the original asm code) and also inspect the contents of registers (like the counter which contains the address of the next instruction to be obeyed).

However - although you can 'patch' your program in hex or asm, and save it as a COM program, to continue testing - you still have to go back to your original asm, and alter that. DDT allows you to alter the object code - but you still have to actually modify the asm yourself - perhaps using ED - and then re-assemble with ASM.

Invoking DDT

DDT stands for the Dynamic Debugging Tool. You load it into memory using the command -

A> DDT< Rt>

and after announcing itself, the DDT prompt (which is a '-', the hyphen or minus sign) will appear on the screen.

Alternatively, you can give DDT a filename for the program which you want to load, at the same time as invoking it, thus -

A> DDT FRED.HEX< Rt>

or

A> DDT FRED.COM< Rt>

83

In the first case, the .HEX file will be converted to binary, and in the second, the program will simply be brought into the transient program area as it is.

In either of these cases, the screen would show the announcement of DDT, followed by two lines of information, like this -

    64k DDT ver 2.0
    NEXT PC
    0120 0100

The number (in hex) under NEXT is the next byte location after the end of the loaded program - the first unused location, in other words. The number shown under PC is the current value of the Program Counter - the address at which the program would start execution if you entered a G (goto) command.

Invoking DDT alone, with no file, suppresses those two items of information. So a sample display could actually show this -

    A> DDT
    DDT ver 2.2
    -

with the cursor sitting immediately after the DDT prompt, the hyphen.

Now to load a program (a file, presumably ending in .HEX or .COM) you first put the name of your program into the 'file control block' with the I command, and then read it into memory with the R command. The equivalent to the command DDT FRED.HEX above would be -

    A> DDT
    DDT ver 2.2
    -IFRED.HEX
    -R

While you are doing this, incidentally, you can use any of the CP/M line editing commands which we mentioned in the first chapter, to correct or wipe-out a line or character.

There are twelve commands which you can use in DDT, and we will cover them in order in a moment, but having mentioned 'display' a few paragraphs back, we will say now that the command for this is D. The 'dump' (D) starts at the current address - or can be given an address - and dumps 256 bytes to the screen. The format is similar to that we showed for DUMP, and also contains sixteen ASCII characters which repeat the content of the sixteen bytes displayed in hex, as if they were ASCII. Where a non-ASCII (or at least, a non-graphic) code is encountered, the D command puts a decimal point in the display. To start from the beginning of the file, which is now in the memory, we need not give D any 'start address' - but if we wanted to, we could say (knowing that the file is in memory starting at 0100H (that is the 257th byte))

-D0100

and the response might be -

```
          Hex                                      ASCII
0100 21 00 00 39 22 15  02 31  57 02 CD C1 01 FE FF C2!..9"..W .......
0110 1B 01 11 F3 01 CD 9C 01 C3 51  01 3E 80 32 13 02........Q.> .2..
etc
```

Not very meaningful at this point in the program we have dumped, but lower down, we come across this line -

```
0200 4C 45 20 50 52 45 53 45 4E 54 20 4F 4E 20 44 49 LE PRESENT ON DI
```

which as you can see contains printable characters - and is one of the screen displays - or part of one - used by that program. The 20 character (that is 20H, in hex) is often a useful one to recognise, even in a DUMP, because it is the 'space' character.

The full list of DDT command characters is

A   Assemble - enter assembler code
D   Dump - display the contents of memory in hex and ASCII
F   Fill - put a specified constant in memory from/to address
G   Goto - Start program execution from address
H   Hex - display hex
I   Input - input the FCB for an R command
L   List - list the dis-assembled contents of memory from/to
M   Move - move a block from/to addresses to a new address
R   Read - read the file specified by I command into memory
S   Substitute - put new content instead of existing at address

T   Trace - execute instruction(s) with register list at each
U   Untrace - execute instructions with register list after last
X   examine - examine or alter registers (all, or specified)

If you get the ? response, it means that DDT cannot obey your command. Likely reasons could be - command incorrect or unknown - file cannot be opened - checksum error found in Hex file - assembler or disassembler has been overlayed and is not therefore accessible.

Several of the DDT commands can be used alone (but not A F or I) or with parameters, so the full details of each follow here.

A command.

A < start-address> Accept assembler code from the keyboard starting at the hex address specified. The DDT system displays each line number (in hex) ready to accept entries, and if you enter an empty line (just a 'Return'), that exits from the A command, without affecting the previous contents of that address. Notice that you are not prevented from over-writing the actual assembler/dis-assembler, and if you should happen to do this (large programs or small memories !), then you will get the ? response, as noted above. Line editing works in the usual CP/M way. Note that the address is specified in hex, but does not have the H after it, as we use in these notes. 03F0 is correct, not 03F0H.

D command.

D Dump from the current address register location to the monitor, in hex and ASCII, for 16 lines. Immediately after R (reading) a file, this will be the first 256 bytes of the file. A second D command displays the next 256 bytes, and so on. If the address register does not contain a multiple of 16, (10H) then the first line will be shortened to make all succeeding lines match the normal 16 byte boundaries.

D < start-add> Dump 16 lines as above, starting from the specified start address, which is in hex, but is simply entered as the number - eg 01F0 correct, not 01F0H.

F command.

F< start-add> , *< end-add>* , *< constant>* Fill both the start-address and the end-address specified, and all the bytes between, with the hex constant specified. The constant must be a 'byte' - that is two hex characters - eg 20 would fill with ASCII spaces, FF would set all 'bits' to 1. Note that the from/to is inclusive, which is not very common. Therefore F0160,0170,20 actually fills 17 bytes with spaces. To fill sixteen, use F0160,016F,20.

G command.

G Start program execution from the address currently in the program counter. This form of the command hands control over to your program, and you can only get it back into DDT if you either have a 'breakpoint' (Assembler language RST 07) in your program (see below) or if you press 'Rubout' or 'Delete'.

G< start-add> This is the simple extension to G - the specified 'start-address' is placed in the program counter, and the program then executes from there.

G,< break1> The comma shows that this is a command to start from the address currently in the program counter, and 'break1' is the address at which you want to stop and return to DDT if that instruction is reached. (If the program counter ever equals 'break1', the G command stops and the '-' prompt re-appears.)

< start-add> , *< break1>* , *< break2>* You may specify a maximum of two breakpoints in the command, and a start address as well, if you wish. There may be many other break points actually in the code (asm RST 07), any of which will interrupt the run, but you can specify a maximum of two additional ones in the G command. The run stops and command is returned to DDT if either of the specified breakpoint addresses is found in the program counter.

G0 This is G (goto) 0 (zero) - in other words, it is a 'warm boot', returning to the first location in memory, which is the start of the CP/M loader. Very useful to get you out of DDT and back to CP/M, but without changing the contents of memory. If you have a 'patched' program in there, it is still there ready to 'SAVE' after the G0 command.

H command.

H,a,b Hex Arithmetic. Display a + b and a-b in hex.

I command.

I < filename> Input to the File Control Block at 005C the filename given, ready for an R (read) command (see below).

L command.

L List in asm (after dis-assembly) the next 12 lines of the program starting at the current position of the Program Counter (PC).

L< start-add> Dis-assemble and display the 12 lines starting at the given address (and including that address).

L< start-add> ,< end-add> Dis-assemble and display from start-add to end-add, both addresses included.

M command.

M< old-add> ,< end-add> ,< new-add> Move the block of program currently in memory, which starts at old-add and ends at end-add, to the storage locations in memory starting with new-add. The addresses given are inclusive (what was at end-add moves). This is the only form of the M command.

R command.

R Read the file identified in the FCB at 005C (put there by the I command) into the memory, starting at location 0100 (hex). After this command has been obeyed, the NEXT and PC values will be displayed, with, as mentioned above, the value under the word NEXT showing the first unused location, and the value under PC showing the 'current address' stored in the program counter. Usually this will say 0100, if the R command has been given no parameters.

R< offset> Read the file into memory starting 'offset' bytes on from 0100. This would allow you to load a part program into unused memory space, higher (numerically) than a part program previously loaded by an R command without parameters. Clearly the NEXT and PC values would be appropriate to the size of the program and the size of the offset. Offset is, of course, stated as a number of bytes, in hex.

S command.

S< start-add> Substitute the value entered at the keyboard, in hex, for the value currently held in the location 'start-add'. After accepting the value (indicated by 'Return'), you are offered the next byte location in ascending sequence, and so on. After typing the command, the byte location and content are displayed, and the cursor stays on the same line, expecting input. If the 'Return' key is pressed (no input), then the byte is unaltered. This makes the S command a 'Substitute or Inspect' facility. If a '.' (period) is entered (followed by 'Return'), control returns to DDT, without affecting the byte then displayed. The display is simply one byte with the address and value shown in hex, thus

0110   1B and if you press return, you get the next, like this
0111   01 and so on until you enter the period (.) and press Return. Pressing two keys (any numbers or A thru' F) stacks the two hex characters into the byte.

T command.

T Execute a single instruction, at the location given by the current value of the Program Counter (PC), and display the contents of the registers after the instruction has been obeyed. See the X command below for the type of display obtained.

Tn Execute 'n' instructions, as above, displaying the register contents after each. ('n' defaults to 1). See the X command below for the register display.

X command.

X Display the contents of various 'flags' and registers. There are five 'flags', which may have values 0 or 1 only, and six registers.

Flags
> C is the carry flag
> Z is the zero flag
> M is the minus flag
> E is the even parity flag
> I is the inter-digit carry flag.

Registers
> A is the accumulator (arithmetic) and is 2 hex digits
> B is the BC register pair, four hex digits
> D is the DE register pair, four hex digits
> H is the HL register pair, four hex digits
> S is the stack pointer, again four hex digits
> P is the program counter, also four hex digits.

In the full display, shown below, the contents of the location in P (program counter) are shown dis-assembled, and follow the counter value. In this example, all the flags are zero (the flag name is followed by the value) A, B, D and H are zero, the stack pointer and program counter are showing the start of program, and the instruction at that location is a JUMP to location 0107 (in hex, of course).

Example of display after entering the X command -

> -X

> C0Z0M0E0I0 A=00 B=0000 D=0000 H=0000 S=0100 P=0100 JMP0107

X< r> Each of the flags and registers can be examined individually, and if required, altered, by following the X with the letter denoting that flag or register, from the list above. As for the S (substitute) command above, the current value is shown, and the cursor is positioned after it. If a valid value is entered (and then Return is pressed), the flag or register will be altered accordingly. If Return only is pressed, the value is unaltered.

7.3.1 An Informative Illustration.

The best way to understand the use of the various DDT commands is to follow an actual run of DDT. The DDT Users Guide which is provided with versions 1.4 and 2.2 of CP/M has a most informative illustration, starting on page 12 of the guide, and finishing on page 19. Pages 10 and 11 also show the process of 'assembling' a program, as you will see, and page 18 shows the use of ED (Chapter 8) to alter the source code before re-assembling.

7.4 SID

The version 3.1 equivalent of DDT is the Symbolic Instruction De- bugger - SID. It works in a very similar way to DDT, amd is loaded using the same command options.

SID	loads SID and it is then in command mode.
SID filename.typ	loads SID and puts the file into the TPA.
SID filename.HEX	loads SID and the file, but converts the file to binary first.
SID filename.COM	loads SID and puts the specified command file into the TPA, ready for de-bugging.

When you are working with SID, it responds to the normal line input editing commands that CP/M 3.1 recognises. Those are defined in Chapter 2.

The SID prompt is the # (the 'hash' or 'number' sign). Some systems use (the 'pounds' sign) instead, if they have been 'anglicised'.

Exactly the same flags and registers, and very similar, though more powerful, commands are available under SID as those used with DDT. However, since you are likely to be working with one or the other, not both, we have included a full summary of the SID commands here.

A - Assemble.

Assss   Enter assembler code starting at address given by ssss.

91

C - Call.

Csss   Call the subroutine whos start address is given by
                        ssss in hex.
Cssss val1,val2   Call the subroutine at ssss with val1 loaded into
                        the register pair BC, and val2 in the register pair
                        DE.

D - Dump. (or Display.)

D   Dump (as the DUMP transient) 16 lines of the
                        content of memory, starting at the current
                        address. The display is in hex and ASCII.
Dssss   Dump 16 lines starting at ssss.
Dssss,eeee   Dump from ssss to eeee (ssss and eeee are 'start'
                        and 'end' addresses in hex).
DWssss,eeee   The W tells SID to use a 16 bit word format,
                        instead of the 8 bit byte.

E - Employ. (Used if you are in SID command mode and you want to load a file or a symbol table.)

Efilename   Load the file for execution/de-bugging.
Efileone,filetwo   Load fileone for execution, and filetwo as the
                        symbol table to be used.
E*filename   Load filename.SYM as the symbol table.

F - Fill.

Fssss,eeee,const   Fill the memory from location ssss (hex) to
                        location eeee (hex) with the constant specified -
                        also in hex. (...,20 would fill with spaces, or ...,00
                        would fill with nulls.) Don't get ssss and eeee the
                        wrong way round !

G - Goto.

                        Start program execution from location stored (or
                        loaded) in the PC.
Gssss   Load ssss into the PC and then G.
Gssss,break1   Start at ssss and stop at address break1.
Gssss,break1,break2   Start at ssss and stop at either break1 or break2,
                        which ever is reached first.

G,break1,break2   Start at location in PC and stop at either break1
                   or break2. Note the comma after G which
                   differentiates this command from the command
                   Gssss,break1. ssss and break1 etc are hex
                   addresses as before.

H - Hex.

H,a,b   Display in hex the values a + b and a-b

I - Input.

(Used to set up an FCB for a file to be read by an R command, or for the
program being debugged.)

Ifilename   Set up an FCB at 005C (the default FCB) for the
                   file specified.

L - List. (disassemble)

L   Disassemble 12 lines from current address.
Lssss   Disassemble 12 lines from ssss address.
Lssss,eeee   Disassemble from ssss to eeee inclusive.

M - Move.

Mssss,eeee,nnnn   Move in RAM the block starting at ssss and
                   ending at eeee to a new position in RAM starting
                   at nnnn.

P - Pass.

(Record the number of times the program executes through a stated
location.)
Ppppp   Set the location pppp as a passpoint for
                   counting.
Ppppp,i   Set the location pppp as a passpoint, and put the
                   value i as the initial value of the counter.

93

R - Read.

R	Read the file specified by the previous I command to the TPA starting at address 0100H.
Roffset	Read the file specified by the I command to the address in RAM given by 0100H + offset.

S - Substitute (or Set)

Saaaa	Set aaaa as the memory address at which the substitution is to start.
SWaaaa	As above, but the substitution will be in 16-bit words.

T - Trace.

T	Execute one instruction, with register dump.
Tn	Execute n instructions, with trace.

U - Untrace.

Un	Execute n instructions with register dump only after the last. (If n is not specified, 1 is the default, so that U alone is identical to T alone.)

V - Value.

V	Display the current values of the SID parameters.

W - Write.

Wufn,ssss,eeee	Write the contents of memory from ssss to eeee to disc, giving the result the filename specified as ufn. (Note that SAVE can be considered as a special form of the W command in SID.)

X - eXamine.

X	Examine (display) the contents of all registers and flags. The names are the same as in DDT, and are listed below.

94

Xr   Examine or alter the content of the register or flag
                            r. Pressing < Rt> after the display leaves the
                            contents unaltered and returns to SID command
                            mode. Enter the new value and < Rt> to alter a
                            register or flag. The five flags and six registers are
                            as follows -

    C Carry flag   Z Zero flag
    M Minus (sign) flag   I Interdigit carry flag
    E Even parity flag

    A Accumulator   B Register pair BC
    D Register pair DE   H Register pair HL
    S Stack pointer   P Program Counter (PC)

Note that the flags are 0 or 1, the accumulator is two hex digits, and all other
registers are four hex digits.

? - The 'eh ?' response.

This means that SID has not understood your command, or that the file you
specified cannot be opened (does it exist ?). You will also get the ? response if
there is a checksum error in a hex file, or if you have overlayed the
assembler/disassembler as a result of previous commands.

All the foregoing refer to SID, the 3.1 debugging tool. the DDT commands
are earlier in the chapter.

7.5 Summary.

DUMP allows you to see, in hex or (3.1) hex and ASCII, the contents of a file
or program which is on disc.

LOAD and (3.1) HEXCOM convert the hex results of ASM or MAC assembly
into a binary COM version, ready to run.

DDT is the programmers main tool for testing, modifying and generally performing 'hands-on' program development at the assembler level in versions of CP/M up to and including 2.2. It happens to include a better dump command (showing the results in ASCII as well as hex) than DUMP itself, though only in 256 byte blocks.

SID is the CP/M version 3.1 equivalent of DDT.

THE CP/M COMPATIBLE ASSEMBLERS

8.1 Fundamentals.

If you are using, or are about to use, an assembler, you are well beyond the fundamental level. If you want a quick overview of programming languages, you should probably skip to Chapter 9. There is also a discussion of assembler concepts in section 8.3.1.

However, if you have turned to this page to find - or remind yourself - how to actually use ASM, MAC or RMAC, we will include them here, together with the error messages on the console and in the file produced after assembly.

We will cover the assembler supplied with CP/M up to and including version 2.2 first (ASM), and then look at the 3.1 assemblers.

8.2 ASM.

You invoke the assembler (ASM) either with a filename alone, or with three parameters added to the filename. Each parameter is a single letter, and is added to the filename after a period (.). This makes it look like a file type extension. Do not be misled.

The assembler produces two files, a copy of the source with line numbers and comments, called PRN, and a HEX file ready for LOADing.

The .PRN file could be used as a .ASM file, by using the ED command (see chapter 10) to remove the first 16 characters from each line, and then renaming it.

To invoke ASM, the command is either

ASM filename or
ASM filename.123 (see details of parameters 1, 2 and 3 below.)

The filename is the name only, not the drive or the type. If you have produced FRED.ASM with an editor, the command is -

ASM FRED

The three parameters allow you to specify the source of the ASM file, the destination of the HEX file and the destination of the PRN file, like this -

1 - a single drive letter (no colon) indicating where FRED.ASM will be found. If the parameter list is not used, FRED.ASM is assumed to be on drive A.
2 - a single drive letter (no colon) indicating where FRED.HEX is o be put. If you put Z as the letter, no hex file will be produced. (Early stages of assembly, looking for language errors.)
3 - a single drive letter as before, indicating the destination of the FRED.PRN file. Z causes ASM to skip the PRN file, or X causes ASM to put the PRN file straight onto the printer.

Thus ASM FRED is exactly the same as ASM FRED.AAA As another example, the first assemble of FRED.ASM might be done with the command-

ASM FRED.BZX

which means that FRED.ASM is on drive B, that you do not want a FRED.HEX at all, and that you want FRED.PRN to appear on the printer.

8.2.1 Successful assembly.

If the assembly is successful (it is a two-stage operation), the assembler signs off with the following messages -

xxxx
yyyH USE FACTOR
END OF ASSEMBLY

xxxx is the hex address of the first unused byte after the program has been loaded. (End of program + 1) yyyH refers to the symbol table space, and if divided by 0FFH, gives the fraction used. So if you convert yyyH to decimal and divide by 2.56 (or multiply by 0.4, roughly), that will give you the percentage of the symbol table space actually used.

8.2.2 Errors on the Console.

The assembler ASM can fail to complete an assembly if one of the following error messages is displayed.

NO SOURCE FILE PRESENT	The file specified in the ASM command is not on the specified or default disc.
NO DIRECTORY SPACE	The directory of the disc is full. Erase files.
SOURCE FILE NAME ERROR	Improperly formed ASM file name.
SOURCE FILE READ ERROR	Source file cannot be read properly by the assembler. Execute a TYPE command on the file to determine where the error is.
OUTPUT FILE WRITE ERROR	Output file(s) cannot be written properly, most likely cause is that the disc is full. Do a STAT to check and erase if necessary.
CANNOT CLOSE FILE	Output file cannot be closed - check to see if the disc is write protected.

8.2.3 Errors in the .PRN file lines.

These errors are displayed on the console during the assembly, and are also embedded in the PRN file.

D   Data error: an element in the data statement cannot be placed in the specified data area.

E   Expression error: expression is ill-formed, and cannot be computed at assembly time.

L   Label error: label cannot appear in this context, or duplicate label.

N   Not implemented: you have attempted to use a feature which requires a later version of ASM.

O   Overflow: the expression is too complicated to compute - simplify it.

P   Phase error: label does not have the same value on two subsequent passes through the program.

R   Register error: the value specified as a register is not compatible with the op code.

V   Value error: operand encountered in the expression is improperly formed.

8.3 An Overview of Assembler.

8.3.1 Format of Assembly code.

Each line of assembly code (source code - see below) can have the following 'fields'. A space separates one field from the next:

    label: opcode operand(s) ;comment

Assembly source code can have line numbers - these are added at assembly in any case. Labels must start with a letter, a question mark (?) or a period (.) and can be up to sixteen characters long, though the first six are significant, and must be unique. Dependent on the command, there may be or there may not be, a label, which must be followed by a colon. However, if the label field is used for a different purpose, the colon must not be present.

Constants in assembler can be entered in Binary, Octal, Decimal or Hex radix (base 2, 8, 10, 16 respectively). If a radix is not indicated, the constant is assumed to be decimal. Indicate radix by following the constant with the appropriate initial letter - viz. - B for binary, Q or O for Octal (Q avoids confusion with zero), D for decimal (the default) or H for Hexadecimal. ASM also expects each constant to start with a valid numeric digit, and since the indicator succeeds the digits, F000H would be an error. Use 0F000H to avoid this (leading zero).

8.3.2 Basic concepts of Assembler level programming.

The basic concepts, and the differences between 'machine code', 'assembler' and 'high level' languages are of fundamental importance, and the following brief explanation will enable a programmer to put the use and manipulation of programs into perspective.

In 'machine code' - which in our terms within CP/M means either the INTEL hex code or the binary equivalent - each instruction performs a specific task, and uses actual memory addresses and registers. The program itself is in the memory, and so are the locations at which data is stored. Any instruction can perform just one arithmetic, sequence change, logic, data movement or input/output operation. That may be 'add the value in memory location pointed to by an address register, to the value currently in the arithmetic register' which would be expressed as a code (for 'add to register'). The address required would have been loaded into the appropriate (HL) address register before the instruction was obeyed.

Programming in machine code is very detailed, and subject to error, and requires the programmer to keep track of every location in memory which is used. Inserting extra code at some point is practically impossible, because every instruction and storage location beyond the insertion would need to be altered. It is usually done, if it is needed, by replacing instructions immediately before the desired insertion with an unconditional branch to a location not previously used, and at that location, the replaced instruction is coded. Then the instructions to be inserted are coded in, and the last instruction is a branch back to the instruction in the main program immediately after the substitution. When that has been done a few times, the actual logic flow of the program becomes almost incomprehensible, very tortuous, and to all intents and purposes, incapable of being enhanced or amended later in the life of the program.

Programming in 'assembly' or 'assembler' language is easier, because symbols are used for both addresses and instruction codes, instead of the actual hex or binary address/code. The symbols used for instructions are usually mnemonics or reasonably comprehensible words. Unconditional branch might be JMP - for 'jump' - add to register might be ADD, and so on. This is much easier to remember, and to read, and is not as subject to error. The symbols used for storage locations can also be short names, which again can be meaningful. Data storage locations might be called GROSPY ('gross pay') or TAXYTD ('tax paid this year-to- date'). Instruction locations are also given names, usually called 'labels'. CALCTX or DISCWR could be labels used at the beginning of the 'tax calculation' and the 'write to disc' instructions. Assembler language is often called a 'Symbolic' language, because of the use of symbols instead of actual codes/addresses.

A program called an 'assembler' (in CP/M terms) translates the instruction mnemonics to the numeric codes, and allocates actual memory addresses to the labels and data locations. If the program is altered, the symbolic code can be easily amended, and the assembler will then be run to produce a new version of the machine code. One other function which most assemblers offer - or have links with - is the definition and incorporation of 'macro-instructions' - "macros" for short. These are sequences of instructions which are labelled and defined as macros, and which can then be used as though the label was a symbolic code for a single instruction. Wherever the macro is wanted in the program, the label is used as an instruction. At assembly, each such use of the macro label is replaced with the appropriate group of instructions. If you use a macro 5 times, then the actual instructions which make up the macro are inserted 5 times in the machine code program. This is, as you can see, different from 'subroutines', which are groups of instructions contained only once in the program, with a mechanism which allows the programmer to 'call' the subroutine (that is 'branch to the subroutine') at any point in the program, and the CPU then stores the necessary address in the 'stack' to enable returning to the next instruction in sequence, after the subroutine instructions have been obeyed.

The use of low-level language, 'assembler language', implies three things. First, there must be an assembler to 'translate' the code into machine language. Second, there must be a program stored in 'assembler' - the 'source' of the program. Third, there must be a translated (assembled) version of the program - the 'object' code.

DDT or SID, discussed in the previous chapter, work with the 'object code' - the assembled program. They allow 'patches' to be inserted in the program, but the patches are only in the version actually in the machine memory, and unless they are 'SAVEd' to disc, they will be lost when the machine is switched off. Patches inserted in that way must be re-introduced at the assembler level, and re-assembled, to preserve the equivalence of 'source and object' program versions.

Writing assembler programs may be, and usually is, done on paper, and the programs are then typed or otherwise fed into the machine using some form of 'editor' (see chapter 10). Then you have a file containing your program, in assembler, which is always required to have the 'type' .ASM Your program called FRED will therefore be put into the machine in assembler called FRED.ASM

That covers the basic ideas. Now we will move on to the actual CP/M assemblers. There are numerous assemblers available, and it is therefore relevant to put them into context before we discuss the details of using them.

8.4 Assemblers available.

The simplest development system available under CP/M is supplied free with CP/M itself (versions up to 2.2). It is -

ASM.COM - the assembler
DDT.COM - the debugger
LOAD.COM - the loader (hex to binary)

This package originated within the Naval Postgraduate School, Monterey, California. Dr Gary Kildall was responsible for some of it, in its original version. Some of DDT and all of the other programs were originally written in PL/M, and have been modified and developed over the years. The assembler itself, in particular, has been developed into Digital's RMAC - the Relocating Macro Assembler. For fairly small jobs, that are not too complex, the basic package is quite adequate, but for more extensive and intensive work there is a better set (supplied with CP/M version 3.1) -

MAC.COM - the macro assembler
SID.COM - the Symbolic Instruction Debugger
LOAD.COM - the same loader as before.

If you do not require object files (that is, files of assembled machine code) which can be put into different parts of the memory at different times - 'relocatable' files - then MAC is a fine tool. Is comes with a good range of macro files to help the programmer with sequential I/O, to provide special instructions, to provide structured assembly constructs and so on.

MAC is an extended version of ASM which can support macros. M80 or PASM offer even more comprehensive macro facilities, but MAC is good. The principal limitation of MAC is that it cannot produce REL (re-locatable) files. Large programs are therefore tedious to develop. When PL1-80 became available, MAC was updated to produce re-locatable output, as RMAC. RMAC and LINK are provided with CP/M Plus - as version 3.1 is being called on 1983 literature.

RMAC.COM - the relocating macro assembler
LINK.COM - the linking loader
SID.COM (or ZSID.COM) - the same Symbolic debugger.

SID is in fact of rather limited use with relocatable files, because it cannot load them as object files, and cannot cope with addresses relative to a relocation base address. If Digital Research were to upgrade SID, the package could very easily become 'state of the art' in 8080/Z80 assembler packages.

103

The TDL package came from a separate line of development. Neil Colvin was responsible for one of the first Z80 assemblers, and this product has now matured. For some time it was a tape based package, rather than disc based, but it did eventually become available under CP/M. A linker and debugger were part of the package. TDL suddenly disappeared, and the package was then sold as -

MACROII.COM
DEBUG.COM
LINK.COM

After Neil Colvin moved to P.S.A. the assembler re-appeared with two new and powerful associate programs.

PASM.COM
BUG.COM
PLINK.COM (or PLINKII.COM)

The P.S.A. package is the most expensive, and probably the most versatile and powerful development package available with CP/M, and even supports overlays. BUG and PLINK are remarkable products, and if BUGII and PASMII eventually appear as promised, assembler level programmers will have a really superb tool. TDL or PASM are more difficult to learn than some of the simpler products, but amply repay persistence.

The third great assembler came from Microsoft. This is a good product which is particularly useful for those who prefer the Zilog mnemonics. It has powerful macro facilities, but does not come with the macro libraries that are so useful with RMAC. The Linker is comparatively primitive compared to PLINK, because it does not link disc to disc, and overlays are difficult to produce. The macro assembler M80 lacks a good debugging tool, but never-the-less, it is probably the best known and most used relocating macro assembler for CP/M. The package is -

M80.COM
L80.COM
LIB.COM

The SD Systems package is yet another, which is unlike the rest in that it uses only the Z80 ops, pseudo ops and macros. It is both robust (reliable !) and quite easy to use, but lacks a debugging tool, and does not produce re-locatable code.

One of the most interesting and unusual development systems is the ML80 package. This is public domain software, fortunately, and it uses completely different ops and pseudo ops. Considering the fact that it is the only relocating macro assembler in the public domain, it is surprisingly little used. Possibly this is because a good manual on it has never been available. It would certainly be more widely used if someone out there wrote a good one ! The complete package is -

ML80 The general macro processor
L81 The structured assembly language parser
L82 The code generator
L83 The linker

There are several more assemblers around, of varying degrees of usefulness. Mostly they can be found in the CP/M User Library. These are the most important of them.

ASMX This assembler recognises extended INTEL Z80 mnemonics which are similar to TDL but not identical. After one or two irritating little bugs are cured or avoided, it works. It is in the US CP/M user library, vol 16
MACASM We have not tried this assembler, and we do not know anyone who has. It uses 8080 mnemonics and processes macros. It is in the US vol 16.
Z80ASM This is available in source as well as .COM form. The assembler recognises Zilog mnemonics. There are a few bugs, and the improved version still has minor problems with drive selection and some of the more obscure op codes. The original is in US vol 16 and an improved version is in UK vol 5.
MILMON80 If you bought Processor Technology equipment, you used to be given this free. It is really only of historical interest, because it didn't work very well. It was a 'monitor- editor-assembler' package, of the type popular before we had discs. The use of an asterisk (*) in the first character of the label field (for a comment line) in this package is actually recognised by ASM, to preserve compatibility. It is in the US vol 17.
RTMASM This will assemble a series of source files into one COM file, and works well, apparently. It is 8080 only. US vol 32.
LINKASM See US vol 36.

That concludes the background, and shows the range of products which are available to the assembly programmer under CP/M. Now we will move onto the actual Assembler language itself.

We can only give a summary of the actual language here, to act as a quick reference guide. If you actually want to learn Assembler Programming, there are other texts, including the INTEL manual "8080 Assembly Language Programming Manual".

8.5 SUMMARY OF CONVENTIONS AND SYMBOLS USED IN ASSEMBLER DIRECTIVES.

The word or symbol(s) on the left are those used in defining the language, the text on the right provides important rules which apply to the directives. Not all the conventions and symbols that were specified by Intel actually appear in ASM, but most of the will be found in RMAC and M80.

There are the three fields indicated earlier, plus the comment field, which starts with a semicolon(;), in each assembler directive/instruction. We will concentrate on the three main fields.

Expression	Numerical expression evaluated during assembly; must evaluate to 8 or 16 bits according to context.
List	Series of symbolic values or expressions separated by commas.
Name	Symbol name which is terminated by a space.
Null	The field must be empty, or an error results.
Oplab	A label may be used, or may be absent, the optional label must be terminated with a colon.
Parameter	Dummy parameters are symbols holding the place of actual parameters specified elsewhere.
String	Series of any ASCII characters enclosed by single quotation marks. (eg 'FRED')
Text	A series of ASCII characters.
&	The ampersand is used to concatenate symbols.
< >	The 'angle' brackets are used to delimit text, such as lists that contain other delimiters.
ii	Used before a comment in a macro definition to prevent the comment going into the code when the assembler expands it to create the HEX file.

!		Placed before what would otherwise be a delimiter, when the symbol is to be passed as a literal in an actual parameter.
%		Precedes actual parameters to be evaluated immediately when the macro is called.

8.5.1 ASSEMBLY DIRECTIVES.

oplab:	DB	exp(s) or string(s)	Define 8-bit data byte(s). Expressions must evaluate to one byte.
oplab:	DS	expression	Reserve data storage area of specified length.
oplab:	DW	exp(s) or string(s)	Define 16-bit data word(s) Strings are limited to 1 - 2 characters.
oplab:	ELSE	null	Conditional assembly. Code between ELSE ENDIF is assembled if expression in IF clause is false.
oplab:	END	expression	Terminate assembler pass. Prog execution starts at expression. If null then starts at 0.
oplab:	ENDIF	null	Terminate conditional assembly block.
name	EQU	expression	Define symbol 'name' with value 'expression'. Symbol is not re-definable.
oplab:	IF	expression	Assemble code between IF and following ELSE or ENDIF directive if 'exp' is true.
oplab:	ORG	expression	Set location counter to 'expression'.
name	SET	expression	Define symbol 'name' with value 'expression'. Symbol can be re-defined.

107

8.5.2 MACRO DIRECTIVES.

null	ENDM	null	Terminate macro definition
obplab:	EXITM	null	Alternate terminator of macro definition.
oplab:	IRP	dummy param < list>	Repeat instruction sequence substituting one character from list for dummy parameter in each iteration.
oplab:	IRPC	dummy param, text	Repeat instruction sequence substituting one character from text for dummy parameter in each iteration.
null	LOCAL	label name(s)	Specify label(s) in macro definition to have local scope (not accesible or used outside the macro).
name	MACRO	dummy param(s)	Define macro 'name' and dummy parameters to be used in macro definition.
oplab:	REPT	expression	Repeat rept block 'expression' times.

8.5.3 RELOCATION DIRECTIVES.

oplab:	ASEG	null	Assemble subsequent instructions and data in the absolute mode.
oplab:	CSEG	boundary spec.	Assemble subsequent instructions and data in relocatable mode using data location counter. (CSEG is 'code segment').
oplab:	DSEG	boundary spec.	Assemble subsequent instructions and data in

		relocatable mode using data location counter. (DSEG is 'data segment').
oplab:	EXTERN name(s)	Identify symbols used in this programme module but defined in a different module.
oplab:	NAME module name	Assigns a name to a program module.
oplab:	PUBLIC name(s)	Identify symbols defined in this module that are to be available to other modules. (see EXTERN)
oplab:	STKLN expression	Specify the number of bytes to be reserved for the stack for this module.

8.6 ASSEMBLER PSEUDO-OPS.

(Note - where we have used < > to enclose an 'op', this denotes equivalence, rather than exact correspondence. eg < .IF> . Where the Z80 assembler uses COND, in CDL/PASM, .IF would be used to form the same construct.)

M80	Z80	CDL/PASM
ASEG		.PABS
COMMON		.LOC
CSEG		.PREL
DB	DEFB DEFM	.ASCII or .BYTE
DC		.ASCIS
DS	DEFS	.BLKB
DSEG		.LOC .DATA
DW	DEFW	.WORD
END		.END
ENTRY/PUBLIC	GLOBAL	.ENTRY
EQU		=
EXT EXTRN	EXTERNAL	.EXTERN
INCLUDE		
$INCLUDE		

109

MACLIB		.INSERT
NAME		.IDENT
ORG		.LOC
PAGE	*EJECT	.PAGE
SET	DEFL	=
SUBTTL		.SBTTL
TITLE		.TITLE
.COMMENT		REMARK
.PRINTX		.PRINTX
.RADIX		.RADIX
.Z80		.Z80
.8080		.I8080
.REQUEST		
IF/IFT	COND	< .IF>
IF[- IFF		< .IFL>
IF1		< .IF1>
IF2		< .IF2>
IFDEF		< .IDDEF>
IFNDEF		< .IFNDEF>
IFB		< .IFB>
IFNB		< .IFNB>
IFIDN		< .IFIDN>
IFDIF		< .IFDIF>
ELSE		<][>
ENDIF	ENDC	]
.LIST		
.XLIST		
.SFCOND		
TFCOND		
.PHASE		
.DEPHASE		
REPT - ENDM		
IRP - ENDM		
IRPC - ENDM		
MACRO		< .DEFINE>
EXITM		.EXIT
LOCAL		

For ASM programmers who are converting to MAC, and who need to beable to use RMAC, we include brief details here.

8.7 MAC (supplied with version 3.1)

The input to MAC is a file of assembly language statements which must be of type ASM. Three files are produced as output, with the same name as the input, and with types HEX, PRN and SYM. The first contains the Intel hex format object code, and the second (PRN) contains an annotated source listing which can be seen at the console or printed out with TYPE and ∧ P or one of the PIP commands. The third file (name.SYM) contains a sorted list of symbols which are defined in the program.

The input sources and the output destinations are controllable, with options, and outputs can be suppressed if required.

There are 15 drive names (A, B, C, up to N, O) plus three pseudo drives. X is a pseudo drive and directs the chosen output to the console. (Another letter is required to choose which output is meant, see below.) P is a pseudo drive and means the printer (the currently allocated LST device). Z is used to suppress the chosen output (Z = zero output).

Two sources are possible, the input file (the name.ASM file) and the macro-library (.LIB) files which may be called by the MACLIB statement. Three destinations are possible, as indicated above.

The basic command without options is this -

   MAC filename

To add options, the dollar sign ($) follows the filename, and then one or more pairs of letters. The first of each pair designates the input or output file as follows -

A   The following letter will be the source drive.
L   The following letter will be the .LIB drive.
H   The following letter will be the drive to which the HEX file is to be directed.
P   The following letter will be the drive to which the PRN file is to be directed.
S   The following letter will be the drive to which the symbol list (SYM file) is to be directed.

After one of these file letters, the letter A to O (for a 'real' drive) or X, P or Z for a pseudo drive will be used.

111

For example, this is the command to take the source from drive B, to suppress the HEX file, put the SYM file to the printer, and put the PRN file on the console. The file is called FRED.ASM.

> MAC FRED $AB HZ SP PX

No disc files will be created with that command, but you will have seen the listing on the screen (interruptible with ^ S) and you will have a printed symbol table.

If a conventional 'assemble' is required, with only the source drive to be specified, the command could be one of -

> MAC B:FRED

or -

> MAC FRED $AB

Those two commands are **not** identical. In the first, all the output will go to drive B, but in the second, the output will go to drive A, taking only the source from B.

The PRN and SYM files can be modified by use of five further options. These are -

+L List the input lines read from macro-library LIB files.
-L (the default) Suppress that listing.

+M List all macro lines as they are processed during assembly.
-M Suppress that listing.
*M List only the hex generated by macro expansion.

+Q List all LOCAL symbols in the SYM file.
-
−Q (the default) Omit LOCAL symbols from the SYM file.

+S Add the SYM file to the end of the PRN file.
-S Do not produce a symbol file at all. (= SZ)

+1 This tells MAC to produce a pass one listing for debugging purposes, to put it in the PRN file.
-1 (the default) Do not produce a pass one listing.

You may introduce controls into your actual ASM file, by putting a $ in the first position of an input line, followed immediately by the desired parameter. If you wanted to switch on the listing of LOCAL symbols part way through a program, one program line would be -

   $ + Q

There are a number of fatal errors which can occur during assembly, several more than with ASM, and these are indicated on the console as follows -

NO SOURCE FILE PRESENT | If you do not specify the correct drive, or if your file is not of type ASM, this will appear. If your drive spec is invalid, (eg - no drive exists with that letter) this will also appear.

NO DIRECTORY SPACE | Note that this refers to **directory** space, not file space. Large files may consume more than one directory entry each (see Part Three, Chapters 11 onwards). Erase some surplus files.

OUTPUT FILE WRITE ERROR | Either the destination disc is full or is write protected. Note that in CP/M 3.1, replaced media are automatically logged on, so this is not a result of changing the medium.

CANNOT CLOSE FILE | Probably arises due to a 'write protected' disc.

SOURCE FILE NAME ERROR | There is an illegal character in your filename. You cannot use an afn.

SOURCE FILE READ ERROR | If the source file is corrupt (did you have a BAD SECTOR error when writing it?) this will occur.

UNBALANCED MACRO LIBRARY | Normally this means that you have omitted the ENDM from a macro definition.

INVALID PARAMETER | You have put in an assembly parameter in the input line, and MAC cannot recognise it. Only use valid parameters !

113

As well as the above errors, there are several 'assemble time' errors which MAC can detect, and will report. Again, there are many more than with ASM, so we have included the full set. They will appear on the console, and will also be embedded in the PRN file. This type of error is denoted by a code as the first character of the line, which is then followed by the line address, the machine code, and your original line, made up of 'label mnemonic operand ;comment'. The single letter codes are as follows -

B   Balance error. MACRO or conditional assembly does not terminate correctly.

C   Comma was not used correctly to delimit items.

D   Data element cannot be placed in the data area. (Too long ?)

E   Expression error. (Too long or ill-formed expression.)

I   Invalid character. (Usually a non-graphic character.)

L   Label error. (Have you defined it more than once ?)

M   MACRO overflow error. The internal macro expansion table has overflowed.

N   You have used a directive which is not implemented. (Is it an RMAC directive?)

O   Overflow. (Expression too complex, or more than 9999 labels.)

P   Phase error. Label has different values on successive passes, or has been defined twice.

R   Register error. The value is not consistent with the op code.

S   Statement/Syntax error. There's a helpful message !

U   Undefined label. (Does not exist, apparently.)

V   Value error. Usually an improper operand - may be just a typing error !

At the end of an assembly run, MAC signs off with the usual message-
```
         eeee
    sssH USE FACTOR
    END OF ASSEMBLY
```

The eeee is the hex address of the end of the program/data. The sss, divided by 0FFH, gives the fraction of the table space actually used.

8.8 RMAC.

RMAC assembles ASM files, just as MAC does, but it creates REL files which you can LINK (see below) to create COM files.

The options are almost identical to those we described for MAC, except that the first letter of an option pair can be R (for the destination REL file) instead of H (for the destination HEX file). So if you wanted the REL file on the disc in drive F, your parameter would be $RF. As for MAC, only one $ sign is needed after the filename and before the list of options.

8.9 LINK.

We have commented on the linking software earlier in the chapter, and for completeness we will include a summary of the version 3.1 linker - LINK-80 - here.

The full description of LINK-80 is included in the programmers Utilities Guide to CP/M 3, but in essence, LINK combines relocatable object modules such as those produced by RMAC, BASCOM, PROPASCAL and PL/I-80 into a COM file or an RSX file or a PRL file, ready for execution.

LINK options follow the file specifications, and are enclosed in square brackets []. Multiple options are separated by commas.

A   Additional memory. Reduces buffers and write temporary data to disc.
B   This is the BIOS link in banked CP/M 3.1 systems. It aligns data segment to page boundary, puts length of code segment in header and defaults to SPR filetype.
Dnnnn   Sets the memory origin to nnnn (hex) for common and data areas.
Gn   Go. Sets start address to label n.
Lnnnn Load.   Change default load address to nnnn. (default for nnnn is 0100H.)

115

Mnnnn Memory size.	Define free memory for MP/M modules.
NL	No Listing of symbol table at console.
NR	No symbol table file.
OC	Output is a COM file. (This is the default.)
OP	Output is a PRL (page relocatable) file for MP/M.
OR	Output RSP (resident system process) file for MP/M.
OS	Output SPR (system page relocatable) file for MP/M.
Pnnnn	Changes default program origin (0100H) to nnnn.
Q	Lists all symbols with leading question mark.
S	Search filename before the S as a library.
$Cd	Put console output to d, where d is X (console, default) or Y (printer, LST device) or Z (no output).
$Id	Source of intermediate files. d is drive A thru P, default is the logged drive.
$Ld	Source of Library. d is drive as for $I. $Od Destination of object file. d is drive A thru P, or Z (no object file). Default is same drive as first file in command.
$Sd	Destination of symbol file. As for $O plus pseudo drive Y (printer).

Some examples will illustrate the uses of the command line and options.

LINK file1,file2,file3

This takes the three separately combined files, resolves their externalreferences and produces a single executable command file called file1.COM.

LINK filename = file1,file2,file3

This is exactly like the previous example, except that filename.COM is produced, instead of file1.COM.

LINK B:filename[NR]

The option specifies 'no symbol table'. There must be a filename.REL on B, and the linker will produce a filename.COM also on B.

LINK file1,file2[S]

The linker will search file2 for the subroutines referenced in file1, and will combine them with file1 to produce an executable command file called file1.COM on the default drive.

8.10 LIB.

The LIB utility will not be defined here, but its purpose is to maintain indexed (type .IRL) or unindexed (type .REL) libraries of frequently used routines in special files. (Or just one file.) There are several options and modifiers for the LIB utility, all defined in the appropriate manual. LIB can delete, replace and select modules in a library, and carry out some simple 'librarian-type' tasks. Names of modules and their contents can be listed and displayed.

8.11 Summary.

There are several CP/M compatible assemblers, from the free ones which come with CP/M, and which (with 2.2 and earlier versions) neither re-locates nor has a macro library - but does have a debugger, to PASM from Phoenix which has pretty well everything an assembly programmer needs. The comparative and other details above will act as a memory aid for anyone who needs a quick reference or reminder. Digital Research took a major step forward in the production of MAC and RMAC with version 3.1.

CHAPTER NINE

THE CP/M PROGRAMMING LANGUAGES

9.1 Fundamentals.

In this chapter, we will run through the main high level languages available under CP/M, and comment where appropriate.

Since CP/M 3.1 (sometimes called CP/M Plus) is upwards compatible with version 2.2 and with MP/M, the following details apply to all implemetations of languages under CP/M. In the places where we refer to a CP/M command, we will cover the different versions where this is needed.

A high level language is an 'English-like' language, which uses Names for data objects (addresses are handled by the software) and which allows the programmer to construct the machine instructions in a format or a language appropriate for the task. There are three forms of language available under CP/M. These are 'interpreted', 'semi-compiled' and 'compiled' forms.

Programs to be run under an interpreter (eg programs in MBASIC) are created and stored in source code (the code the programmer writes) and at run time, each instruction in turn is 'interpreted' by the MBASIC software into the appropriate machine code, which is obeyed. The program never exists as a completely 'interpreted' version - it only exists in source form. The implication of this way of running is that it is slow. However, it may be quite fast enough for programs which require considerable operator interaction, because the delays in 'interpretation' are completely or partially masked by the slow speed of even a fast keyboard operator.

At the other end of the scale are programs which have been 'compiled'. These are written in a language (which could still be MBASIC) and then submitted (like assembler programs) to a compilation process which translates them into actual machine code. Then you do not need to have the compiler or interpreter resident in the memory, you can load the 'compiled' (and probably 'linked') program directly, just as though it was a 'transient command' to CP/M.

Between these two are programs which are written in languages for which either interpretation (large memory usage) or full compilation is impractical, so an 'intermediate' version ('semi-compiled') is produced, first, with part of the complex translation process completed. Then a different piece of software (the 'run-time' program) is loaded with the intermediate code of your program, and that interprets the intermediate code at run time.

9.2 The common languages.

We will consider several dialects of BASIC (Beginners All-purpose Symbolic Instruction Code), ALGOL/M, (ALGOrithmic Language for cp/M), CIS COBOL (the Micro Focus version of COBOL called the Compact Interactive Standard for the COmmon Business Oriented Language for microcomputers), versions of PASCAL, FORTH, ALGOL-60, the C language and PL/I.

Since there will be minor differences in implementations of languages on different hardware systems, we cannot replace the manuals supplied with the language for your system. However we can provide a quick reference to major features.

9.3 BASIC-E.

This is a subset of CBASIC, and is a 'semi-compiled' language in a single piece of software called EBASIC. (cf CBASIC, which is in two separate parts.)

A program is created using an editor (see next chapter) or even using MBASIC, and the program is filed with the file extension '.BAS'. BASIC-E is invoked with a selection of options, and the command is -

119

EBASIC filename $o

Where 'filename' is the source code (with .BAS type) and 'o' is one or more of the following options - (only use the $ sign if you do want to specify one or more options)

A   list code produced (for compiler debugging); this is not normally done unless called for, i.e. it is OFF

B   List only the source statements with errors; normally OFF

C   Check syntax only, do not produce the .INT file; normally OFF. (useful to check quickly for errors in source code.)

D   Convert lowercase to uppercase; this is normally ON so unless you specify, convertion will take place.

E   Generate line numbers for code; normally OFF

The result (unless option C is taken) is that a filename.INT is produced, ready to run with the command -

ERUN filename

Statements valid in BASIC-E:

FOR	NEXT	FILE		GOTO	LET	CLOSE
GOSUB	INPUT	ON		PRINT	READ	RESTORE
RETURN	OUT	RANDOMIZE		STOP	DATA	DEF
DIM	END	IF		REM	ELSE	THEN

Functions contained in BASIC-E:

ABS	ASC	ATN	CHR$	COS	COSH
FRE	INP	INT	LEFT$	RIGHT$	MID$
LEN	LOG	POS	RND	SGN	SIN
SINH	STR$	SQR	TAB	TAN	VAL
EXP					

Functions in CBASIC but not in BASIC-E.

PEEK	POKE	PRINT USING	LPRINT
CALL (to machine code program)			

120

Error messages in BASIC-E.

Most of the error messages, including the 2-letter codes, are those produced by the CBASIC compiler, which we cover next in this chapter. See CBASIC for the details.

9.4 CBASIC.

Like BASIC-E, this is a semi-compiled language, and it may be executed on any floppy disc based CP/M system having at least 20k bytes of memory.

The major difference between CBASIC and BASIC-E is that with CBASIC there is a separate run-time monitor which must be loaded, and therefore you can **either** use CBASIC - the interpreter - **or** use CRUN - the run time monitor. With BASIC-E, both the interpreter and run-time monitor are in EBASIC.

There are two versions of CBASIC which are in common use - the original one and the 'Version 2' - which is called CBASIC2, with the monitor called CRUN2.

Code written for CBASIC can be interpreted by either CBASIC or CBASIC2, but once interpreted, the correct monitor must be used. An interpreted file produced by CBASIC will not run under CRUN2.

Another point worth noting is that if software is supplied to a customer including CRUN or CRUN2, that customer must have a current licence for the monitor, or must pay the (reduced) licence fee for the monitor.

The enhancements which were added when CBASIC2 was issued in May 1979 were the declaration of Integer variables, the ability to specify variables as 'common' when chaining from program to program, some extra pre-defined functions and a capability for cross referencing using XREF.

Although, as we said, CBASIC is an interpreted language, because it requires a run-time monitor, the CBASIC program itself is actually referred to in the documentation as a 'compiler' - so to avoid confusion, we will continue the fiction. We will refer to CBAS2 - the version 2 'compiler' in these notes. (Version 1 was issued as CBASIC.)

121

First, as with COBOL and most languages other than interpreted BASIC (MBASIC), you need an editor to get your program code into the machine in a file, which should be a .BAS file. The next chapter contains details of the main CP/M editors. Having got a BAS file with the code, you can then invoke the compiler, which **must** be done with CBAS2 filename

The filename, without extension, (because .BAS is assumed) must follow CBAS2 in the command. There are six switches which you can set at the time you invoke the compiler, by following the filename with a space, then a dollar sign ($) and one or more of the letters for the switches. All the switches are 'toggles', that is they refer to an on/off switch, which has an assumed (default) value, and will take the other value if the toggle name is entered after the $.

Drive name may be used in the command, as normal, either to point CP/M to the disc where CBAS2 is (if not the logged drive), or to indicate where the BAS file is. With toggle G and with XREF which we shall cover shortly, we will note a special use of the drive name.

The basic command to compile a filename.BAS is this -

A> CBAS2 filename< Rt>

The toggles are B, C, D, E, F and G, so examples of commands are these -

CBAS2 JOBCOST
B:CBAS2 A:JOBCOST
CBAS2 JOBCOST $B
CBAS2 JOBCOST $GEC
CBAS2 JOBCOST $G(D:)

9.4.1 The CBASIC Toggles in detail.

B   Suppresses the display of the compiled listing at the console during compilation, except that errors will still be displayed. If toggle B is omitted, the listing will be displayed during compilation. Note that this toggle refers only to the console output, not the printer or disc output (see F and G).

C   Suppresses the generation of an INT file. This allows the compiler to check syntax and display errors without producing a file for use with CRUN2 (which takes time !)

D   Suppresses translation of lower-case letters to upper-case. Without this toggle, any lower case variable names will be preserved in lower case, and will be different from any variable with the same name in upper-case. So with the D toggle set, Amt, amt and AMT are three different variables. Without the D toggle, they are all AMT.

E   This is a toggle which is actually carried into the INT file for use by CRUN2. If you used toggle E at compilation, then an error message at run time would be accompanied by the CBASIC line number at which the error was detected. Without toggle E, CRUN2 messages do not give the line number in the CBASIC code. If you use TRACE in your program, E must be on - included at compile time.

F   This tells CBAS2 to output the compiler listing (in CBASIC) to the current LST: device, during compilation. If you omit the F, then no printing takes place during compilation.

G   This tells CBAS2 to put the compiler listing out onto diskette, and to call it filename.LST (the same filename as your original BAS file). This would allow you to list the file later, without delaying the compilation significantly. If the G toggle is followed by a drive letter and colon, in parentheses - for example - $G(B:) then the LST file will be sent to that drive.

9.4.2 More examples of toggles.

CBAS2 JOBCOST $BCDG - this compiles without an INT file output, without a printed listing, with the display of errors only on the console, but with a LST file so that you could print the compiler output later, if you wanted to. Note that upper/lower case conversion is suppressed.

CBAS2 JOBCOST $BE - this is the fastest compilation, with minimum output, but with the INT file and the TRACE option set for run-time use. You might use this if you had had a 'clean' compilation, with a listing, at a previous run, and wanted to progress to CRUN2.

123

9.5 XREF

There is a separate program called XREF.COM which produces a listing which can be invaluable. It fulfils the same function as the 'symbol table' in assembler programming. The program produces a list, in alphabetical order, of all the variable names used, of what they are used for (eg Function name or Parameter or Global variable), and also lists every line number on which each appears. Note that you will need a 132 column printer, unless you use the D toggle (see below).

The command can also include a 'title' to be output at the head of each page of the listing. The title will be truncated to 30 characters (if it is longer) or to 20 characters if the D toggle is used. The title must be the last item in the command line, and must start with a single quote - the apostrophe (').

XREF assumes that you want a disc file with the stated filename and with the type XRF (filename.XRF). The toggles allow you to modify this assumption. You can also tell XREF to put the disc file on a specified drive (other than the logged drive) by putting the driveletter, colon before the $toggles.

The command is therefore like this -

A> XREF filename driveletter $TTT 'title------'

The filename may have a drive letter - and the type defaults to BAS, as for CBAS2. Up to three toggles may be used (see below), and the title if present must be the final part of the command line.

9.5.1 The XREF toggles.

A Produce a listing (on the LST: device) as well as the disc file.

B Suppress disc output. Dont use B on its own, or there will be no output at all !

C Produce a listing and suppress the disc file. That is the same as toggles A and B together.

D Format the output to fit into 80 columns, instead of the default of 132 columns.

E Produce only an identifier list, with usage, not including the functions, parameters.

9.5.2 Examples of XREF commands.

XREF JOBCOST $CD 'PRODUCED ON 12,1,83' - that produces an 80 column listing, no disc file, with the title shown as the heading.
XREF JOBCOST B: $AE- that produces a disc file on drive B, a listing at the same time, and includes only the identifiers. The listing (and the disc format) assume 132 column width printer (or wider).
XREF JOBCOST $CD '12/1/83' - that is possibly the most common usage, giving a printed listing only, at 80 column width, and with the date on each page. You put the correct date in, of course.

9.6 RESERVED WORDS in CBASIC.

This is not a language manual, but it may be useful to note the following list of reserved words which have specific meanings to the compiler.

ABS	AND	AS	ASC	ATN	BUFF
CALL	CHAIN	CHR$	CLOSE	COMMAND$	COMMON
CONCHAR%	CONSOLE	CONSTAT%	COS	CREATE	DATA
DEF	DEF	DELETE	DIM	ELSE	END
EQ	EXP	FEND	FILE	FOR	FRE
GE	GO	GOSUB	GOTO	GT	IF
INITIALIZE	INP	INPUT	INT	INT%	LE
LEFT$	LEN	LET	LINE	LOG	LPRINTER
LT	MATCH	MID$	NE	NEXT	ON
NOT	OPEN	OR	OUT	PEEK	POKE
POS	PRINT	RANDOMIZE	READ	RECL	RECS
REM	REMARK	RENAME	RESTORE	RETURN	RIGHT$
RND	SADD	SGN	SIN	SIZE	SQR
STEP	STOP	SRT$	SUB	TAB	TAN
THEN	TO	UCASE$	USING	VAL	WEND
WHILE	WIDTH	XOR			

The symbols ( ) ∧ * / + − < = > have the usual meanings and hierarchy.

125

Note that CONCHAR% (read one character from the CON: device), CONSTAT% (return TRUE integer if the console is in the 'ready' state) and the definition of a series of user functions starting with DEF and ending with FEND (must be numbered line) are the main additions to the more familiar forms of BASIC. Also the GE operator ("Greater than or Equal to") and GT etc are useful aids to legibility.

A CBASIC listing will often look unfamiliar to a user of the less powerful forms, because of the inclusion of line numbers only when needed, and because of the use of the above - and one or two more - unfamiliar operators.

9.6.1 Error messages from CBAS2.

Both CBAS2 and CRUN2 have a substantial set of error messages, some of which are text, others merely two-letter codes. The set here lists the text ones first, then the two-letter codes.

SOURCE FILE: filename.BAS
Either the CBASIC command line or an INCLUDE command was unable to find the specified file on the disc. (Wrong disc ?)
PROGRAM CONTAINS n UNMATCHED FOR/WHILE STATEMENTS
There are n FOR statements or n WHILE statements (whichever is stated) without the appropriate NEXT or WEND.
WARNING: INVALID CHARACTER IGNORED
The compiler has found a character which it does not recognise and has replaced it with a question mark (?). This message is included on the line below that containing the error.
OUT OF DISK SPACE
Either the INT or the LST file (or both) is incomplete, because space was not found on the disc. Note that a horrific number of error messages could cause that (or other) message to be output which may in fact simply be the compiler giving up. Use STAT to check on this.
OUT OF DIRECTORY SPACE
The compiler cannot insert a filename in the directory, because the directory is full. In version 2.2 and earlier, check with STAT DSK: for the number of

directory entries permitted. In version 3.1, SHOW [DIR] tells you the number of free entries. If that is not the problem - it could simply be the sheer volume of errors found.

DISK ERROR

This could be a 'bad sector' error on read/write, or a disc or file could have been set to R/O, or any of the 'hardware type' errors.

INLUDE NESTING TOO DEEP NEAR LINE n

An INCLUDE statement in the program being compiled at some point adjacent to the line number specified, exceeds the maximum number of levels of nesting permitted. Reduce the number of source files nested in this way, by writing the code differently. Note that 'near line n' is the closest the compiler can get, since it is busy with source file handling at that point, not with interpreting the code actually written into your program.

BF - You have attempted to Branch into a multi-line Function from outside it.

BN - A Bad Number (invalid numeric constant) was found.

CE - *Close Error - the INT file could not be closed (DIR or DISK full possibly).*

CI - Close Include - an invalid filename was found in a %INCLUDE statement.

CS - Common Statement - COMMON statements must be at the start of the program, one has been found lower down.

CV - Common Variable - A reference to a subscripted variable in a COMMON statement is not valid.

DE - Disc Error - this is an error during the read of the filename.BAS file. (The text message DISK ERROR described above could be any file, read or write.)

DF - Disc Full - The INT file has not been satisfactorily created, because either the disc or the directory is full.

DL - Duplicate Line number - You have used the same line number twice **or** the compiler is confused and **thinks** you have ! Some error has caused this, but it may not actually be DL.

DP - A variable in a DIM statement was Defined Previously. (ie nearer the beginning of the program.)

EF - A number in Exponential Format was input without any digits following the E. (Therefore the power is Zero - so the multiplier of the mantissa - the digits before the E - is one.)

FA - Function Assignment. The function name is on the left side of an assignment statement, but is not in the function itself.

FD - Function re-Definition - You have already defined that function name, and now you have used it again in a DEF statement.

FE - 'FOR' Error - you have a 'mixed mode' expression in a FOR statement which the compiler cannot 'unravel'.

FI - 'FOR' Index - the loop index (the counter) in a FOR loop must be numeric, and must not be subscripted. The variable or expression found disobeys the rules. (String variables, or expressions which evaluate to string variables, cannot be used, nor can you use an 'array' variable which is subscripted.)

FN - Function Number of parameters. The number of parameters you have provided to the function is too many or too few. That is an error when the function is used, not when it is defined.

FP - Function Parameter type. You have used a parameter of the wrong type (string when it should be numeric, or vice-versa).

FU - Function Undefined. This indicates that you have attempted to use a function earlier in the code than the 'DEF' for that function - or more likely that you have used a variable name beginning with FN. (eg DNAME$, ENAME$ and FNAME$ might be logical to you, but the last would give rise to an FU error !)

IE - *IF Expression* - the expression following an IF evaluates to (or is) a string, but only numeric or logical 'conditions' are allowed. You can use a string comparison in the expression, of course, because the result of a string comparison is TRUE or FALSE. For example, the expression INSTR("YyNn",Q$) evaluates to zero if the content of Q$ is not one of the quoted characters, or to 1 if it does.

IF - In File. A variable used in a FILE statement is numeric, where a string variable is required.

IP - Input Prompt. What the compiler takes to be an input 'prompt' string is not enclosed in the double quotation marks, as it should be. (eg "Enter Date"; not Enter Date;)

IS - Invalid Subscript has been used - usually because you have not DIMensioned the variable, or not early enough in the program.

IT - Invalid Toggle. A compiler switch (toggle) is not valid. The valid directives are B to G, as specified above.

IU - Invalid Use. You are not permitted to use a variable name which you have defined as an array, without subscript. (MBASIC does allow this, assuming that the use without subscript is a separate and different variable. CBASIC does not allow it.)

MF - Mixed Format. An expression evaluates to type string, when the context requires a type numeric.

MM - Mixed Mode. An expression contains both string and numeric variables, in a way the compiler cannot interpret. For example, X% + LEN(X$) is valid, but X% + X$ is not.

MS - Mixed String. The reverse of MF. You have used an expression which evaluates to numeric, where a string is required by the context.

ND - No DEF FN. A FEND was encountered without a preceding DEF.

NI - 'NEXT' Index. The variable in a NEXT statement does not match any of the preceding FOR indices which are still 'open'.

NU - 'NEXT' Unexpected. There is no FOR statement running at the point where this NEXT was encountered.

OF - Out of Function. A branch in a multiple line function attempts to branch outside the function.

OO - 'ON' Overflow. Not more than 25 ON statements are allowed in one program - you have exceeded the limit.

PM - Perform Miracles. (Well, it must stand for something !) This error code tells you that a DEF statement has been found within a multiple line function. You cannot 'nest' function definitions in this way.

SE - Syntax Error. All this tells you is that the preceding line contains a syntax error of a type not covered by one of the other error codes.

SF - SAVEMEM File. SAVEMEM needs a string expression to denote the name of the file. This is numeric. (Would be valid with "quotation marks" round it.)

SN - Subscripts, Number of. Too many or too few subscripts.

SO - Syntax Overflow. You are pushing the compiler too hard, your expression is too complex for a single expression. Split it between lines to simplify it.

TO - Table Overflow. Not what you might think - it means the program is too big for the system. Either cut the program down and use chaining, or add memory and MOVCPM.

UL - Undefined Line number. You have referenced a non-existant line number.

US - Undefined String. Strings must be terminated with quotation marks. The Return at the end of the line might be sufficient for MBASIC, but not for CBASIC.

VO - Variable name Overflow. Variable names are too long for the statement. (CBASIC ought to be able to cope, this error message was left in the system, but should not occur.)

WE - 'WHILE' Error. This is the same as IE (above) - the expression after the WHILE does not evaluate to numeric.

WU - 'WHILE' Undefined. The compiler has found a WEND without an associated WHILE.

9.6.2 Error messages in CRUN2.

These will occur during program testing, but most of them should be avoided by the way a program is constructed. Two are text messages, the rest are codes. The codes fall into two groups, those which are warnings that something has gone wrong - but the run continues - and those which indicate why the run has stopped. The text messages are first, then the warnings, and last the list of actual error codes.

9.6.3 Text messages in CRUN2

NO INTERMEDIATE FILE. Either you forgot to put in the name of the file (program) you want to run, or there is no such file of type .INT on the logged/specified drive.

IMPROPER INPUT - REENTER. This really should not be allowed to occur. It is the CBASIC equivalent of MBASIC's 'Redo from start'. If you input to a string variable, using LINE INPUT or if you use INPUT$, this will accept any input key(s). The error occurs if the operator puts in more or less fields separated by commas than he/she should, or puts letters instead of numbers. If a single field is expected, and the input contains a comma, you will get this error message.

9.6.4 Warning error codes in CRUN2

DZ - Divide by Zero. The result is set to the largest CBASIC number valid on your hardware.
FL - Field Length. More than 255 bytes have been found during a READ LINE. The field is truncated to 255 bytes, losing those at the right.
LN - Logarithm error. The argument in a LOG function must be positive and non-zero. This one is not. The result returned is the actual argument, unconverted.
NE - Negative number. A negative number follows the ^ (raised to the power of) operator. The absolute value is used (-2 found, 2 used etc).
OF - OverFlow during a calculation. The number which was too large was replaced by the largest CBASIC number.
SQ - SQuare root error. A negative number was specified in the SQR function. The absolute value was used (-3 specified, 3 used).

9.6.5 Error codes in CRUN2

AC - AsCii error. The string as the argument in an ASC function evaluated to a null string.
BN - 'BUFF' Number. The value following the BUFF option in an OPEN or CREATE statement is not between 1 and 52 inclusive. It must be.

CC - Chain Code. A chained program (the code area of it) is larger than the main program. Not permitted.

CD - Chain Data. The Data area in a chained program is greater than the data area in the main program.

CE - Close Error. An error occurred during the attempt to close a file. You cannot assume that the file is correctly closed.

CF - Chain Function. The constant area of a chained program is larger than the constant area of the main program.

CP - Chain Variable Storage. The variable storage area of a chained program is larger than the corresponding area of the main program.

CS - Chain 'SAVEMEM'. The chained program reserves a different amount of memory with the SAVEMEM statement than the main program.

CU - Close Undefined file. The file number specified in a close statement was not allocated to an open file.

DF - Defined File. An attempt was made to OPEN or CREATE a file with a number that was already 'active'.

DU - Delete Undefined file. The file number in a Delete statement was not active.

DW - Disc Write error. Either the Directory or the actual storage space was found to be full when a 'write' was attempted.

EF - End of File. No IF END statement was specified, and a read has taken place past the end of file.

ER - Error in Record. You have tried to write a longer record than the maximum you specified.

FR - File Rename. The name to which you were attempting to change a filename already exists.

FT - File Toggle. A FILE statement was executed when there were already 20 files active.

FU - File Undefined. A read or write statement included an inactive file number.

IF - Invalid Filename. This would have been picked up at compile time if it had been a specifed string, so it must be an expression which evaluates to an invalid name.

IR - Invalid Record number. Record numbers must be positive and non-zero. This one was not.

IV - Invalid Version. You are using CRUN2 but the .INT file was created using CBAS, not CBAS2.

IX - Invalid Function nesting. A FEND statement was found immediately before executing a RETURN. You cannot *do* that !

LW - Line Width less than 1 or greater than 133 was found in a LINEPRINTER WIDTH statement.

ME - 'MAKE' Error. The disc directory is full, and you are attempting to create or extend a file.

MP - 'MATCH' Parameter. The third parameter in a MATCH function must be positive and non-zero. This one was not.

NF - Number of FILE. File numbers must be between 1 and 20 inclusive. This one is outside the limits.

NM - No Memory. The program is larger than the memory available. It will not load. Split it and use chaining.

NN - No Number field. A PRINT USING command has no numeric data fields in it, but you are trying to print a number.

NS - No String field. The reverse of the above. The USING command string has only numeric data fields, and you are trying to print a string.

OD - Overflow Data. A READ was executed for which there was no DATA available. (forgot to RESET ?)

OE - 'OPEN' Error. An attempt was made to open a file which does not exist, and for which no IF END statement had previously been encountered.

OI - 'ON' Index. The expression in an ON ... GOTO or an ON ... GOSUB is either less than one or greater than the number of line numbers in the list. Put a 'trap' in to guard against that.

OM - Overflow Memory. During execution, the program ran out of memory. Watch those subscripted variables, they can soak up space.

QE - Quote Error. You are not allowed to PRINT to a file a string which contains a quotation mark, but you tried to.

RB - Random 'BUFF'. The BUFF option specifies more than one buffer, so you cannot attempt random access to that file.

RE - 'READ' Error. An attempt was made to read past the end of a record in a fixed format file.

RG - 'RETURN' without 'GOSUB'. You have allowed the program logic to GOTO or simply to progress into a subroutine. Trap this by ensuring that all subroutines are preceded by an unconditional GOTO (or a THEN and an ELSE).

RU - Random Undefined. The file from or to which you are attempting a random READ or PRINT is not fixed format and therefore is unsuitable for random access.

SB - SuBscript. You have attempted to address an array with a subscript outside the range for which the arrray was specified.

SL - String Length. A concatenation (eg A$ + B$) resulted in a string longer than 255 bytes.

SO - SAVEMEM nOt found. The file specified in a SAVEMEM could not be found on the drive specified (or the default drive).

SS - SubString error. The second parameter of a MID$ function was either zero or negative (the start of the select).

TF - Too many Files. As for the FT error, there are already 20 files active, you cannot have more.

TL - 'TAB' Length. If you want to TAB, your parameter must be greater than zero and less than the line width which is current. This is outside limits. (Check for WIDTH statements.)

UN - UNdefined edit string. PRINT USING must have a string of edit characters. This has none. Insert the string or change to PRINT.

WR - WRite error. You have read from the file, but not to the end, and now you have attempted a write. You can only do this at end of file (to extend it) or at the beginning (and overwrite the whole).

That completes the error code list from CRUN2.

9.7 MBASIC.

MBASIC is the Microsoft version of BASIC which allows you to create BASIC programs which can then be run under the interpreter which is loaded when you type MBASIC, or can be compiled with BASCOM. This is a full compiler, not a 'semi-compiler'.

MBASIC is also referred to a BASIC-80, and is often renamed BASIC when creating development discs. We will use MBASIC.

The language derives from the Beginners All-purpose Symbolic Instruction Code, which was a very limited, easy to start using, language. Many different forms of BASIC exist, particularly in the low-cost micro market, and each has its own foibles and methods of approach. It is a measure of the quality and range of MBASIC that you will often find other versions compared with MBASIC as 'the standard'. Because it is easy to learn, easy to use and very widely available, MBASIC is often looked down on by the professional programmer or software house. The main criticisms are that it runs much more slowly as an interpreted language than a 'proper' compiled language, and that it is all too easy to write programs that are very badly structured, badly annotated, difficult to modify safely, and generally unprofessional. All these criticisms are true, but it is equally true that a good programmer can write programs in MBASIC which stand up to rigorous inspection.

There are many good reference guides to BASIC in general and MBASIC in particular, so we will approach this discussion of MBASIC in a somewhat

133

different way from that which we adopted for CBASIC and (see later) COBOL. We will take each part of MBASIC in turn - the editor, then the interpreter, and finally the compiler. We will see that there are some special elements of MBASIC under CP/M, which a programmer needs to know, and there are also some commands available under the interpreter which will not compile.

9.7.1 Loading MBASIC under CP/M.

The command MBASIC alone will load the interpreter and editor. All the available memory (that which CP/M refers to as the TPA, or Transient Program Area) is made available to the programmer, except the part of it which is actually occupied by MBASIC, of course.

The response to MBASIC will be a statement of the version and serial number of your particular program, followed by a statement of the number of bytes of TPA available after MBASIC is in the memory. The command may be extended in several ways. If you have a program in MBASIC called START.BAS (for instance), the command -

MBASIC START< Rt>

will load MBASIC, and will then load and run the program START.BAS. If you wish to restrict the amount of memory available, you can extend the command with /M:hhhh and the value which is in hhhh will be the highest memory location which MBASIC will use for your subsequent work. (Omitting /M:hhhh allows use of all TPA up to the start of FDOS.) This will most often be used when you have assembler subroutines to slot into the memory, and these will be loaded into the highest available memory, so MBASIC needs to be restricted.

Also, MBASIC assumes by default that you will not want to have more than 3 files open (file numbers 1, 2 and 3) at one time. If you use file number 4 or greater, you will get an error. To tell MBASIC that you will require more files, extend the command with /F:nn, where nn is the total number of files that will be used. The maximum number allowed (in version 5.n) is 15. For each file assumed or required, an area of 166 bytes of memory is reserved, so the 'memory available' response will be reduced by the appropriate multiple of 166.

Finally, there is an assumed random record size of 128 bytes. You can specify less than this in your program, and the random records will be the size you specify. If you do not specify a size, 128 is assumed. If you need a longer random record, then you must extend the original command invoking MBASIC with a 'size' parameter - /S:250 (if 250 was the size you needed). However - this new size will also be the default if you do not specify a size when you open a random file - so it is good practice - and much safer - always to include the record length as the last entry in an OPEN"R"... statement - like this -

  1250 OPEN"R", #3,"B:KEYFILE.DAT",124

(The 124 is the sum of the characters allocated in the 'FIELD' statement for that file)

The full command for loading MBASIC with 5 files, all memory, and random records up to 180 bytes long, and loading and running the program START.BAS on the disc in drive B, say, is

  BASIC B:START /F:5 /S:180< Rt>

The sequence of the /M:, /F: and /S: extension is not important, except that they must follow any program name, and must be separated by a space.

9.7.2 The MBASIC editor.

Every line in an MBASIC program is numbered, usually in tens, but not necessarily, and line numbers can run from 0 to 65529. The programmer can key in the line numbers as he/she keys in the program, but there is an automatic line-numbering facility which is invoked with AUTO. AUTO used alone assumes you want to start with line 10, and step the line numbers in tens. To start AUTO at line 2550 and step in multiples of 5, the command is -

  AUTO 2550,5< Rt>

If AUTO offers you a line number which has already been input - say you have a program of 170 lines, starting at 10, already in memory, and you carelessly enter AUTO instead of AUTO 1710, then there will be an asterisk (*) after the line number and before the cursor - thus

  10*■

Either escape from AUTO with ⌃ C (which does **not** re-boot CP/M), or simply press Return, and you will be taken onto the next number without affecting the content of the previous one.

The MBASIC prompt is OK, and it is displayed, and the cursor positioned below the O of OK, ready to accept entries.

Editing your program in MBASIC is slightly longwinded - it owes much to ED (next chapter), but it does work.

First, you must invoke the editor by typing (when you are in MBASIC) EDIT nnnn, where nnnn is the line number you wish to edit. You will next see the line number stated on the left of the screen, with a space, and the cursor immediately after it. To see the line, press L (for 'list'). The line will be displayed in full, the number repeated and the cursor repositioned ready for your command.

The four most used editing commands are the space bar, which moves the cursor along one character (and displays the one 'uncovered'), The I which means 'start inserting characters here' (and its terminator, the Escape key - 'stop inserting'), the command nC - 'change the n characters for the ones keyed in next' and the command nD - 'delete the n characters from the cursor onwards'. This last one displays the deleted characters enclosed in \ (back slash) characters. However, the X 'go to the end of the existing line and enter insert mode' (X = eXtend), the H 'delete all characters from the cursor onwards and enter insert mode to allow replacement', and the nSc 'find the n'th occurrence of character c in the line from the cursor position, and stop with the cursor before the character' are all very useful.

The full set of commands available in EDIT mode are these -

A	Abandon. Restore the line as it was, and re-start edit
nC	Change n characters from the cursor to those next keyed in. This is 'over-write'
nD	Delete the n characters from the cursor position
E	End the edit, save the changes made, do not type out the rest of the line
H	Hack off the line at this point and enter Insert mode - deleting any characters which followed the cursor position. See I for exiting from I mode.

I	Insert characters at the cursor position until either the ESCape key is pressed (leaving you in edit mode) or the RETurn key is pressed (displaying the line and exiting from EDIT)
nKc	Kill (delete) all characters up to the nth occurrence of the character c (do not delete that occurrence of c)
L	List out the rest of the line and re-enter edit at the start of the line
Q	Quit the edit and restore the original line (note that A above restores the original line, but leaves you in edit mode at the start of line)
nSc	Search for the nth occurrence of character c and leave the cursor immediately before it (not displayed)
X	eXtend the line by displaying the whole line and entering Insert mode at the end of it
< DEL>	backspace (opposite of 'space-bar'). Can be used in Insert mode to delete inserted characters
< ESC>	Escape from insert mode, remaining in edit
< RET>	Escape from edit or insert mode to MBASIC, saving any changes which have been made

There is one pretty little use of the edit mode keys which is not immediately obvious, but which can be useful when creating programs. You can, if you wish, duplicate a line which exists, with a different line number. This allows you to move a line to a different place, or to duplicate almost identical lines. Commonly, one might have a subroutine which contains the detailed instructions to display some data on the screen, with PRINT USING and a variety of ; and : characters. You probably entered it by using the ? key instead of typing PRINT, and now you want the subroutine reproduced with LPRINT instead of PRINT in each place. If the line you want to reproduce is, say, line 1230, and you want a copy of it at line 1500, then proceed like this.

Type EDIT 1230< Rt> When you get 1230 and the cursor on the screen, immediately press E Now press ∧ A (control and A) and you will get a ! prompt. Press I (for insert) and type in the new number 1500. Press < Rt> . That is it - one line copied. Now repeat for the other lines.

Go through the new lines in turn with EDIT 1500 etc, L (list) each line out to check it, use SP to move the cursor to just before the first P, press IL< ESC> , then SP again and so on until you have changed the PRINT commands to

LPRINT. If SP finds a P which does not want an L in front (like in P% or P$) then SP again will skip on.

That little sequence EDIT olnum < Rt> E∧ Alnunum< Rt> is probably worth remembering if you do much MBASIC coding. (One of the editors such as WordStar, described in Chapter 10, will also help, but can take time to set up, as we will see.)

We introduced∧ A without explaining it - so now we will say that∧ A allows you to enter edit mode on the line you are typing, if you suddenly realise that you have skipped something or made some error. It saves re-typing the whole line, or going through the process of typing in EDIT linenumber.

There are some more special characters which apply to the use of the MBASIC interpreter, and this is the list -

∧ A	Enter EDIT mode on line being typed or last line typed
∧ C	Interrupt program execution (re-start with CONT) or exit from AUTO without saving the current line number
∧ G	Ring the bell at the terminal (!)
∧ H	Delete last character typed
∧ I	Tab (tabs every 8 columns) if you haven't a TAB key
∧ O	Halts/Resumes program output
∧ S	Suspends program execution (also suspends LIST, LLIST)
∧ Q	Resumes program execution after ˜S (any key resumes LIST, LLIST)
∧ U or ∧ X	Deletes line being typed
< Rt>	End of current line
< Lf>	(Line Feed) Breaks logical lines into separate physical lines on the screen
< Esc>	Escape from sub-commands (I,H,X and nC) in edit
.	(a space followed by a full stop/period) refers AUTO, EDIT, RENUM, LIST and LLIST to the current line. Do not omit the space. The manuals say 'EDIT.' but they should say 'EDIT .'
?	shorthand for PRINT when preceded by space or punctuation. (L? is not LPRINT)
name$	a string variable containing up to 255 chars
name%	an integer (whole number) variable -32768 to 32767

name   (old form name!) 'single precision' variable. Held as a
                        floating point number with 7 digits or less and one digit as
                        the exponent. Effectively, up to seven digits including the
                        decimal point.

name #   'double precision' variable. Held as floating point with up
                        to 17 digits and an 8 digit exponent.

NOTE that the fact that MBASIC uses floating point numbers can give rise to strange results, and lack of precision in the last digit. For instance multiplying 234.567 by 23 gives 5395.04, not 5495.041 as it should. Or you may find a number printed out with a string of zeros and a 3 (or something) after it. When you output numerics using the PRINT (or LPRINT) command, you need to be aware that numerics are printed with a space before and after them unless you use one of the PRINT USING editing characters And you may get some very strange numbers, again unless you use PRINT USING. Be careful when using integers - although they speed up processing, holding a value as a whole number of pence is very limiting indeed - less than 327.00 can be held in an integer.

9.7.3 The MBASIC interpreter.

Any reference manual and most instruction texts will give you sufficient detail on the instruction set, so we will confine ourselves to some of the less obvious area.

For obtaining a password which you do not want 'echoed' to the screen, use INPUT$(n) where n is the number of characters. n need not be a literal, it could be an integer variable, which can be altered. For example -

```
4560 N% = 6
4570 PRINT "ENTER PASSWORD";
4580 PASSWORD$ = INPUT$(N%):PRINT
```

The final PRINT moves the cursor down to the next line.

For obtaining a 'MENU' type response, use a single character length, perhaps like this -

```
3450 PRINT "IF CORRECT PRESS 'C', OR PRESS 'R' TO RE-ENTER";
3460 Q$ = " "
3470 WHILE INSTR("CcRr",Q$) = 0:Q$ = INPUT$(1):WEND:PRINT Q$
```

The final PRINT in this case provides the 'echo'.

For all other input from the keyboard, you are strongly recommended to use LINE INPUT to a string. That will avoid the 'Redo from start' message which would spoil a good screen layout and could be confusing to a user. (LINE INPUT accepts commas and any keyboard character except < Rt> and ^ C. < Rt> indicates end of input and ^ C suspends program execution.)

Random files are often a source of confusion to beginners particularly if you read from a record to which you have not previously written. You will get some very strange characters if the disc space has been used before. KILLing or ERAsing (in CP/M) a random file also has its moments. You do not actually touch the file itself with those commands, only the Directory entry. So if you KILL a random file, and then re-open it, you'll possibly find that everything is still there, where it was before the KILL. Random files do not always PIP as one expects. If there is any doubt, a genuine 'track for track' copy program written in assembler, or the slower approach, reading and writing every record from one disc to another, is an alternative approach to security copying.

Since MBASIC does not allow you to extend a serial file (other than by reading and writing it, then adding to the end of the written version), random files are sometimes used for this. You will need a separate file - or the first record of your file - to hold a counter of the record number which you last used. Then you can write to the 'counter + 1'th record and step the counter.

Program chaining in MBASIC is very simple. Your statement is for instance

    1230 CHAIN"START"

or

    1230 CHAIN"START.BAS"

which is equivalent to an END statement, followed by keying in

    LOAD"START"
    Ok
    RUN

or the shorter alternatives

RUN"START"
or
LOAD"START",R

You can tell the interpreter where to start a program by including the line number. If you were to use

1230 CHAIN"START",50

then you would enter the program at line 50. Watch this, though if you are in the habit of defining functions early in your program. Do not enter after the DEF FN... statement, or your program will halt if the function is invoked.

There are no restrictions on sizes of the programs, you can go from a short to a long and vice-versa. You can also carry the values in variables from a program to a chained program. There are various possibilities, but the one we will mention here is the one which you can use with the BASCOM compiler. In each of your programs which are to be CHAINED together, you can include a COMMON statement. You follow this with the list of names of the variables you wish to hold their values through a CHAIN. Use commas to separate them, and specify arrays as below, with nothing between the brackets.

COMMON V$,CLIENT$,MONVAL #(),ANNVAL #,JD%

You can have several COMMON statements, provided the same variable is not named twice, and the statements can be anywhere (before CHAIN) in the program. One word of warning. The variable names in the COMMON statement must actually have been used - must have values in (even if they are zero or a space) - before you CHAIN. Otherwise, even though the first program will happily accept a COMMON statement with empty (and that means effectively non-existent) variables, the second and subsequent ones will not ! Once a value is in there and the location has been 'activated', so to speak, the program need not address the variable(s) at all, but may simply hold them to pass on to the next CHAINed program.

The other ways of passing variables are the extensions to the CHAIN statement, such as ALL. CHAIN"START",ALL means preserve the values of all variables, and does not need any COMMON statement(s).

It is very common practice - and good practice - for programmers to build up libraries of subroutines which they have developed These are usually

141

RENUMbered up in the high numbers, and SAVEd as short programs in ASCII. Then they can be retrieved and merged into subsequent programs.

You might have developed a routine to convert a date to an integer, useful for date-checking and for storage in 2 characters on a random file, and you might refer to it as JULIAN. When you have DELETEd any other code from memory, you could renumber it

RENUM 65000,1

and then put it on disc as ASCII with

SAVE"JULIAN",A

Then, provided that you do not use the 65000 series of numbers in your program, you can copy it into the program which you are developing with the command

MERGE"JULIAN"

Merge commands are sometimes slow, so do not be surprised (or panic!) if the disc drive access light goes out intermittently during a MERGE. Now you can GOSUB 65000 in your program.

The MBASIC functions all work exactly as the manuals say, but there is sometimes confusion about the string returned by the STR$(numeric-variable) function. VAL(X$) returns the numeric value of X$ as stated, but STR$(X) returns a single space character and **then** the characters which represent X. Check it if you like, with this program -

```
10 INPUT"ENTER NUMBER";X
20 PRINT X,STR$(X),LEN(STR$(X))
30 GOTO 10
```

The number returned for the length of the string is always one more than the length of the number you input. So if you have a number, and you want the string representation of it, without stray spaces, the function is RIGHT$(STR$(X),LEN(STR$(X)) − 1). The space is for a ' − ' sign.

Error trapping is an important feature of good MBASIC programs which can otherwise be somewhat inappropriate for use by non- programmers. If the first statement of your program is

10 ON ERROR GOTO 65500

and at 65500 you have a series of traps, ending in

65529 ON ERROR GOTO 0

then your program will not only be robust, in so far as you trap the errors, but it will be informative if an error should occur because that 65529 statement tells MBASIC to be as informative as possible about the error when the program is terminated.

You can trap errors with either the error codes (see below) or with the line number in your program at which they occur.

65500 IF ERL = the line number in your program at which you are trapping the error, will be followed by some imperatives to get out of the problem, and then a RESUME nnnn - the line number at which you want to carry on.

For example, if you need /F:5 in your programs, it makes sense to have an early test for five files like this -

30 OPEN"R", #5,"X"
40 CLOSE #5
50 KILL"X"
.
.
.
65500 IF ERL=30 THEN PRINT"YOU MUST ENTER/F:5. RE-START":SYSTEM

And that introduces the method of getting from MBASIC to CP/M   The conventional ∧ C does not work, that, is a command to MBASIC. The corresponding command is SYSTEM< Rt>, which can be used either in direct or indirect mode.

Another useful command is FILES. That will display the directory of the currently logged drive. To display the directory of another drive, you need FILES"B:*.*" for drive B. In a program you may want to display to the user, all the files of type EST which exist on drive A. The statements would be

2450 PRINT"Estimates currently on file are:-"
2460 FILES"A:*.EST":PRINT:PRINT

The FILES statement leaves the cursor after the last item in the list, unless there happens to be a full line, hence the extra PRINT statement.

The error codes in the MBASIC interpreter are as follows (the asterisk * before the message means that the error number and message also apply to run-time errors in compiled programs) -

Code	Number	Message
BS	9	* Subscript out of range (or too many/few)
CN	17	Can't continue (attempted CONT)
DD	10	Redimensioned array. (Two DIM statements or perhaps the DIM follows a default of 10 which has occurred because the array has been addressed)
FC	5	* Illegal function call. (Parameter out of range)
ID	12	Illegal direct. (can only use in indirect mode)
NF	1	NEXT without FOR
OD	4	* Out of data when READ attempted (forgotten to RESET ?)
OM	7	Out of Memory. Too big or too many loops/GOSUBs
OS	14	* Out of String space. (CLEAR in versions before 5.n will allocate more. 5.0 on allocates dynamically - so this means OM - code 7.
OV	6	* Overflow - too big a number.
SN	2	* Syntax error. (Not very helpful !)
ST	16	String formula too complex. Break it down.
TM	13	Type Mismatch - string/numeric or vice-versa
RG	3	* RETURN without GOSUB (preface subroutines with unconditional GOTOs)
UF	18	Undefined user function (or a name which you have started with FN... without realising)
/0	11	* Division by zero. Warning issued and run continues.

The above are in all versions of MBASIC - large, small, stand-alone etc. The next set are in extended and disc versions only.

	19	No RESUME in an error trapping statement
	20	* RESUME without error
	21	* Unprintable error ! (No code exists)
	22	Missing Operand - operator but no operand
	23	Line buffer overflow -(> 255 chars)
	26	FOR without NEXT
	29	WHILE without WEND
	30	WEND without WHILE

These folowing next are disc errors.

50	* Field Overflow (too many characters for length of record stated/implied)
51	* Internal error (Shout for help to MicroSoft)
52	* Bad file Number (not open or too big)
53	* File not found (LOAD, KILL or OPEN"I")
54	* Bad file mode (wrong file commands)
55	* File already open (attempted OPEN or KILL)
57	* Disc I/O error. (fatal to your program)
58	* File exists (NAME exists)
61	* Disc full (no more file space)
62	* Input past end (use EOF or other trap to avoid)
63	* Bad GET/PUT record number (usually 0, or >32767)
64	* Bad file name (eg too long)
66	Direct Statement in your ASCII program file. You cannot have that - the LOAD terminates and you are back in MBASIC command mode
67	* Too many files (directory full)

9.7.4 The MBASIC Compiler.

The MBASIC compiler is called BASCOM, and generates a '.REL' file,which then needs to be linked to the system using L-80, which produces the '.COM' file which runs as a CP/M transient.

If you are this far down the line, all you need are the instructions for running BASCOM, and the details and meanings of the switches. You will find that BASCOM is more pedantic than MBASIC - for example, MBASIC would understand PRINTFND$(X%) but BASCOM would require PRINT FND$(X%).

When you are ready to compile, RENUM the program and SAVE it as ASCII. (SAVE"PROGNAME",A) Exit from MBASIC to SYSTEM.

Invoke BASCOM with the command BASCOM, and wait for the * prompt.

A suggested command line to get you going is -

*PROGNAME,TTY: = PROGNAME/N< Rt>

145

If you hear the bell and see an error on the screen, ^ S, if you are quick enough, will allow you to inspect the program, note the area of the fault and the fault code (see below), and then press any key to continue. At the end it will tell you how many errors you have. Correct and re-compile until it is clean. You will now have a file PROGNAME.REL

Now invoke L-80 with the appropriate command (L80 on many discs). You will again see the * prompt, and a suitable starter command line for L80 is -

      *PROGNAME/E,PROGNAME/N< Rt>

When you have your '.COM' file (ie PROGNAME.COM) you can save space by erasing the '.REL' file (ie ERA PROGNAME.REL), and your program is ready to run. If you have several programs which CHAIN together, you need all of them compiled, of course.

Now for the BASCOM command line switches. The switches follow the source file name after the = sign. Each letter has it own /.

/E	If your program includes ON ERROR GOTO with RESUME and a line number, then you need the module which this switches in. (It is left out if no switch).
/X	If you have used RESUME 0 or RESUME NEXT, then you'll need this module.
/N	This switches off the listing of generated code (and is the one we used above). You get the display of the source code on the screen.
/D	This switches on the generation of debug/checking code at run time
/S	With this switch, quoted strings of more than 4 characters are written as they are encountered.
/4	The compiler is told to recognise MicroSoft Basic ver 4.51 conventions (not 5.n)
/C	If line numbers are not sequential, accept this. You may not use /4 and /C together.

If you get compile-time warnings, they will be one of these two -

ND	Array not dimensioned (a default array has been assumed)
SI	Statement ignored - not compiled.

146

Compile-time Error messages (which are fatal, and you cannot Link your '.REL' file) are as follows -

SN	Syntax error
SQ	Sequence error
TC	Too complex a statement - simplify
LL	Line Length too great
OV	Overflow - arithmetic statement invalid
OM	Out of Memory
TM	Type Mismatch (string/numeric)
BS	Bad Subscript
UC	Unrecognisable Command
/0	Division by zero
DD	Array already DIMensioned
FD	Function already Defined
WE	WHILE/WEND error
FN	FOR/NEXT error
UF	Undefined Function
/E	You should have used the /E switch
/X	You should have used the /X switch

And that is it. Terse, perhaps, but probably adequate.

At run-time, there may be errors. These will be reported with numeric codes, and they are exactly the same codes as we listed for the Interpreter. In fact, we put an asterisk against each one which is also a Compiled Run Time error.

Details of L80 - the linker - switches are listed below, but the important point is that you must include the /N if you want a filename.COM Without the /N, the program will be in memory, and you may then save it to disc with

      SAVE nn filename.COM

where nn is the response you will get from L80 after it has successfully created the memory image. In CP/M 3.1, the SAVE command is entered first, see Chapter 2.

Switch Function

/R	Reset - initialise the loader
/E or / E:label	Exit from the linker. If label included, that will be taken as the program start address

147

/G or /G:label	Go. Start program execution (at label address)
/U	List all undefined references
/M	Map. List all references and if they are defined, give their values, otherwise asterisk
/S	Search the filename preceding this switch to satisfy references
/N	New program 'SAVE'd with a default type of '.COM'when the linker exits. Note that /E and /G both give three numeric responses at the console-

       aaaa bbbb nn

Where aaaa and bbbb are the start address and next free byte (beginning and one after the end) and nn is the number 256 byte pages occupied. That is the source of the nn in the SAVE command which you will need if you do not use the /N switch.

Now you can see that the command line we suggested was

       L80 relfilname/E,comfilname/N

which means, load the linker, locate the program relfilname.REL in memory, making the necessary address adjustments, exit from the linker. Then SAVE the memory image onto the disc and file.COM specified in comfilname.

This linker is used for .REL files produced not only by BASCOM, but also those produced by F-80 (FORTRAN) and M-80 (the MACRO language compiler). These are mentioned later in the chapter. LINK is the version 3.1 equivalent of L-80, and was discussed in Chapter 8.

9.8 ALGOL/M (Public domain software in the CP/M Users' Group)

This version of ALGOL (the ALGOrithmic Language) produces a semi-compiled program which is referred to as 'pseudo-code'. An editor has to be used (see next chapter) to create a source code file (with extension

.ALG). This is then semicompiled using ALGOLM and run by using RUNALG. The semicompiled form is called 'pseudo-code'.

Although ALGOL/M is based on ALGOL-60, which is the published language, and for which a very large library of software exists, it was not created as a formal sub-set. This short decription fulfils three tasks. First, it gives the new ALGOL/M user a quick guide to the compiler options and the compile and run commands. Second, it provides all ALGOL/M users with a list of compile and run-time error and warning messages. Third, for the ALGOL-60 user, it provides a summary of the Reserved Words and of the general structure and capability of ALGOL/M.

9.8.1 ALGOL/M Compile and Run.

You need an editor (see ED etc in the next chapter) with which to create a source code file called filename.ALG

To compile it, use -

    ALGOLM filename $AE   (or $A or $E or blank)

This produces the Algol intermediate file filename.AIN. The options are $A to generate a listing at the terminal and $E to set Trace mode for execution under RUNALG. Neither, one or both may be used.

To run your filename.AIN program, enter -

    RUNALG   filename

9.8.2 ALGOL/M Errors and Warnings

ALGOLM compiler errors

AS   Function or Procedure on left side of assignment statement
BP   Bound pair subtype must be integer.
DE   Disc Error - program/system cannot recover.
DD   Double declaration of identifier, label, variable etc.
FP   Wrong file open statement
IC   Special Character which is invalid
ID   Incompatible subtypes (you cannot assign decimal values to integer variables etc)
IO   Integer overflow (too large, more than 16383)

IT   Identifier is not declared as a simple variable or function
NG   No file '.ALG' found.
NI   Not integer subtype - and it should be
NP   No applicable production exists
NS   Not string subtype - and it should be
NT   In a For..Step..Until, clauses and expressions must be of same type - all integer, or all decimal. These aren't
PC   Parameter count in call does not match declaration
PD   Parameter not declared
PM   Parameter does not Match declared type
SO   Stack overflow (no more memory)
SI   Subscript must be of subtype integer
TD   Subtype must be integer or decimal, not string
TM   Subtypes do not match or are incompatible in context
TO   Symbol Table overflow
TS   You have subscripted a variable wihout declaring it
UD   Undeclared Identifier
UF   Undeclared File/Function
UL   Undeclared Label
UP   Undeclared Procedure
US   Undeclared simple variable
VO   Varc table overflow - possible caused by too many long identifier names

RUNALG Error Messages

AB   Array subscript out of specified range
CE   Disc file Close error (important - not closed, no file)
DB   Input field length greater than buffer size
DW   Disc file Write error.
ER   Variable block size write error
IO   Integer overflow (> 16383)
IR   Incorrect Record number - or random file not initialised
ME   Disc file creation error (of some kind)
NA   No '.AIN' file found
OV   Decimal register overflow
RE   Attempt to read past end of record on blocked file
RU   Attempt to random access a non-blocked file
SK   Stack Overflow (no more memory space)

RUNALG Warning Messages

AZ   Attempt to allocate zero length decimal or string. System gives you a default length of 10 digits/chars

DO   Decimal overflow - variable set to 1.0 - run continues. Before next run, increase variable size allocation

DI   Disc file variable format error

DZ   Decimal division by Zero - result set to 1.0

EF   End of file on Read

IA   Integer addition or subtraction under or overflow. Result set to 1.0

II   Invalid console input - re-input

IR   Record number incorrect or random file not initialized

I   Integer division by Zero - Divisor set to 1 and division continues (not like DZ see above)

NX   Negative exponential - exponentiation not done

SO   String overflow - characters lost

9.8.3 ALGOL/M General description

Three types of variable are supported - integer (-16383 to +16383), decimal (up to 18 digits of precision, default 10) and string (up to 255 characters, default 10). Decimal and string variable lengths can be given integer variables allocated values at run-time. Arrays can be declared with up to 255 dimensions, each dimension can be 0 to +16383. The maximum address space will naturally limit arrays to something less than the maximum theoretically possible. The contents of arrays can be any of the three types, and the dimensions can be integer variables, with values assigned at run-time.

Arithmetic is either integer or binary-coded decimal. Integers can be used in decimal expressions, and are converted to decimal at run-time. The comparators < => are available, used singly, or in combination. Logical AND, OR and NOT are available.

Control structures are BEGIN..END, FOR, IF..THEN, IF..THEN..ELSE, WHILE, CASE and GOTO. Function and procedure calls are supported. Block structuring uses BEGIN..END and nesting up to nine levels is allowed. Local variables declared within a block are only available within the block. Storage is re-allocated if control moves out of a block in which local variables

151

are used, so that values are not preserved. Recursion is allowed, and Functions return an integer value, while procedures do not return a value. Parameters of all types may be used with procedures or functions.

WRITE (new line) and WRITEON (continue on same line) output to the console, the write list being contained in parentheses (). The write list may contain string constants which are enclosed in quotation marks. Any combination of variable types and expressions evaluating to different types can be included in a write list. When WRITE or WRITEON fill an 80 character line, new line is given automatically. TAB and the displacement is supported.

READ is the console input statements. The read list is enclosed in parentheses, and contains any combination of variables. A space in the input indicates that the next character keyed starts the next variable entry. To enter spaces to a string variable, the actual keyboard entry must be enclosed in quotation marks. Thus THIS WEEK would be put in two string variables, and you must input "THIS WEEK" to put it into one. Wrong type/number of inputs gives the II error (see above) and the program remains halted until a matching set of inputs is provided. < Rt> is the end of input to a READ.

READ and WRITE are also available for disc I/O. READ/WRITE folowed by a standard CP/M filename.typ, with or without drive letter and colon, is the method. Random files are accessed by following the filename by a comma and the integer or integer variable containing the record number. Such files must be blocked by including the record length in the file declaration. Files not so declared will be unblocked serial/sequential.

The Reserved Words in ALGOL/M are these -

AND	ARRAY	BEGIN	CASE	CLOSE	DECIMAL
DO	ELSE	END	FILE	FUNCTION	GO
GOTO	IF	INTEGER	NOT	OF	ONENDFILE
OR	PROCEDURE	READ	STEP	STRING	TAB
THEN	TO	UNTIL	WHILE	WRITE	WRITEON

9.9 CIS COBOL

CIS COBOL produces semi-compiled programs. An editor (see next chapter) is needed to create the program source on a file with the extension .CBL The compiler has several overlays, and loads in each overlay as required from the logged drive. The complier consists of the following programs -

COBOL.COM
COBOL.IO1
COBOL.IO2
COBOL.IO3
COBOL.IO4

There is a separate run time system which runs the intermediate code produced by the compiler, called -

   RUNA.COM

CIS COBOL is also usually supplied with CONFIG.COM to configure COBOL to match the terminal and other peripherals in use, and with simple demonstration programs which show ways of screen handling, which may be unfamiliar to 'main-frame COBOL' programmers. There is also a run-time subroutine, named CALL, which is suplied in .ASM .HEX and .PRN forms.

Optionally, there is also a FORMS-2 package which allows screen creation and the handling of files which contain the screen content without actually writing the data and procedure divisions to do this. This comes in 13 programs, plus CONFIG.

The COBOL command line format is -

   COBOL filename directives

where 'filename' is the name of the .CBL source file (eg WRSCGDAT.CBL) and 'directives' are none, one or several of the valid compiler directives, which are simply entered after the filename in any sequence, with at least one space between them and before the first. 'Return' completes the command line. Note that the use of '.CBL' as the type is not actually recognised as a default by the COBOL program, and must be specified in the command line, but it is recommended for ease of recognition in a STAT or DIR display.

In the explanation of the directives which follows, "source-name" is the name of the .CBL file created with the editor. Where rounded brackets are used () they and their content must be present.

Some directives are mutually exclusive, and these will be listed after the explanation of the directives themselves.

The directives are -

FLAG(level) This specifies the output of validation flags at compile time, relating to the features at different levels of compiler certification of GSA (General Services Administration)

The 'level' can be one of the following -

LOW Produces flags for all above Low Level
L-I All above Low-Intermediate
H-I All above High-Intermediate
HIGH All above High Level
CIS Only for CIS extensions to standard COBOL 1974

NOFLAG No flags are listed by the compiler - this is the default if FLAG is ommitted.

RESEQ If included, the compiler will generate sequence numbers incrementing in 10s, and re-numbering if necessary. If this is omitted, line numbers are ignored and treated as documentation only.

NOINT No Intermediate file is produced. Used for syntax checking.

NOLIST No list file is produced. Default is that a full listing is produced. Used for fast compilation of a 'clean' program.

COPYLIST The contents of any file nominated in a COPY statement are included in the program listing.

NOFORM No form feeds or page headings are included in the list file. The default is that the listing is paginated for 66 line pages, and each page is headed.

ERRLIST Only lines containing errors are included in the listing. The default is that all lines are listed.

INT(name) The 'name' will be the name of the intermediate file. The default is source-name.INT

LIST(name) The 'name' will either be the name of the .LST file or can cause direct listing using LST: (to the printer) or CON: (to the console). Example - LIST(CON:) LIST(LST:) will show the compiler output on the console and simultaneously print it on whatever device is the current LST: device.

FORM(integer) This 'integer' specifies the number of COBOL lines per page of the listing (minimum 5, default 60).

NOECHO Error lines are echoed on the console unless this directive is included.

NOREF The four-digit location addresses which are normally printed on the right hand side of the listing will be suppressed by this directive.

DATE(string) If the program being compiled has the DATE-COMPILED entry, then the information following it will be replaced by the contents of the string. This is then printed at the head of each listing page.

The directives that exclude others are listed below. If the first is included, the ones following may not be.

Directive	Excluded directives
NOLIST	LIST NOFORM FORM RESEQ COPYLIST ERRLIST NOREF
ERRLIST	RESEQ COPYLIST NOREF

Numbering your COBOL source can be achieved by using the three directives NOREF NOFORM RESEQ. This will give a list file which is exactly the same as your source, but with the sequence number field in columns 1 to 6. The first is 000010 the second 000020 and so on.

During a compilation run, the console will show the following information -

155

COBOL filename directives

**CIS COBOL Vv.r (version and release)

directive ACCEPTED   (or REJECTED)
directive ACCEPTED   (or REJECTED)

for each directive in turn.

filename COMPILING

will then appear, and if the source-file specified as file-name cannot be opened (does not exist, for example) the message -

filename FAILED TO OPEN

will appear, and the compiler aborts and returns to CP/M.

After completing the compilation, the console contains the following details -

**ERRORS = nnn DATA = nnn CODE = nnn DICT = mmm:nnn/ppp GSA FLAGS = nnn

ERRORS denotes the number of errors found
DATA denotes the size of the data area required
CODE denotes the size of the program area (not including data)
DICT has three values.
    mmm is the number of bytes used in the data dictionary
    nnn is the number of bytes remaining unused
    ppp is the total of mmm and nnn
GSA FLAGS gives the number of flags encountered, or shows OFF if he NOFLAG directive was given (or assumed by default)

A list of the error codes which may be printed in the listing after an erroneous line is included below, and the command structure for a "RUN" follows the list.

156

9.9.1 CIS COBOL Error Codes

(note that 'missing' could simply mean 'mis-spelt')

01	Compiler Error (fault in the compiler!)
02	Illegal format of data-name
03	Illegal format of literal
04	Illegal format of character
05	data-name declared twice
06	Too many names (data and procedure)
07	Illegal character in col 7
08	COPY is nested (illegal) or file not found
09	'.' missing
10	statement starts in wrong area of source line
22	'DIVISION' is missing
23	'SECTION' is missing
24	'IDENTIFICATION' is missing
25	'PROGRAM-ID' is missing
26	'AUTHOR' is missing
27	'INSTALLATION' is missing
28	'DATE-WRITTEN' is missing
29	'SECURITY' is missing
30	'ENVIRONMENT' is missing
31	'CONFIGURATION' is missing
32	'SOURCE-COMPUTER' is missing
33	There is an error in one (or more) of the MEMORY SIZE, COLLATING SEQUENCE or SPECIAL-NAMES clauses
34	'OBJECT-COMPUTER' is missing
36	'SPECIAL-NAMES' is missing
37	SWITCH clause is in error
38	DECIMAL-POINT clause is in error
39	CONSOLE clause is in error
40	Illegal currency symbol
42	'DIVISION' is missing
43	'SECTION' is missing
44	'INPUT-OUTPUT' is missing
45	'FILE-CONTROL' is missing
46	'ASSIGN' is missing
47	'SEQUENTIAL' or 'INDEXED' or 'RELATIVE' is missing
48	'ACCESS' is missing on indexed or relative file
49	'SEQUENTIAL/DYNAMIC' missing

50	Illegal combination ORGANISATION/ACCESS/KEY
51	SELECT clause phrase unrecognised
52	RERUN clause syntax error
53	SAME AREA clause syntax error
54	file-name missing or illegal
55	'DATA DIVISION' is missing
56	'PROCEDURE DIVISION' is missing, or unknown statement
62	'DIVISION' is missing
63	'SECTION' is missing
64	file-name not specified in SELECT statement
65	record size integer is missing
66	illegal level number - (01-49) - or 01 level required
67	FD qualification contains syntax error
68	'WORKING-STORAGE' is missing
69	'PROCEDURE DIVISION' is missing, or unknown statement
70	data description qualifier or '.' missing
71	SIGN/USAGE is illegal with a COMP data item, or with unsigned PIC data, or is incompatible with other qualifier
72	BLANK is illegal with non-numeric data item
73	picture clause is too long. Max numeric 18, max numeric edited 512, max alphanumeric 8192
74	VALUE clause not allowed with non-elementary data item, or truncation, or wrong data type
75	'VALUE' in error, or illegal for data type
76	FILLER/SYNCHRONISED/JUSTIFIED/BLANK not allowed for non-elementary item
77	level has more than 8192 bytes or zero bytes.
78	REDEFINES of unequal fields or different levels
79	data storage exceeds 64k bytes
81	data description qualifier is inappropriate or repeated
82	REDEFINED data name not declared
83	USAGE must be COMP, DISPLAY or INDEX, no other
87	BLANK must be replaced by ZERO
88	OCCURS must be numeric, non-zero and unsigned
89	VALUE must be a literal, numeric literal or figurative constant
90	PICture string has illegal precedence or character
91	INDEXED data-name missing or already declared
92	numeric edited PICture string is too large
101	unrecognised verb
102	IF...ELSE mismatch
103	Wrong data-type or data-name not declared

104	Paragraph name used twice
105	Paragraph name used as data-name
106	Name required
107	Wrong combination of data types
108	Conditional statement not allowed in this context, must be an imperative statement
109	Subscript wrongly formed
110	ACCEPT/DISPLAY wrong
111	Illegal syntax for I-O
116	Too deep nesting if IF statements (too many levels)
117	Incorrect structure of procedure division - for example, sections out of order.
118	Obligatory reserved word missing
119	Too many subscripts in one statement
120	Too many operands in one statement
141	Inter-segment procedure name duplication
142	IF...ELSE mismatch at end of Source Program input
143	Wrong data-type or data-name not declared
144	Paragraph name not declared (eg GO TO unknown paragraph)
145	Index name declared twice
146	Faulty cursor control. AT clause wrongly specified
147	KEY declaration missing
148	STATUS declaration missing
149	Faulty STATUS record
150	Undefined inter-segment reference
151	PROCEDURE DIVISION in error
152	USING parameter not declared in linkage section
153	USING parameter is not level 01 or 77
154	USING parameter used twice in parameter list
157	Incorrect structure of procedure division - for example, sections out of order
160	Too many operands in one statement (as 120)

In addition to any of the above errors, which are reported during compilation and inserted in the listing after the offending line, the compilation may be terminated by a 'disc full', 'directory full' or other input/output error condition.

If that does happen, the message

FATAL I-O ERROR: filename

159

will be displayed. If you get that message, you will not have a useable intermediate (.INT) file.

One other important, but far from obvious, condition which will cause the FATAL I-O ERROR message is if you have a line in your source program which is longer than permitted. You may have 72 characters of 'sequence, continuation, areas A and B', followed by the 'Carriage Return and Line Feed' characters, but no more than these. If you have allowed your line to be overlong, you will get 'FATAL I-O'.

You should also take note - you'll soon find problems if you don't - that CIS COBOL only accepts **simple** conditions. That means just one comparison. IF A-1 > B-1 OR A-2 > B-2 GO TO — is not allowed. That particular example will 'fall out' at the OR - because the rule is that a simple condition must be followed by an imperative. When you have a 'clean' compilation, you are ready to attempt to 'run' the program.

9.9.2 COBOL 'RUN' command line.

There are several options available to the programmer at run time, including the linkage of the .INT file to the Run Time System, so that the program name can simply be entered as though it was a fully compiled program.

The items in the square brackets are optional.

The full command format is -

RUNA [load param] [(switch param)] [link param] filename [progpars]

The simplest form is just -

RUNA filename

but the parameters allow you to add considerably more to your run-time command.

[load param] is either + D or -I ('add Debugging' or 'omit the Index-sequential module')

When you load the Run Time System, you can choose whether or not to include the optional 'Debug' module, which invokes the interactive debug facility. The default is **not** to include it.
If you want it, enter, say, -

RUN + D filename

There is a list two pages further on of the options available under interactive debug.

There is a module which handles Indexed Sequential files, which is normally loaded with the Run Time System, but which can be omitted (saves space and time) if you do not require it for the program in work. To omit it, type

RUNA-I filename

The choice is threefold. You can have neither optional module, or the I-S one but not the Debug one, or both.

RUNA-I   neither Debug nor I-S
RUNA I-S   but not Debug (the default)
RUNA + D   both.

[switch param] is the way in which you set switches at run-time which can then be tested by the program. According to the settings, the program will carry out the tasks coded for that circumstance.

These switches are on/off only, and are all 'off' (negative value) by default. They may be set 'on' (positive value) by entering the switch number and a + sign. As many of the switches, which are numbered 0 to 7, may be set as desired. For example, (+ 1 + 2 + 3) sets the three switches 1, 2 and 3 'on' and the rest remain 'off'.

As well as the 8 numbered switches, there is a D switch, switched 'off' by default, and switched 'on' by entering D on its own. This is the standard ANSI COBOL 'debug', not the 'CIS COBOL interactive debug'. You may have either of the debug facilities, or both, or neither. They are quite independent.

Examples of load and switch parameters are -

RUNA + D (D + 1 + 2) filename   CIS debug and ANSI debug are both on, also switches one and two. The rest are off.

161

RUNA (+1, +2 +0) filename   Switches 0, 1 and 2 are all on, the rest are off. note that sequence is not important, and that spaces may be used for clarity. Commas are ignored, but are better omitted.

RUNA-I (+1 -1) filename   Switches may be switched off with the - sign, and the last occurrence of the switch number is effective. That is just the same as having no switch parameters. Index Sequential module is omitted.

[link param] has just one value, the 'equals sign' = . What it does is to tell the run-time system to SAVE onto disc a binary image of the run-time system as loaded, together with your (.INT) program. When you enter -

    RUNA = filename

the memory image is dumped to disc, with the filename 'SAVE'. If you want to re-run, you must now re-name that file as a .COM file, and you will then be able to re-run as though it was a fully compiled program. If we had our filename FRED, we started by creating FRED.CBL (and probably FRED.BAK) with the editor of our choice (see next Chapter).

Then we entered COBOL FRED.CBL, and that produced FRED.INT and FRED.LST - the intermediate code and the listing. Now we can type -

    RUNA = FRED

and the program will be loaded, but before the run actually takes place, the memory will be dumped to disc as SAVE. After the run, we re-name SAVE as FRED.COM with the command -

    REN FRED.COM = SAVE

and we have the full set of files like this -

FRED.BAK   the previous version of our source code
FRED.CBL   the version we compiled
FRED.LST   the annotated listing produced by COBOL
FRED.INT   the intermediate code
FRED.COM   the simulated 'COM' program made up of the run-time system and the INT program.

This last file allows us now to enter FRED as a command to CP/M as though it was a transient command, but remember that FRED.COM actually contains

RUNA with or without the optional modules, so watch the copyright situation. It is very convenient for an installation developing programs for use on that installation only.

Clearly, the 'link' parameter will not be used until there is a clean, fully tested program.

[program param] is the place in the command line (after the filename) where you enter values expected by the ACCEPT verb. This is very similar to the XSUB facility with SUBMIT. If the first two data items required by the program, and asked for with ACCEPT, are the day and month, then you could enter the two values in the command line, separated by spaces and separated from the filename by one or more spaces. For example -

   RUNA filename 27 7

would give your program the values 27 and 7 for the first ACCEPTs. Subsequent ACCEPTs would still require keyboard entry as usual.

9.9.3 Interactive Debugging.

The D switch simply treats line with a D in column 7 as statements in the program, whereas omitting the D treats them as comments. This is the ANSI debug facility.

The + D parameter invokes a rather more powerful module. If you use it in the command line, then you are entered into a system roughly like DDT. The interactive Debug prompt is ?. Fourteen different command keys are offered, and the following is only a brief summary of the functions. See the CIS COBOL mabual for full details.

P	Display the current program counter (in hex)
G hhhh	Execute from current program counter to the breakpoint specified as hhhh (an address in hex)
X	Execute one CIS COBOL statement
D hhhh	Display the contents of the specified byte and the next fifteen bytes, in hex and ASCII (if printable)
A hhhh nn	Replace the content of hhhh with the hex character nn or the ASCII character after the " (eg "A or 41 are the same.)
S hhhh	Set a working register with address hhhh

/	Display the first byte at the address held in the working register (and add 0001 to the register)
.nn	Replace the content of the address held in the working register with hex nn (and add 000 to the register)
T hhhh	Execute from current program counter to hhhh and print the address of each new paragraph encountered
L	Output a single 'Carriage Return/Line Feed' on the CRT
M $	define the start and end of a macro (see manual)
C	allows a macro to output a character to the console
;	is the macro comment marker (put before the comment)

9.10 Pascal/MT.

Pascal, like COBOL above, comes as a semi-compiler with several overlays, and a Run-Time System. Unlike COBOL, it also comes in two versions, dependent on the type of arithmetic that is performed. REAL numbers are implemented internally in either floating-point or binary-coded-decimal, dependent on the version chosen. The sets of program are as follows -

Floating point.

Compile time -

FLTCOMP.COM
P2/FLT.OVL
P1ERRORS.TXT
P2ERRORS.TXT

Run time -

PASCAL/F.RTP

Binary coded decimal.

BCDCOMP.COM
P2/BCD.OVL
P1ERRORS.TXT (same)
P2ERRORS.TXT (same)

PASCAL/B.RTP

In either case the source file (yes, you need an editor) must have the type '.SRC' OR '.PAS', since one of these is the assumed type which is not input in the command line. Line lengths must not exceed 80 characters and must end in the < Rt> character (which is Carriage return and Line Feed)

Options are not specified in the command line, but incorporated into the source file (see below). Two directives can be used in the command line, either of which has the value Y or N. N is the default assumed for both - so in the second is required as a Y, the first must also be stated explicitly.

The first directive controls the inclusion of the debugger in the compiler output file (which is a '.COM' file). The second controls the production of a '.PRN' file (which is a listing).

Valid command lines for the source file called MYPROG.PAS (or MYPROG.SRC) are these -

FLTCOMP MYPROG	neither debugger nor list file
FLTCOMP MYPROG.Y	debugger but no list file
FLTCOMP MYPROG.NY	no debugger but list file req'd
FLTCOMP MYPROG.YY	both debugger and list file

Note the period (decimal point) before the directives. If the BCD version is required insted of FLT, that would be invoked in exactly the same way. It is common practice to re-name the Compiler program as PASCAL (for the FLT version).

9.10.1 Compile-time Options.

These are indicated in the source program as special comments of the form

   *$opletter details or $opletter details

The opletter (option letter code) and relevant details if any are listed here -

$Ifilename	Include filename.SRC into the source stream
$L+ or $L-	Turn listing on (the default) or off
$P	Insert form feeds into the .PRN file
$D+ or $D-	Debug code on (the default) or off
$C+	Use CALL instruction for real operations
$Cn	Use RST n for real operations (n = 0 to 7)
$O $hhhh	ORG (origin) of program at run time at address hhhh (default origin is 100H)
$R $hhhh	ORG RAM data at hhhh
$Z $nn00	Set run-time size to nn (hex) pages of 256 bytes
$X $ssss	Set run-time stack space to ssss (default 200)
$S+ or $S-	Turn on or off (default) recursion handling
$Q+ or $Q-	Enable (default) or disable verbose output

165

9.10.2 Input and Output in Pascal/MT.

READ, READLN, WRITE and WRITELN statements are standard for the console device, and in addition WRITE and WRITELN can address a built-in file called PRINTER to access the CP/M list (LST:) device. For instance, you could say WRITE(PRINTER,'Hello').

There are extensions for file handling, which are summarised below, using the conventions -

```
fcbname      =   variable of type TEXT (array 0 to 32 of CHAR)
title        =   ARRAY [0 to 11] of CHAR with -
                 title[0] = disc select byte (0 = logged, 1 = A etc)
                 title[1 to 8] = filename (normal CP/M)
                 title[9 to 11] = type (note absense of '.')
result       =   integer to contain returned value
buffer       =   ARRAY[0 to 127] of CHAR
relativeblock =  optional integer 0 to 255
extent-number defaults to 0
```

The extensions are -

```
OPEN(fcbname,title,result{ ,extent-number} );
CLOSE(fcbname,result);
CREATE(fcbname,title,result);
DELETE(fcbname);
BLOCKREAD(fcbname,buffer,result{ ,relativeblock} );
BLOCKWRITE(fcbname,buffer,result{ ,relativeblock} );
```

9.10.3 PASCAL/MT special routines.

The following routines are supported in PASCAL/MT, and more details will be found in the PASCAL/MT 3.0 Guide (pp32, 33).

```
PROC MOVE(source,dest,length-in-bytes);
PROC EXIT;
FUNC TSTBIT(16-bit-var,bit #):BOOLEAN;
```

166

PROC SETBIT(VAR 16-bit-var,bit #);
PROC CLRBIT(VAR 16-bit-var,bit #);
FUNC SHR(16-bit-var, #bits):16-bit-result;   (shift right)
FUNC SHL(16-bit-var, #bits):16-bit-result;   (shift left)
FUNC LO(16-bit-var):16-bit-result;
FUNC HI(16-bit-var):16-bit-result;
FUNC SWAP(16-bit-var):16-bit-result;
FUNC ADDR(variable-reference):16-bit-result;
PROC WAIT(port-num:constant; mask:constant; polarity:boolean);
FUNC SIZEOF(variable-or-type-name):integer;

9.10.4 Pascal Debugging facilities.

There are two categories of debugging facility. You can control program
flow, and you can display the content of variable(s).

While the debugger is executing, there is a ?< Rt> command which will
display all the commands available.

The debugger works at source statement level, and program controls allow
the usual go/continue with/out breakpoint, trace and
setting/clearing/displaying of breakpoints embedded in the program. The
following summary will allow ready reference.

T{ integ r}	Trace - execute 'integer' lines of the program
{ -} E	Engage display of names of procedures/functions entered. -E disengages it. Disengaged on entry
{ -} S	Slow execution. Allow set of Fast/Medium/Slow speed. -S disengages (normal speed)
-P	clears permanent breakpoint
Pline-number	
Pproc/func	set permanent breakpoint at line number or name
Dglobal-var	
Dproc/func:local-var	
Dfunc	
Dpointer	Display the name(s) listed as encountered
*	Display last variable requested (with D etc)

+n	Display variable n bytes forward from last
−n	Display variable n bytes backward from last

9.10.5 Reserved Words in PASCAL/MT

ABS	ADDR	AND	ARRAY	BEGIN	BLOCKREAD
BLOCKWRITE		BOOLEAN	CASE	CHAIN	CHAR
CHR	CLOSE	CLRBIT	CONST	CREATE	DELETE
DISABLE	DIV	DO	DOWNTO	ELSE	ENABLE
END	EXIT	EXTERNAL	FALSE	FILE	FOR
FUNCTION	GOTO	HI	IF	INLINE	INPUT
INTEGER	INTERRUPT	LABEL	LO	MAXINT	MOD
MOVE	NIL	NOT	ODD	OF	OPEN
OR	ORD	OUTPUT	PACKED	PRED	PRINTER
PROCEDURE	PROGRAM	RANDOMREAD		RANDOMWRITE	
READ	READLN	REAL	RECORD	REPEAT	RIM85
RND	SETBIT	SHL	SHR	SIM85	SIZEOF
SQR	SQRT	SUCC	SWAP	THEN	TO
TRUE	TSTBIT	TYPE	UNTIL	VAR	WAIT
WHILE	WRITE	WRITELN			

Additional notes about the PASCAL/MT variants from Pascal.

Hex values may be specified as in the option list above, $hhhh. For example 1AH may be specified as $1A in PASCAL/MT.

All standard type definitions are supported with the exception of ARRAY, which has a special form. Instead of ARRAY...OF ARRAY... you specify ARRAY[...,...,...] with a maximum of three dimensions. Type TEXT is ARRAY[0 to 35] OF CHAR

PROCEDURE INTERRUPT[i] proc; is supported, where i is the re-start vector number (0 to 7).

CP/M V2.x random file access is supported by RANDOMWRITE and RANDOMREAD.

Pages 37-39 of the Guide explain the use of INLINE to insert machine code, constant data and assembler code.

CHAIN(filename); is supported, as is re-directed I/O (Guide pp 42-43)

9.11 The language C

Several versions are available, BDS C is one of the better ones.

Under CP/M, the C language produces actual object code. The compiler is a genuine compiler, and CLINK produces a '.COM' file which is a genuine 8080 machine code file.

The following general comments about C will explain the process of compilation, give a very brief comment on the content of the language. You are referred to the C Manual for more details.

Although there appear to be two passes of the compiler, there are actually about eight, in two main phases. There are 4 executable programs in C, a standard library file, and a skeleton run-time subroutine file.

The first half of the compiler (CC1.COM) loads the entire source into memory at one go, and produces an encoded version of the source, together with the symbol table, as a file. The name will be the same as your original, with the type '.CCI'. Your source file may have any name and type, and must be stated fully in the compiler call (unless you are using a SUBMIT file which assumes type '.C'). If any errors are detected during that first phase, the '.CCI' file will not be written.

There are options which can be introduced after a '-' in the command line, such as the '-s' which allows the compiler to set undeclared variables as integer where possible. Normally C does not accept defaults. Also the size of the symbol table can be set by following the s (or the -) directly with a hex digit (from 4 to F), the digit being the table size in K bytes. -A is 10K, and -sF is 15K, and default to integer variables.

If a drive letter is specified as the location of the source file, the '.CCI' file will also be put on that drive.

The second half of the compiler (CC2.COM) expects a '.CCI' file as input, and writes a '.CRL' file if no errors are found. (CRL is the equivalent of REL, and means C ReLocatable.) If the CRL file is written, the CCI file is deleted automatically.

Once the re-locatable code exists in a CRL file, it is submitted to the linker CLINK. If this succeeds, the result is a '.COM' file ready to run as a CP/M

169

transient command. Linkage offers the opportunity to combine several CRL files, and/or library routines. You can also rename the combined program (-o option), leave clear space between BDOS and your program (-t), print out sizes and other load statistics (-s) and indicate that chaining between programs will be required (-c).

There are other useful routines available to C programmers, such as a librarian, to maintain .CRL files and allow transfer of functions between files. To see the full list of librarian commands, invoke CLIB and reply 'h' to the prompt, which is an *.

The C language has gained importance recently, since Digital Research have announced that they will be using it for some CP/M work, to improve portability.

9.12 FORTRAN under CP/M.

The most commonly used FORTRAN compiler under CP/M is F80 - and is, as the C compiler, a true compiler producing a relocatable file which only needs to be linked using L80 to produce a true '.COM' file.

The L80 linker was describer earlier in this chapter, under MBASIC, where the BASCOM compiler was described. That description applies equally here, and will not be repeated.

The F80 compiler is invoked with (or without) an argument list which refers to the places where the various outputs are to be directed. There are also (as in BASCOM earlier) a number of switches, each of which is preceded by a /, and must be at the end of the command line. If F80 is invoked without argument list, the * prompt will ask for details.

The arguments are

a,b = c

where a is the '.REL' file, b is the '.PRN' file and c is the '.FOR' source file. The comma is needed if b is included, and the equals sign must be present.

You may specify a disc drive (A: or B: only - no other) and filename, or a device such as TTY: or LST: or HSR:

If you omit the entry **before** the comma, no '.REL' file will be produced. Omit the entry **after** the comma, and no list file will be produced (fast compile of a clean program) . Omit both and it falls off the perch !

For example, you can enter

*NEWNAME,B:MYLIST = OLDNAME

and that will tell F80 to compile OLDNAME.FOR on (probably) drive A:, calling the relocatable file NEWNAME.REL also on A: and putting the program listing out as MYLIST.PRN on drive B:.

There are seven switches which may follow the arguments, and **each** switch is preceded by a / (eg /N/L)

The switches are -

O	All addresses on the listing in Octal
H	All addresses on the listing in Hex (that is the default)
N	Do not list the generated code.
R	Force generation of an object file (even with errors)
L	Force generation of a Listing file
P	Each /P allocates an extra 100 bytes of run-time stack space
M	Tells the compiler to produce the generated code in a form which can be loaded into ROM

Logical Unit Numbers

Each LUN in FORTRAN below LUN 11 is pre-assigned. 11 up to 255 are user assignable.

1, 3, 4, 5	assigned to CON:
2	assigned to LST:
6, 7, 8, 9, 10	assigned to disc files (these are re-assignable)

9.13 MACRO-80

The MACRO-80 compiler (M80) is invoked in exactly the same way as F80 above, has the same arguments and switches, produces '.REL' files for submission to L80 in the same way, and is therefore not discussed further.

9.14 Summary.

There is little that can sensibly be said to summarise all the foregoing, except that it is always worth-while really exploring the potential of your particular language and its implementation. There is the school of thought which says - don't push the limits, the compiler might go wrong. There is also the opposing school which says - try it, and if it works, use it !

If the version of a language which you are offered under CP/M is not up to the standard to which you think you are entitled, then look around for another version, produced by someone else. There will almost certainly be one !

If you use MBASIC (for instance), and you want to edit your program with a full text editor (next chapter), then your program will have to be saved in ASCII. The command is SAVE"MYPROG",A and the save and load will be slower, because the binary form of your program which MBASIC usually produces is smaller. Small changes to a program will probably not justify the time to load the program, save it in ASCII, exit to CP/M, find and invoke the editor, and so on. Global changes, and searches, however, usually do justify the use of a good editor. Watch your line lengths and formats if you use an editor, it is easy to go over the limits, and this may give rise to some rather obscure error messages.

CHAPTER TEN

THE CP/M EDITORS

There is always a need to enter text into a file, either for program entry, ready for compilation, or for a SUBMIT file, or for simply typing in text which can be retained on file, displayed or printed out, used as a data file by a program, or whatever is required.

It is appropriate to differentiate between 'text editors' - which can be pretty basic, with the absolute minimum of facilities - and 'word processors' - which have most if not all of the facilities that typists expect.

As in the previous chapter, there is no need to differentiate between the various versions of CP/M. The editors work in the same way, under whichever version they are available.

We will look at the extremes, ED, which is the basic text editor which comes with the CP/M system (very basic) and WordStar, the MicroPro word processing software which has become almost as much of an 'industry standard' as CP/M has. Many reviews of new or different word processing systems and packages actually take WordStar as the 'standard' against which the other is compared. We will also look at developments of ED such as TED and PEDIT.

10.1 ED - the CP/M text editor.

This can be somewhat confusing, unless you have understood how it works, and therefore what happens when you give a command or enter text.

First, you can only enter ED by including the file name of the file you want to create or alter. The command is -

ED filename

(A small diversion here. If you have CP/M 86 or CP/M 3.1, the command could include a second filespec which would be the identity of the newly edited file. (eg ED oldspec newspec.))

You can give the file a .typ extension if you want to (or if you are editing an existing file which has a 'type'), and you may specify any drive for the file. ED assumes that it is on the logged drive unless you give a drive letter.

If this is a new file, then NEW FILE will appear on the screen. This is a useful check, because if the file exists on a different drive, and you omitted the drive letter, ED would look on the logged drive only, and if your filename was not there, it would open a new file. Similarly if you forget the 'type'.

Then you will get the ED prompt, which is an asterisk. The screen so far looks like this -

ED filename
NEW FILE
: *█

If you want to give ED a command, you **must** have the * prompt on the screen to the left of the cursor. If you are in the middle of entering text, the way to get back to ED is to enter ^ Z (Control and Z).

10.1.1 Simple command set.

ED uses a 'character pointer' (CP), which moves around the file in memory according to your commands. You cannot see it, and it will often not be in the position of the cursor, in relation to the text shown on the screen. For instance, if you tell ED to display a page of text, the cursor will be at 'the end' of the text, but the character pointer will be at the beginning of that page ! If you gave the insert command as the next command, the insertion would be before that page, not after it as you might perhaps think. To get you started there are three or four simple commands which you can use. We will cover these in detail, first, and then go through all the commands, afterwards.

Commands can be given to ED one at a time (when the asterisk is on the screen, remember), or in a string of commands, as we will see.

The # symbol means that you want 'the largest number available'.

174

Commands.

B   This command moves the character pointer to the beginning of the file in memory.

-B   This command moves the character pointer to the end of the file in memory.

(Neither of these commands actually put any of your file on the screen.)

#T   This types the specified number of lines onto the screen, starting from the character pointer. Because you have specified 'as many as possible', the whole file in memory (from CP onwards) will be displayed, and you can stop and start the scrolling display with ⌃ S.

I   This command says 'insert the following characters into the file starting from the CP'. To add to the end of your file, combine two commands, like this -

-BI   That moves the character pointer to the end of your file, and puts you into 'insert mode'. The asterisk will have disappeared.. Now any characters, including carriage returns, which you type, will be put into your file. To get back to ED, so that you can give a command, you type ⌃ Z.

#A   A means 'append'. If the file you specified to ED was an existing file, then you want to bring the file into memory before you start using it. #A means 'bring all the file into memory' or 'fill the buffer'. The CP will still be at the beginning of the file.

#A # T-BI   As a first command, to add to the end of an existing file, this will read the whole file into memory, type it all on the screen, move the CP to the end, and put you into insert mode, ready to enter your additional text.

E   This is the command to 'end the edit' and it will write everything in the memory to your new file, including the changes/insertions, and close the file. ED is terminated, and you are back in CP/M.

At the simplest level, to alter a line, you can give the line number, followed by a colon (:),and then give the K (kill line) and I (insert line) command and re-type it, including the carriage return. You use ^ Z after the carriage return to get back to ED. So if you want to change line 23 (say) to contain the words " DATA DIVISION." instead of what it now says, you would type the following (< Rt> means 'carriage return') -

    23:KI DATA DIVISION.< Rt> ˜Z

And you could then check this with the type command, either with

    23:0T (zero T means 'the current line to left of the pointer.)

or

    23:0TT (0TT means current line to left and right - whole line.)

or, to see the whole file,

    B ‖T

Notice that you insert a line before an existing one, by using

    26:I

which will give you a new line 26 (assuming that you end the insertion with a < Rt>) and push the rest down. The text which was line 26 becomes line 27 when you enter < Rt> .

Now you have enough to allow you to create a new file, save it, re-open it to alter or add to it, and save the alterations. There are many more, and more powerful, commands, which you can experiment with as you need them.

10.1.2 Back-up Files.

ED does not actually alter the file you start with, if it is an existing file. What it does do is to open a new file with your filename and the type $$$, and write from the memory into that file (when you use 'E' for instance). Then it will delete any existing file called filename.BAK, rename the original file to the name filename.BAK, and rename filename.$$$ to the filename.typ which you originally specified to ED. (In later versions of ED you may actually supply an output filespec as well as a source filespec, in which case these would be used, and the source file would not be renamed '.BAK'.)

The biggest single difference between ED and a word processor is that **you** have to tell ED to 'append' the existing file to memory, and **you** have to tell ED to write the contents of memory out to a file. A word processor usually assumes that you want to do both those things, and simply keeps a memory buffer for you, with space to add what you type. As that buffer fills, the word processor writes some of the contents to your file, releasing more space. It also keeps the character pointer where the cursor is. So if you move the cursor, the character pointer moves with it. More about that shortly.

10.1.3 Line numbers in ED.

In the later versions of ED, which you probably have, whenever you are in insert mode, the screen displays a line number. If the character pointer is within the file (not right at the end, that is) then the line number where it is is also shown, just before the asterisk. If no line number appears, try 'switching on' the line number facility with the V command. (-V switches it off.) In the earliest versions of ED, there is no line number facility.

That line number is not part of your file. It is only a line count maintained by ED during the edit. Your file is only the text which you put in through the keyboard, or from existing files. If you want line numbers in your file, then you have to put them there. You can do it as you enter text, or you could do it using the N parameter of PIP (see chapter 4). If you are typing a program for CIS COBOL (see previous chapter) then the compiler has a numbering facility built in (the directive is RESEQ).

10.1.4 The full set of ED commands.

Now we can look at all the commands which ED obeys. Some have been added in later versions, so not all the commands work for the earliest issues of ED. Try them out for yourself, they are not quite as logical as you might expect, and you will get some results which may surprise you ! Remember the CP !

nA	Append n lines from the file to the memory buffer. If n = 0 half the buffer will be used. If n = # this gives all the file.
B	Move the CP to beginning of file
-B	Move the CP to the end of file
nC	Move the CP forwards n characters (towards end of file)
-nC	Move the CP backwards n characters (towards beginning)

177

nD	Delete n characters forwards
-nD	Delete n characters backwards
E	End the edit, close file, return to CP/M
nFstring^ Z	Find the n'th occurrence of 'string'
x::yFstring^ Z	Find the first occurence of 'string' between line numbers x and y (both inclusive)
H	End edit, move CP to start of file in buffer ready to continue with a new edit, having saved the work so far.
I	Insert characters following the command at the position of the CP until a ^ Z is encountered.)istring^ Z)
x:I	Move the CP to the start of line x and enter insert mode
nJastr^ Zbstr^ Zcstr	Find astr, put bstr after it and erase until cstr is encountered, n times.
K	Kill the current line
nK	Kill n lines, starting at CP
x:K	Kill line x leaving the CP where line x was
x::yK	Kill lines between and including x and y
x: #K	Kill line x and all following lines
nL	Move CP n lines forwards (opposite direction to B, note)
-nL	Move CP n lines back (opposite direction to -B, note)
0L	Move CP to start of current line (zero L)
nM commands	Execute commands n times (M = multiple)
M commands	Execute commands until error or end file
x::yM commands	Execute commands repeatedly between x and y
nNstring^ Z	Find n'th occurrence of string or end of file
O	(letter O) Ignore all editing done this run and restart the edit
nP	Display (print) n pages starting from CP. A page is 23 lines long.
-nP	Display previous page and n subsequent ones
Q	Quit the edit without altering the original input file and return to CP/M
R	Read temporary file (see X command) into buffer at CP
x:R	Read temporary file into buffer at line x:

Rfilename	Read filename.LIB into buffer at CP. If you end the filename with < Rt>, the 'read' is performed. If you want to continue with more commands on the same command line, use ^ Z to signal 'end of filename' and continue with the command line.
x:Rfilename	Read filename.LIB into buffer at line x
nSoldstr^ Znewstr	Substitute newstr for next n occurences of oldstr
nT	Type n lines on the screen
-nT	Type the n lines before the CP
0T	Type from start of current line to CP (zero T)
T	Type from the CP to the end of the current line
0TT	Type the whole of the current line
x:T	Type line x
x::yT	Type lines from x to y inclusive
#T	Type from CP to end of the file in the buffer
U	Change lower case to upper case for all future entries
-U	Disable the case change. (Note that U #A changes lower case to upper case while appending a file to the buffer)
V	Enable line numbering
-V	Disable line numbering
0V	Display free space/buffer size (zero V)
nW	Write n lines from start of buffer to file
nX	Append the next n lines to the temporary file X$$$$$$$.LIB creating the file if necessary, and leaving the lines also in memory.
0X	Delete the temporary file X$$$$$$$.LIB (zero X)

(Note that the temporary file allows block movement within a file by allowing 'write block to file' and 'read from file', as stated in the R command above. The lines still have to be deleted if they are not required in their original place. This is 'block copy', rather than 'block move'.)

nZ	Pause for n/2 seconds. (Snooze !)
n	Move forward n lines and type one line
< Rt>	Move forward one line and type a line (Return only)

179

-	Move back one line and type a line
x: commands	Move to line x and obey commands
:y commands	Perform commands from CP to line y
x::y commands	Move to line x obey commands until line y

10.1.5 Further examples of combination commands.

B #T	Type the whole buffer (CP left at start)
-B-T	Type the last line of the buffer
-3L7T	Type the line you are at, plus the three lines above and below it
-UV#	
AB #T-BI	Disable upper case conversion, enable line numbering, append whole file to buffer, type it, move to end and enter insert mode.
BMSoldstr⌃ Znewstr⌃ Z0TT	
	Move to start of buffer, replace oldstr with newstr in all file and type each amended line. (If used with ⌃P the command also prints the lines)
BM0L5D0TTL	Erase the first 5 characters of each line throughout the buffer, displaying the result.
x::yXBzLR	Copy lines between x and y to z (do 0X first !)
x::yMX0TTK	Transfer all lines between x and y to the temporary buffer file, typing and then deleting each line as it is transferred.
BM-B-LX0TTK	Copy the buffer to the temporary file in reverse line sequence and read it back, thus completely inverting the line order, and type each line as it is processed !
B73M0LI ⌃Z0TTL	This allows you to key in a COBOL program as though columns 1 to 7 did not exist, and then run through all 73 lines of your program inserting the seven spaces (before the ⌃Z) before you submit your program to the compiler. If you omit the 'no of lines' - 73 in the illustration - then a new last line will be added to your program which will be repetitively loaded with 7 spaces, and then 7 more and so on until you stop it with⌃ Z. If you do this, you can easily nn:K that superfluous line.

And so on - now try developing your own concatenated commands.

10.1.6 ED error indicators.

?	You have typed an unrecognised command
>	The buffer is full, write some lines to the file (W)
#	ED cannot obey the command the number of times specified
O	Cannot open the .LIB file in R command (not there ?)

10.1.7 ED control characters.

^ C	Abort, re-boot the system and lose all text in buffer
^ E	Physical < RtLf> sequence (obeyed on screen, not put into command - use for long commands)
^ H	Delete last character typed (destructive backspace)
^ I	Logical tab.
^ J	New line (line feed)
^ L	Logical < RtLf> used in search (S) and find (F) string specifications to match with the actual < RtLf> in the text.
^ M	New line (carriage return)
^ U	Delete a line (command line)
^ X	Delete a line and backspace
	String terminator ('escape' to ED)
Rubout	Character delete and echo the deletion
Break	Discontinue the ED command now being obeyed

10.1.8 Summary of ED.

Since ED is provided free with CP/M, and since on most machines a word processor costs a significant amount of money, many people use ED whenever they need an editor for their program or for a '.SUB' file or whatever, and through familiarity, can make use of the commands in a powerful and flexible way. There is no need for any other editor. The shortcomings of ED, when compared with a word processor, are that the screen does not automatically display the 'environment' of the character pointer - though with the right commands it will do so - and the system does not either automatically read from your input file or write to your output file. Neither of these represents a real problem when writing programs, since a program normally fits completely within the memory buffer (particularly an interpreted program) and since a programmer is quite capable of memorising and using the edit commands. However, for large text files, ED does not offer quite the facilities needed.

10.2 WordStar.

The word processing package which is used by more people than any other, under CP/M, is WordStar, the MicroPro package. It has features which are the envy of operators of 'dedicated' word processors, and can 'drive' practically any printer which can be attached to your machine.

The programs which make up WordStar are as follows -

WS.COM	The main program and loader
WSMSGS.OVR	The overlay which contains all the 'help' text
WSOVLY1.OVR	One of the processing overlays
WS3.COM	The program which allows you to run other programs within WordStar
WSU. COM	The basic WordStar from which your WS is installed
INSTALL.COM	The program which installs WordStar for your terminal and printer
MAILMRGE.OVR	
	The overlay which allows you to use a file as the source of additional text to be incorporated in the printed results, the merging being done at print time. (Earlier version called MERGPRIN.OVR) There is also a spelling dictionary and program, which allows you to build up a list of your own terminology.

WordStar requires all the programs to be on drive A, but files can be on drive

A or any other. (To be precise, WordStar requires all the programs to be on the same drive and requires you to log onto that drive before you enter WS.)

Two types of file can be created with WordStar, one of which is entirely under the control of the operator, with no 'format' implied, and the other of which contains various 'defaults' which allow the operator to type a document without consideration of the various requirements for margins and pagination.

WordStar, in the 'document' mode, recognises two kinds of 'carriage return'. Since margins are set (either by default, or as changed by the operator) WordStar can handle 'word wrapping' from the end of one line to the start of another, quite automatically, with no need for the operator to decide when to start a new line. WordStar inserts 'soft' < Rt> characters, which it can move or remove as necessary if the text is revised at a later time. At the end of a paragraph, however, the operator does need to indicate where this is to be, and this is shown by pressing the < Rt> key. This is a 'hard' return, is retained in that position by WordStar, and is shown on the right edge of the screen as a < symbol.

Word-wrapping, hyphenation, 'find' and 'find and replace', tabbing, margin setting, justification or non-justification are just some of the many things which WordStar handles. Text can be entered at draft spacing and printed that way, and then with a single command, altered and reprinted at final spacing. Margins can be set and re-set before, during or after an edit, as can other features, such as print character width, line height, page offset, page numbering and so on.

There are four levels of 'helpfulness' which WordStar offers, from the most helpful (Level 3) to the fastest (Level 0). At level 3, part of the screen displays the most commonly used commands all the time, and displays other descriptive text at any time the operator wants to see it, during editing. At level 0, all the screen is used to show the text being input, and there are no delays caused by overlays being fetched from disc.

WordStar can be entered exactly like ED, with the command -

    WS filespec

or alternatively the operator can simply enter -

    WS

and the 'no file' menu will be offered. This gives various file handling facilities as well as the edit and print selections.

You can have WordStar printing one file while you are (rather more slowly than normal) editing another file. However, you cannot use ^ P in WordStar to echo your keystrokes to the printer. ^ P is actually a WordStar 'part command'. Also, you cannot print the file you are actually editing. To be absolutely precise, you can print the last completed edition of it, but not the one containing the changes you are currently making.

WordStar commands fall into three types. There are 'single letter' commands all of which (except 'delete' or 'rubout') require the Control key as well as a single letter. There are 'two letter commands', in five groups, each of which starts with one of the five letters P Q O K J. And finally there are 'dot commands', so called because they start with a dot (.) in the leftmost column of the screen (column 1).

Many commands are called 'toggles' or 'switches', because the features they control are 'binary', so a single 'switch' command either enables or disables the facility, according to its previous state.

The following list covers each group of commands in turn.

10.2.1 Single letter commands.

Cursor movement. (these are in a diamond shape on the keyboard, and are ofter referred to as the 'cursor control diamond')

^ S	Character to left.
^ D	Character to right.
^ A	Word to left.
^ F	Word to right.
^ E	Line up.
^ X	Line down.

Scrolling. (moving the text on the screen)

^ Z	Text one line up.
^ W	Text one line down.
^ C	Text moves one screen up.
^ R	Text moves one screen down.

Deleting.

DEL	Delete character to left of cursor.
^ G	Delete character at the cursor position.
^ T	Delete the word or part word at and to right of cursor.
^ Y	Delete whole line containing cursor.

Miscellaneous one-letter commands

^ I	Tab (used if your keyboard has no TAB key).
^ B	Paragraph reform from the cursor to after the next hard carriage return (used after margin changes, or deleting or adding text, also to get you to the end of the text in the current paragraph).
^ V	Switch insert ON or OFF (toggle). When OFF, new text entered where text is already displayed will over write that displayed text. When ON, the line will be moved along to make space for the inserted keystrokes.
^ L	Find/replace again. This allows repetition of a previously entered find or replace command, without going through the entry again in detail. (see ^ QF,^ QA)
RETURN	End of paragraph - 'hard' return.
^ N	New line. Insert a return, and leave the cursor to the left of the return so that new text can be entered in that line. (Pressing the RETURN key leaves the cursor to the right of the return.)
^ U	Interrupt a command and return to the previous state. (This is useful if you start to give a command with several steps, or give a command which has a 'global' effect, and then change your mind, or remember something you should have done first.)

10.2.2 Two-letter commands.

With all the two-letter commands following, using the space bar as the second 'letter' cancels the 'prefix' (the first letter).

The 'Q' commands. (Q = Quick - commands which speed up other 'single step' commands, or perform 'global' actions.)

^Q   Display 'Q' menu, at help levels 3 and 2 only.

^QE   Cursor to top of screen (cf ^ E - up one line).
^QX   Cursor to bottom of screen (cf ^ X).
^QS   Cursor to Start of line.
^QD   Cursor to enD of line.
^QR   Cursor to start of file (^ KS is quicker for long files).
^QC   Cursor to end of file.
^Q0 to ^Q9   Cursor to numbered place marker (set with ^ K0 to ^ K9).
^QB   Cursor to start of marked Block (set with ^ KB).
^QK   Cursor to end of marked blocK (set with ^ KK).
^Q   Cursor to Position before last command.
^QV   Cursor to last BlocK handled, or last Find/replace.
^QF   Find. Cursor to first occurrence of string (the actual string
                       is entered in response to a question, and also search
                       parameters are put in, to search back/forward and to
                       ignore case, search for whole words only etc).
^A   Find And replace. Strings and parameters are entered in
                       response to questions displayed.
^QY   Delete character at cursor position, and all characters to
                       the right hand end of the line.
^Q 'DEL'   Delete all characters to the left of the cursor on line
^QQ   Repeat the next keystroke (command or text entry) until
                       the space bar is pressed. (eg ^ QQ^ B reforms to end file)

The 'O' commands. (O = Onscreen. These commands control some of the
functions visible on-screen during editing - eg Margins)

^O   Display 'O' menu, at help levels 3 and 2 only.

^OI   Set tab at position keyed in. If position is preceded by the
                       # sign, a numeric tab stop, for alignment of decimal
                       points in columns of figures, is set. If the ESC (escape)
                       key is pressed, instead of the entry of a column number,
                       the tab will be set at the column position where the cursor
                       was before the ^ OI command, and which is shown in the
                       prompt line at the top of the screen.
^ON   Clear tab at position keyed in. A for position means 'clear
                       All tabs currently set'.

^ OF	Sets ruler (margins) from length of line containing cursor. Any ! or # characters in the line are set as tabs. Space characters at the start or end of the line are ignored when setting the margins.
^ OC	Centre text in the existing line (for headings etc)
^ OLn	Set Left margin to column number n
^ ORn	Set Right margin to column number n (can be outside screen width - early WordStar showed 2 screen lines for each text line, later WordStar scrolls screen sideways)
^ OSn	Set line spacing (n = 2, double - n = 3, treble)
^ OX	Margin release toggle. Margins relock when cursor re-enters margins (exactly as typewriter key)
^ OJ	Toggle for justification (right justified/ragged)
^ OT	Toggle for 'ruler' display (margins/tabs) ON/OFF
^ OH	Toggle for Hyphen-help (during para reform ^ B)
^ OP	Toggle for page break display ON/OFF
^ OW	Toggle for Word-wrap
^ OV	Toggle for vari-tab (logical/physical tab)
^ OG	Set paragraph tab one tab position to the right, temporarily changing the left margin until a < Rt> is hit. Indenting to second tab position is ^ OG ^ OG and so on. This does not affect the right margin.
^ OE	Soft hyphen toggle. Any hyphen (minus sign) entered when soft-hyphenation is on will appear on the screen, but will be suppressed at print time unless it is needed for word-break. This allows long words to be used in text which may be subsequently reformed, and the words can contain one or more suitable break points to avoid wrapping the whole word, and giving an untidy layout.
^ OD	Toggle for print display. Some commands enter extra characters in the text, to be obeyed at print time. If this obscures the appearance of the document, they can be suppressed with ^ OD to allow the actual layout to be studied.

The 'K' commands. (K = blocK. All commands which refer to a block of text - either a whole file or just part of a file are in this group.)

^ K	Display the 'K' menu at help levels 3 and 2 only.
^ KD	Done this edit. Save the work done but stay in WordStar

^ KX   Done edit. Save work done and exit to CP/M (= E in ED)

^ KQ   Quit the edit. Do **not** save the current editing, but return to the state before this edit started. Asks the question 'ABANDON EDITED VERSION OF filename (Y/N)' if any changes have been made. Stays in WordStar.

^ KS   Save and continue/resume edit. (= H in ED) Allows return to point where the command was given with ^ QP or to end of file with ^ QC. USE FREQUENTLY WITH LONG DOCUMENTS. Avoids possible loss of text if disc or hardware malfunction, or if disc space becomes full.

^ KP   Print a file during the edit. (Generally takes priority of cpu/disc access over an edit, so edit slowly !)

^ KJ   Erase file during edit (as CP/M ERA command)

^ KL   Change logged drive during edit.

^ KE   rEname file during edit.

^ KO   cOpy file during edit (names prompted for).

^ KF   Display (part) directory during edit. Toggle.

^ K0 to ^ K9   Insert place marker (numbered) at cursor position.

^ KB   Mark start of Block at cursor position (or remove mark).

^ KK   Mark end of blocK at cursor position (or remove mark).

^ KV   moVe marked block to cursor position.

^ KC   Copy marked block to cursor position.

^ KY   Delete marked block.

^ KH   Hide (un-display) or re-display block markers.

^ KN   Set/release columnar move toggle (see note below).

^ KR   Read whole of file (name prompted for) to cursor posn.

^ KW   Write marked block to file (name prompted for)

Note on ^ KN. Earlier versions did not offer this facility. When columnar move is OFF, the **whole** of the text between the < B> and < K> markers (or the highlighted text) is affected. If columnar move is ON, the < B> marks the top left of the block, and the < K> marks the bottom right. Any text to the left of the < B> position, even on lines between the < B> and < K> is left unaffected. Any text to the right of the < K> is similarly unaffected. If a column is moVed or deleted (Y), text to the right is moved over to the left to join up with any text on that side, and so on. Try it.

The 'P' commands (P = print-time. These commands are inserted into the text, but not obeyed until the document is printed. Often called the 'print enhancements'. Where these are 'toggles', they are used twice, once before the text to be enhanced, and once after. The ¯P itself is not put into the file, but the second letter of the command is, with the '∧' symbol. Some of these commands have no effect on 'matrix' printers, and only work on 'daisy-wheel' printers.)

∧P	Displays the 'P' menu at help levels 3 and 2.
∧PS	underScore (underline) toggle. Does not underscore the space character.
∧PB	Boldface toggle. Each character is struck twice, and the print head is moved slightly between strikes.
∧PD	Double strike toggle. As boldface, but no movement between the two (or more) strikes.
∧PX	Strike-out toggle. (eg ~~Strike---out~~)
∧PV	Subscript toggle.
∧PT	Superscript toggle.
∧PY	Ribbon colour toggle.
∧PC	STOP print at this point (allows change printwheel etc).
∧PA	Change to Alternate pitch (usually 12 cpi).
∧PN	Change to Normal pitch (usually 10 cpi).
∧PK	Left/right heading/footing control. (Omit following spaces if page number is even.)
∧PF	'Phantom space' - depends on printer or printwheel, sometimes a currency sign - pounds or cents.
∧PG	'Phantom rubout' - depends on printer/printwheel.
∧PO	'Non-break space' prints as space, but will not allow word separation at line end.
∧PH	Backspace. Allows multiple printing in same position.
∧PQ ∧ PW ∧ PE ∧ PR	allow and need special definition for your system
∧ P< Rt>	Set overprint line. Useful for embedding a non-print ruler in text, and for continuous underline.

The 'J' commands. (J = jog your memory. This set of commands allows you to display on the screen, during editing, an abbreviated form of the WordStar manual, with explanations and hints about all the facets of WordStar.)

∧J	Display the 'J' menu at help levels 3 and 2 only.
∧JH	Displays help menu and asks for selection of level.
∧JF	Explains flags (at right edge of screen).

^ JI	Displays command index (not on menu).
^ JB	Displays details of reforming text (^ B).
^ JD	Details of print directives and 'dot' commands.
^ JM	Details of margin controls and settings.
^ JS	Explanation of 'status' line (top line of screen).
^ JR	Explanation of ruler line (^ O commands).
^ JV	Details of how to move text (^ K commands).
^ JP	Explanation of 'place' markers (^ Kn and ^ Qn).

10.2.3 The 'DOT' commands.

Each starts with a full stop (dot) in column one at the left edge of the screen. Even if the left margin is at some other column, the 'dot' holds in column one. These commands occupy a line on the screen, but not in the text. They take effect at print time, but they do also affect the screen display. For example, the dot command for page length (.pl nn) affects the position of the page break display as text is entered or edited.

There are default settings for all these commands.

The commands for character width and line height set the character size, and all other commands relating to page size are calculated from these two. The page length is stated as a number of lines, the margin at the top is a number of lines **within that page length**, as is the bottom margin. Headings and footings are within the top and bottom margins, and can be positioned with the heading and footing margins, which state the space between text and heading/footing. The page offset adds the stated number of columns to the left margin position, so that paper can be loaded in the printer with the left edge on column 1, and the text will be offset to the right to give a blank filing margin.

..comment	Any characters after the .. are ignored.
.IGcomment	As above.
.CWn	Character Width in 1/120" (default 12 = 10cpi).
.LHn	Line Height in 1/48" (default 8 = 6 lpi).
.POn	Page Offset in columns (default 8).
.PLn	Page Length in lines (default 66).
.MTn	Margin at Top in lines (default 3).
.MBn	Margin at Bottom in lines (default 8).

.HMn	Heading Margin in lines between text and heading Margin in lines between text and footing (def 2).
.HEtext	Text printed every following page as heading, with # as page number (see also ∧ PK).
.FOtext	Text as footing. Page number is default text.
.OP	Omit Page numbering.
.PNn	Page Numbering on, starting with n as page number. If n is omitted, starts at 1 at beginning of file, or at page number in status line at that point. This number can be used to select pages to be printed at print time.
.PCn	Page number column position (defaults to centre).
.PA	PAge change now (unconditional).
.CPn	Change Page if less than n lines remain on this page.
.SRn	Sub/superscript Roll in 1/48" (default 3).
.BPn	Bidirectional Printing OFF (n = 0) or ON (n = 1).
.UJn	Microspace Justification at print time OFF/ON (0/1).

Merge-Print DOT commands. There is a further set of dot commands which are ignored by the WordStar print routines, but which are handled by Merge-Print. A data file may be specified, and it must be created so that all records have exactly the same number of fields. Wherever a field is to be printed, it is placed in the text using the name given in the .RV command, with an ampersand (&) at each end of it. Spaces may be used between the field name and the &'s. Merge-print automatically reforms text to suit variable length insertions either from the file or through the keyboard, unless you suppress this.

.DFfilename	Data File to be used.
.RVnamestring	Read Variables into names in string (commas used to separate names). eg - .RV A, B, C reads three fields from file. These are used in the text as &A& or &B& or &C& or & C &.
.RP	Repeat reading the data file to end. Only required if several reads needed in one document. If one read per printed letter (say), then the .RP is not needed.
.SVname, text	Allows you to set the name and the value of the variable in the document. Wherever &name& appears, the text will replace it. Text can also include variables read from file.

.AVname	Ask for Variable to be input from the keyboard at print time. The input will then replace &name& where it appears in the document.
.DMtext	Displays the Message in text (which can include names read from file or keyboard) on the screen at print time.
.CS	Clear Screen. Clears any .DM or other screen messages previously displayed.
.FIfilename	File will be printed in the position of the command at print time. Can be used to make the printing 're-entrant', by calling the document which contains the .FI command.
.PFxxx	Print-time re-Form (xxx = ON/OFF/DIScretionary). Allows control of re-forming at print time. Default is DIS.
.IJxxx	Input Justification (xxx = ON/OFF/DIS). Allows control of justification at print time. If DIS is entered, the justification which was set at input of the text is preserved. Default DIS.
.OJxxx	As above for Output text at run-time.
.LSn	Line Spacing reset at print time. (as ^ OS)
.LMn	Left Margin reset at print time.
.RMn	Right Margin reset at print time. None of the above five commands or this one affects the stored files.

Any name included in ampersands for 'content printing' may be extended by /O (alpha O). This will suppress the whole line if the name is empty and nothing else needs to be printed on that line. (eg in an address, &district/O& with nothing else on the line will not print a blank line if 'district' is blank, but will omit the line altogether.)

For record purposes, you can take a print of your file with embedded dot commands and names in ampersands, with the commands actually printed, not obeyed, by answering Y to the question SUPPRESS PAGE FORMATTING (Y/N) which appears during the specification of the ordinary WordStar print command.

Two commands which can speed up processing are ^R and the ESC key. When you are asked for a filename, use of ^R will enter the last filename used for that purpose (= Repeat). After entering a filename for printing, instead of pressing the RETURN key, which will initiate a series of questions, you can 'escape' from the questions by pressing < ESC>. The later versions of WordStar also allow you to 'escape' part way through the list of questions.

10.2.4 WordStar Summary.

There are clearly very many more commands in WordStar than in ED. However, this requires no feat of memory, because the only command you need to know is ˄ JH3. Using this command allows you to bring up any of the menus, and in particular the 'help' menus, during text editing. It must be re-stated that the preceding sections are not a replacement for the manual, or for a training course, but will help as a quick reference summary, if you use it irregularly, or are not yet familiar with the system.

10.3 BASIC line editors.

Within MBASIC and some other languages, there are simple - rather crude-line editors. These require you to specify the line to be edited (MBASIC is 'EDIT linenumber'). Then you have a small set of edit commands which allow you to change your existing text. The set below is the MBASIC set - others tend to be very similar. (See also the section in chapter 9 on MBASIC.)

L	List the line on the screen and return to the start for editing.
X	eXtend the line. List it, put the cursor at the end of the line and enter 'Insert mode'.
nC	Change the next n characters to the ones keyed in.
nD	Delete the next n characters and show them within the 'back slash' symbols (\.)
I	Insert characters from the keyboard until either the ESC key or RETURN is pressed.
RETURN	end line edit - display the remainder of the line and return to MBASIC command mode.
E	As RETURN but do not display the rest of the line.
'space'	pressing the space bar steps along one character at a time, displaying the character 'uncovered'.
nSx	Search along the line for the n'th occurrence of the character x, and stop with the cursor to the left of it.
nKx	As search, but deleting all characters passed over.
A	Start the line edit Again, ignoring what has just been done.
Q	Quit the edit, do not save changes, return to MBASIC comand mode.

H   Delete all characters to the right of the cursor and enter
                        'insert' mode.

To enter EDIT during the original entry of text, use ⌃ A. This puts you in
editmode in the line you are/were typing.

One warning, attempting to 'insert' (I) long strings of underline
characters(___) can confuse the MBASIC editor, and you may find that you
have succeeded in actually truncating lines, rather than extending them. List
the line again if in doubt.

10.4 Other Editors.

There are numerous derivations of the basic editor (ED), such as TED and
PEDIT. If you have one of these, you will find it's operation very similar to the
operation of ED itself - and you'll also find considerable overlap in the
commands and how they perform. Once you know how the different levels of
editor work, the precise operation of a particular one should be reasonably
transparent.

10.5 Spooling the Printed Output.

It is relevant here to make a brief mention of the availability of print spoolers
and de-spoolers. These are programs which reside up near the top of
memory, and which can intercept LST: device outputs, transferring them to
one or several files. They can also be set up to empty 'spool' files onto the
printer during the gaps when the system is doing nothing else.

There is a de-spooler from Digital Research, which resides in the memory just
below the FDOS, and which will copy a file to the LST device whenever
CP/M is waiting for input. (DESPOOL)

If you use MP/M, you will find that there is a spooler and de-spooler provided
with the system - obviously much more necessary when several users are
working at once, and all may be calling for the LST device

There are also proprietary products which work quite happily, but some of
them require that you make some modifications to your CBIOS. The detailed
instructions are provided - and even the most rudimentary understanding of

DDT will suffice to enable you to perform the mods. There is sufficient information on the use of MOVCPM and DDT within these pages to enable you to follow the instructions.

Why might you want such a utility? If your system is print-bound, because you have a lot of output or a slow printer or both, then the printing can continue while you get on with someting else. If your printer is not only slow but noisy, you might want to print at times when it will not distract you or other people. Essential? No. But it might be very useful.

10.6 Summary

Some languages contain editors which allow you to key in your program and manipulate it before submitting to compilation or interpretation. Most, however, do not. Therefore you need an editor. ED comes free with CP/M, and with a little practice is acceptable and perfectly usable. WordStar costs money, as do the other CP/M word processors, but offer vastly enhanced facilities. When considering the purchase of an editor/word processor, check the facilities offered. Some, for instance, have all the commands embedded in the text, and do not show the actual 'page layout' until print time. This is less easy for a typist, but can easily be learned.

Many systems are now available which attempt to bridge the gap between the word processing package and the dedicated word processing system. They do this by providing additional keys on the keyboard which are wired to give one of the single or two-letter commands. Interestingly, most seem to choose Wordstar as the software. There is always a disagreement between those who like to use the commands directly from the main keyboard, and those who prefer special 'function' keys. the function keys are faster, when you have found the right key. Using the main keyboard is fast, for mnemonics, because the typists fingers fall naturally on the keys. The argument is usually resolved by the marketing organisation which says 'pretty keyboards sell better'.

Spooling and De-spooling is a useful adjunct to any system which handles extensive amounts of text to be printed. WordStar contains a limited form of de-spooler, in that it allows you to edit one file while printing another. In effect - the way WordStar handles its files is just like a sophisticated spooler!

CHAPTER ELEVEN

The structure of CP/M.

11.1 FUNDAMENTALS

All of this chapter is fundamental to the rest of the book - but it might help if we started with a very brief verbal description, before we get down to details.

First, the internal storage of your microcomputer may be referred to with a variety of names - 'core' is one which comes from the use of magnetic cores strung together in a matrix, this was one of the first electronic, non-volatile, storage methods. We will use 'memory', because it also covers current microcomputer storage, which needs power to retain the content.

CP/M is the operating system, and some of it is resident in the memory at all times. We will talk principally about CP/M 1.4 and 2.0, for clarity, and introduce the CP/M Plus (3.1) variants as they arise later in the chapter.

At the 'bottom' of the memory - in the bytes with the lowest numbers, starting from 0000H - is a page (256 bytes, up to 00FFH) which is reserved for the 'system parameters'. The program which you load - either a 'transient command' or a program or whatever - sits above that in the 'transient program area', which usually starts at 0100H - the start address of many programs. The system parameters are the link between your program in the TPA (the 'transient program area' - starting at 0100H) and the resident programs of CP/M. These - the resident CP/M routines - are at the other end of the memory, in the highest numbers.

Right at the top is the BIOS - the Basic Input Output System. This is the one which conforms to the CP/M 'skeleton form' - but actually contains all the routines needed to handle your particular hardware. Next to it - below it in the memory - is the BDOS - the Basic Disc Operating System. This is standard.

The two parts we have just mentioned - BIOS and BDOS - are often referred to as one, under the name FDOS - the Full floppy Disc Operating System. FDOS (BIOS + BDOS) must be resident in the memory while you are using the system.

Below FDOS in a smaller area of the memory is the CCP - the Console Command Processor. This is a complete program - in fact in CP/M 3.1, it is actually a file on disc called CCP.COM - and it has the group of instructions which handle your keyboard editing commands, the resident commands like DIR, and one other simple routine. That routine looks for any keyboard entry, signalled by the pressing of the < Rt> key, and picks out the first word - the characters up to the first space. If that word is not a command built into the CCP, it assumes that it is the name of a file on the logged drive (or the stated drive if d: is at the front of the word) called by that name with the extension (.typ) of '.COM'. Any other words - following the first - are not handled by the CCP, they are left for the program to deal with. The file with the stated name and the '.COM' extension is loaded into the bottom of the TPA. The words following the transient name are moved to location 0080. CP/M attempts to 'format' them into filenames at 005C and 006C. Then, control is passed to location 0100H (the 257th byte).

From that moment, the CCP can be overwritten, if need be - because it will have no further part to play until the A> (or B> etc) is on the screen. And the action of re-booting reloads the CCP - as well as one or two other things we will mention soon. One other point about the CCP - it assumes a *default* extension of '.COM' - you must *not* supply it. If the '.COM' file is not found the word is echoed back to the keyboard with a ? after it. Of course, if you call one of your programs or files a '.COM' file, and enter it as a command to the CCP, them CCP will try to load and run it. Users of CP/M 3.1 will note that we covered the SETDEF command earlier - which allows the CCP to search for .SUB as well as .COM files, and on more than one drive.

That is the introduction over. You now have the picture. System parameters in the very bottom page of memory, FDOS at the top, and CCP just below it. Pressing < Rt> invokes the CCP which searches for a file who's name is the first word typed after the 'prompt' and who's type is '.COM'. The memory between the Parameters and the FDOS - including that occupied by CCP after each re-boot - is available for your invoked program to use, and is called the

197

TPA - Transient Program Area. If your command (COM filename) also includes a drive letter, the disc on that drive will be searched for the command.

Now let us go into a little more detail.

11.2 CP/M in memory.

CP/M 1.4 up to 2.x can be installed in any memory size from 20K bytes up to 64K. 1K bytes, to be precise, is 1 X 1024 bytes, not 1000. The majority of implementations actually have the full 64K, so we will assume that. Smaller implementations work in the same way, but leave less space available in the 'centre' of the memory for the TPA, as we will see. Memory is usually numbered from 0 (zero) up to 64 X 1024 - 1 (= 65535). One byte is eight 'bits', each capable of representing only 0 or 1. References to the 'top' of memory refer to the high numbered bytes. The 'bottom' of memory starts at byte 0. (We will indicate the way CP/M 3.1 uses banked memory with more than 64K, shortly.)

One byte (eight bits) may contain an alphanumeric character according to the ASCII code (The American Standard Code for Information Interchange), or may contain a pure binary number from 0 up to 255, or may be used in other ways. If two bytes are considered together, they can be regarded as forming four groups, each of four 'bits'. Each group of four bits can hold from 0 to 15, or one of the digits used to count in 'hexadecimal'. The hexadecimal digits from (decimal) 10 to (decimal) 15 are usually represented by A to F. Counting in hexadecimal ('hex') goes like this :-

```
 0  1  2  3  4  5  6  7  8  9  A  B  C  D  E  F (single digit)
10 11 12 13 14 15 16 17 18 19 1A 1B 1C 1D 1E 1F
20 ....
   ....
E0 ....
F0 F1 F2 F3 F4 F5 F6 F7 F8 F9 FA FB FC FD FE FF (two digits)
```

and so on .

The addresses of the 'bottom' and 'top' of a 64K memory are often referred to as 0000H and FFFFH - the 'H' indicating that 'hex' is being used.

CP/M contains some *resident* software, which stays in the memory, or which is re-loaded at every 'boot', and some *transient* software which is held as separate programs, and is loaded on demand, as we will see. The memory map of the resident software in a 64K machine looks like this.

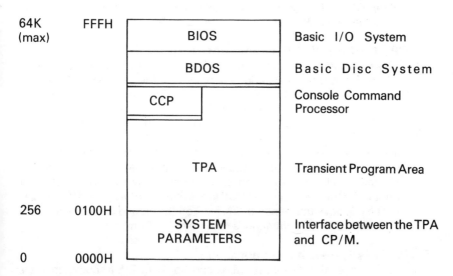

64K (max)	FFFH	
		BIOS — Basic I/O System
		BDOS — Basic Disc System
		CCP — Console Command Processor
		TPA — Transient Program Area
256	0100H	
		SYSTEM PARAMETERS — Interface between the TPA and CP/M.
0	0000H	

STRUCTURE OF CP/M IN A 64K MEMORY

The five regions of the memory shown above are used as follows:

1. BIOS - Basic I/O System

The BIOS sits between the BDOS and the hardware, and contains the lowest level interface between the standard commands and data handling of the BDOS (basic disc operating system) and the special requirements of the peripherals of the computer. A standard BIOS is supplied by Digital Research, together with explicit and detailed instructions for re-configuring the BIOS to match practically any hardware environment. Defining and implementing this part was the principal reason behind the current success of CP/M.

2. BDOS - Basic Disc Operating System

This, as implied above, is the standard part of CP/M which is the real 'heart' of the system. The two parts together form a logically complete

199

unit, called FDOS by Digital Research. FDOS is the resident part of the operating system which is in memory while a users program is being executed. If parts of FDOS are not required, they may be 'overlayed' by user code, but the program which does so must 're-boot' on completion, to re-instate the resident FDOS. The FDOS - and in particular the BDOS - will be examined in detail later.

3. CCP - The Console Command Processor

This is a distinct program which uses FDOS to allow the operator to access information held and catalogued on the backing storage. The CCP reads a user command put in through the console. The CCP contains some built-in commands, which execute programs fully contained in CCP, and it recognises transient commands and uses FDOS to get them from disc and loads them into the transient program area. It then executes them. This is one of the standard parts of CP/M, and we have studied the resident and some transient commands in Chapter 2. It is also worth noting that when the system is re-booted - or booted for the first time - the CCP looks first for a partly used 'SUB' file - which will have the filename $$$.SUB on the logged drive. If such a file is found, the next command is taken directly from it.

4. TPA - The Transient Program Area

This area is where user programs and transient CP/M commands are executed. It includes the CCP, which may be over-written, (and re-loaded at program completion), since CCP is never required during program execution. In version 3.1, resident system extensions (RSX files) are loaded at the top of the TPA.

5. System Parameters Area

This region is the first 256 bytes at the bottom of the memory (from 0000H to 00FFH) and is a reserved area for system information (it contains the 'jump to warm boot' instruction, for instance). It contains the numbers of locations in FDOS which are needed by the user program, and it also has information put into certain locations by either FDOS or a user program for the use of the other.

In this and subsequent chapters, we will study the content, alteration and use of these areas in more depth.

The System Parameter Area is the first 256 bytes of memory - from 0000H to 00FFH. The transient program area starts at 0100H, and runs right through to the start of the FDOS. FDOS is BIOS and BDOS considered as a unit, and must be resident when it is used, it cannot be invoked and loaded when required, like a transient command.

We have repeated that information in several ways, and in at least three places, because it really is essential to your further comprehension. Now we can move on to consider elements of CP/M directly.

11.2.1 The System Parameter area.

You can inspect the content of this area by loading DDT, and then entering D0< Rt>. You will also need a D< Rt> to show the full 256 locations.

The main areas that we are concerned with are the first 8 bytes and the last 164. In the first byte (00) and the sixth byte (05) you will find the machine code JMP instruction. This requires an address in the following two bytes, and the addresses you will find in bytes 01,02 and 06,07 are the address in BIOS of the 'warm start', and, usually, the lowest numbered location of FDOS - the part immediately adjacent to the CCP. However, as we will see in a moment, if you have loaded DDT to look at the addresses, then you will get an unusually low number.

These are the contents of the first 8 bytes

00H	the JMP instruction
01H	the first byte of the address of the warm start
02H	the second byte as above
03H	the IOBYTE (maps logical to physical peripherals)
04H	the current default disc drive number (0 = A,1 = B etc) and user number
05H	the JMP instruction
06H	the first address byte of FDOS (but see below)
07H	the second

The warm start routine is in BIOS - that is the part of CP/M which is tailored to the hardware. BIOS is not re-loaded when a warm start takes place. BDOS and CCP are re-loaded.

We will discuss the IOBYTE later in this chapter.

201

The current default disc drive number is fairly clear - CP/M 1.4 only accepted 0 to 3 for this (drives A: to D:) but 2.x accepts 0 to 15 (F in hex) as A: to P:. Version 3.1 also accepts 16 logical drives, of course. ('Logical', because you can treat one physical drive as two or more logical drives, for example with a Winchester.)

The address in 06H and 07H has two purposes. First, and obviously, it is the address in the BDOS to which all calls to CP/M from a transient program are made. (As we will see, the code currently in register C is inspected by BDOS, to find out what it is supposed to do !) Second, it is a higher address than any TPA program is allowed to use - to prevent a program from overwriting the BDOS. However, DDT is aware of that, and the authors of DDT decided to stack a lower value in there, to prevent the user of DDT from overwriting DDT itself, while 'charging about in the memory'. That is why, if you use DDT to inspect the first 8 bytes, you will get a false value in 06H/07H.

The area between 07H and 5CH need not concern us here.

From 5CH to 7FH inclusive - 36 bytes - are the default FCB's, or File Control Blocks.

From 80H to FFH inclusive - 128 bytes - is the Default disc buffer. The content of a File Control Block, and the reason for a disc buffer of 128 bytes will be developed in the next few pages.

11.2.2 The Bootstrap.

A hardware facility - possibly invoked with a particular key depression or just by 'power on' - reads the first sector of the first track on the first drive (A:) into the bottom of the memory, and transfers control to whatever is in there. What is in there will be a small program to read the CCP, BDOS and BIOS from the disc into the memory, and to transfer control to the CCP.

That is 'cold boot' - everything from the lowest location of CCP to the top of (assumed) memory is loaded. If you are wondering why we put 'assumed' memory, remember what we said earlier about MOVCPM (Chapter 6) which can take a smaller or larger version of CP/M and re-organise it for the memory size you want. Now that you understand what goes where in the memory, you can get a better idea of what MOVCPM does. If you 'boot' a 32K version of CP/M into a 64K memory, the FDOS is loaded in the bytes up to 7FFFH -

and bytes 8000H up to FFFFH are inaccessible to the programs and the system.

'Warm boot' is somewhat different. For one thing, the content of the TPA is unaltered (which would not be the case if you powered down and then powered up again) and for another - the program which performs 'warm boot' is in BIOS - at the top of the memory. So the 'warm boot' reads a reduced number of sectors off the disc, and only re-loads CCP and BDOS before handing over control to the Console Command Processor, CCP.

You may find, for instance, that your screen is blanked out by a 'cold boot', but left unaltered by the 'warm boot'. This is logical, since the handling of your screen must be contained in BIOS, and that is the area of the memory which is not reloaded with a 'warm boot'.

11.2.3 The Disc Directory.

In order to discuss the File control block, we will first establish how files are actually recorded and controlled by CP/M.

If your discs are 'soft sectored' - see disussion in the next chapter - you will have had to 'FORMAT' any new discs. This is the process of writing special sector start/end markers before and after each sector of 128 byte capacity which will be used for your data. In the process of 'formatting', the 128 bytes are filled with E5 hex characters. Hard sectored discs do not need to be 'formatted' - but the E5 character is still significant, as we will see.

All discs have a fixed number of sectors following the 'system track(s)' for a directory of the disc - rather like the contents pages in a book. Each CP/M sector has 128 bytes, as we said, and each directory entry needs 32 bytes. Thus, if you have a disc which allows for 64 directory entries, that means that the directory of that disc is the first 16 sectors after the 'system'.

Whenever you 'manipulate' either a file itself, or just its directory entry, the 32 bytes of the directory are copied into the memory, and 'manipulated' there. Only after the file is closed, or the manipulation is complete, is the entry written back onto the disc from the image in memory.

If you are using one of the transient commands like REN or STAT - then you only handle the directory entry. If you are reading from or writing to a file -

such as a data file - then the directory image in memory is kept up-to-date with what you have done - but the directory on disc is not - not until, as we said, the file is closed. Then, and only then, is the directory on disc replaced with the image from memory.

Now you can see why it is so vital that you close a file properly before unloading a disc.

If we look at the content of the directory entry, much of the detail of how ERA works, how files are identified, how they are marked for user areas and/or with $SYS attributes and so on will become clear. This applies to all versions of CP/M, including 3.1, unless you have invoked the password/date stamping. We noted earlier that password/date stamping in version 3.1 requires the use of INITDIR to reformat and extend the directory space first, and then you may use SET to actually initiate passwords/date stamps as required.

If you have looked at a published table of ASCII codes and their meanings, you will have seen that the table which is presented is always eight rows by sixteen colunms - and that therefore the binary coding requires only three bits by four, not the four by four which are actually available in a byte. That missing bit - called the 'high order' bit, is used by CP/M.

The directory entry is in two halves - the file identity half - called FNT or File Name Table, and the half in which actual disc sector allocation is recorded - the RBT or Record Block Table.

11.2.4 The File Name Table

This table contains the following data:

Byte	Name	Content
00	ET	Entry type. If this contains E5, the directory entry has not been or has been ERAsed. If it contains 00, the file exists in USER 0. Any other number is a USER number. (eg 03 is USER 3.) To 'unerase' a file after an unintentional ERA - before you do anything else, find the entry and stack 00 in this byte instead of the E5. You can write a program for this. Entries other than E5 or 00 are only found in CP/M 2.x + . 1.4 did not support USER.

01-08   FN   File name. Up to eight characters supplied by you, made up to eight with 20H - the blank or space character. If CP/M has created the filename, it will be in upper case only. If you created it with, say, a SAVE command in MBASIC, it may include lower case as well, but then will not be found as a ufn by any CP/M command - since CP/M translates l/c to u/c.

09-0B   FD   File Type. Up to three characters, with 20H filling any gaps at the right. The high order bits of these three characters are used for signals. The 'h-o-b' of the first character is normally zero, but if set to 1 means that the file is set to 'Read Only'. In the second character of type, the 'h-o-b' set to one means that the file has the $SYS attribute. See chapter 3. These only apply to CP/M 2.x, because CP/M 1.4 did not have the $SYS facility.

0C   EX   Extent number. Here any additional 'extents' - which are units of 128 by 128 bytes (16K) - which may be needed for files larger than 16k are recorded. Each directory entry is thus, actually an 'extent' entry, not a 'file' entry. This is usually 0.

0D   Not used in CP/M 1.4 or 2.x

0E   S2   Not used in CP/M 1.4, but used for part of the 'extent count' by 2.x (how many extents).

0F   RC   Record Count. An extent can have up to 128 of what CP/M calls 'records' - 128 byte units. The number of records which are used in the extent represented by this directory entry is included here. When you look at a STAT listing, this is the number (for a single extent file) listed under 'Recs'. If this is the first entry for a two extent - or larger - file, the value here will be 128. (represented by 7F in hex.)

Notice that we have slightly over-simplified the 'extent' picture. What we have said is correct for a standard 8" IBM format single sided disc. Higher capacity discs may have a slightly different way of handling the extents, which results in a single directory entry for more than one extent.

Although you must always enter a filename with extension with a full stop (period) between the two parts, this is automatically translated into a full eleven characters by CP/M, by padding either or both parts with space characters at the right as needed. What you enter as FRED.COM is actually held in the directory as FREDßßßßCOM (where the 'ß' is a space).

That completes the description of the FNT - File Name Table - and you will already have seen how many of the commands we discussed in earlier chapters actually work.

11.2.5 Record Block Table

Now for the RBT - Record Block Table. These are the bytes, continuing on from 0F. (We are still numbering them in Hex.)

Byte	Name	Content
10-1F	DM	Disc Map. This is a table of bytes or words which are a list of those CP/M logical blocks which are in use by the file. If a particular block contains part of the file, it is listed in the table.

That is the end of the directory entry, but one further character is held in the File Control Block - the FCB - held as the memory image for that file. In CP/M 2.x, there are four more bytes used in the memory image.

Byte	Name	Content
20	NR or CR	Next Record. The next record number to be read or written in a sequential file. In a closed file, this will be zero.
21-23		Three bytes added to the Directory entry which we have described above - these are used for random access record number.

11.2.6 The IOBYTE - Input/Output Device mapping.

There are four logical devices (CON: RDR: PUN: and LST:) understood by CPM. Each of these can be allocated to one of four values - as we saw in chapter 4 - the four physical devices available for each.

This byte is best considered in four parts, with each pair of bytes in the part taking values 00 to 11 - four values. As you will see from the table, if bits 2 and

3 are set to 01, that means that the PUN: device (bits 2&3) is set to PTP: (the second possible value).

Bits	Ref to	Values 00	01	10	11
6&7	CON:	= TTY:	CRT:	BAT:	UC1:
4&5	RDR:	= TTY:	PTR:	UR1:	UR2:
2&3	PUN:	= TTY:	PTP:	UP1:	UP2:
0&1	LST:	= TTY:	CRT:	LPT:	UL1:

11.2.7 Sector Allocation by CP/M.

All disc reads and writes are actually direct access - though they look like sequential access because of the way CP/M handles it. If a disc write instruction is received by the BDOS, then it looks at its table of space allocation for that disc, and allocates the next available sector. The block containing that sector is marked in the FCB for the file (in memory) and will eventually be written out to the disc directory as the entry for that file.

Although it appears to you that all files are simple sequences of sectors, in fact, CP/M will allocate 'next available' space to your file, and thus your file may be scattered through the area of the disc. If a file is deleted, this allows re-allocation of sectors which were used for it, to other files, when a 'write' is carried out.

One of the effects of this that you can see for yourself is in the display of entries by the DIR command. The entries are listed on the screen for you (without the '.' between name and type, and if you look back a couple of pages, you'll see that the '.' is not held in the directory) in the sequence in which they appear in the disc directory. Deleting a file not only makes space available in the file area of the disc, but it also makes space available in the directory. So your newly written file may appear in the directory, not at the end, but in the first available space.

That is not the whole story, however. Much CP/M software makes use of a '.$$$' file type. If, during development in MBASIC or during a PIP command, for instance, you indicate that you want a file to be overwritten, what actually happens is that a new directory entry is created in the next available space, the new file is written with filename of name.$$$, and when it has been completed and the new file closed, the old file is then deleted, and the new one re-named to name.BAS or whatever. As a result, repeated SAVEs of a

BASIC program will not only keep shuffling the location of the file name in the directory, but will probably also use different areas of the disc each time.

11.3 Memory Disc - MDISC.

While we are in this introduction to CP/M, we need to introduce the concept of 'bank switching' to allow the use of more memory than the 64K which CP/M can use with its two-byte addresses. The way we will do this is to discuss the advantages and disadvantages, and the method of implementation, of MDISC. Then we will look at version 3.1, which incorporates 'banked memory handling'. If you use non-banked CP/M 3.1 in a 64K memory, everything works in the way we have described so far. With a banked system 3.1 contains the necessary routines, and the banked memory is not handled as 'pseudo disc', as we will now describe for MDISC.

There are various names for the 'device' - MDISC, SILICON DISC, RAM DISC for instance - but they all have two things in common. They are handled by CP/M as a disc, but the 'medium' is actually Random Access Memory - RAM.

The costs are higher than comparable storage on 'floppies' - but the speed advantages are breathtaking. The price of a floppy disc drive of, say 500k bytes would probably buy not much more than 100k bytes of MDISC. The costs are certainly higher - byte for byte - than the costs of Winchester storage - but there are benefits which may outweigh the extra costs.

For example, on a Winchester disc, it is very tempting to use lots of USER areas in different drive numbers to partition the disc amongst different development jobs - and very rapidly indeed, the development programmer will find he has the most enormous labelling and indexing and accessing problem. The advantage of a 'floppy' is that you can quickly and easily label and re-label it. What can you do with a Winchester ? That doesn't apply to the user who simply needs large file space for large files in a stable, running system, of course - but it could apply to you.

Have you tried handling a 60 page file, using WordStar ? If you have, you'll know just how long it takes to do a 'Save and Resume'. And of course, the longer the file gets, the more important it is that you do keep an up-to-date back-up. With MDISC, that process takes only a second or two.

Another important benefit of MDISC, which might seem a disadvantage at first, is that it is volatile, and it will be cleared by a 'power-off' or even a cold boot. That means that the development programmer gets into the habit of taking a 'floppy copy' of any updated program or whatever, before attempting to run it. That is, of course, good practice, but it is easy to get slip-shod. When a program under test runs wild and crashes the system, and you realise that a) the only copy you have of the program as it is, is in the MDISC, still, and b) that the only way to regain control of the machine is to 'cold boot' - which will wipe the MDISC, then you will realise that absolutely rigorous archiving and security copying are valuable.

The main uses to which you will be able to put MDISC - though perhaps not all at once unless funds are available for a large MDISC - are these -

a) Simulate large arrays in MDISC which can give very fast handling of large volumes of data. This becomes a sort of 'pseudo virtual memory'.

b) Spool files, submit files, work files of all kinds will be handled very quickly indeed in MDISC. The WordStar example was such a one as this.

c) High speed access to discs. If you first copy a disc file to MDISC, and then access it there - that will be much faster than accessing on the floppy. It does not take a large amount of file accessing to outweigh the 'overhead' of having to copy in (and perhaps copy back out).

11.3.1 Adding MDISC to a CP/M system.

Clearly, what is needed is a way of adding memory and of paging that memory. Systems which use bank switching normally use fairly large pages - typically 16k - but memory-mapped systems tend to work with smaller units - typically 4k, called 'granules'. 4k is common because, apart from any other reason, one byte can address 256 locations, and if each location is a granule identity, you have $256 \times 4K = 1$ Mega Byte.

In a memory mapped system, what tends to happen is that the processor address (two bytes, remember) is split into two parts, the bottom 12 bits being unaltered, but the top four being used to address a high speed memory bank which returns a single byte for the four bit address. The address is thus the 12 original 'low' bits, plus the new 8 bits retrieved by the four original 'high' bits.

If you have version 3.1, you have all the necessary routines. If you do not, how you actually do the job is a matter of choice, convenience, cost and competence. One way is to buy the add-on complete, another is to write your own code for the disc addressing. If that sounds a formidable task - do not be put off the idea, because the actual code itself occupies less than 256 bytes. The concept and the idea of what you are trying to achieve is the difficult part - the code is not so difficult.

We will include, here, a summary of what will be required - but this will only make sense if you understand about customising a BIOS, and are reasonably familiar with the activity. Never-the-less, though it may be out of sequence (see following chapters), this is the logical place for it.

First, define the disc parameter block for the MDISC. Because you are simulating a disc drive, you need to define 'sectors' and 'tracks'. The obvious sector size is the standard 128 bytes. Anything else would require some 'de-blocking' code which would waste space and execution time. (As well as being more code for you to write !) The most convenient track size is the 'granule' size, as we used it a moment ago. The granule is the smallest amount of memory which can be addressed in the bank switching or memory mapping. Each granule then resembles a track, and a change in track corresponds to a change in memory bank. Also, as a bonus, the track number then becomes the memory bank or granule number, when you are writing your BIOS code. The disc parameter definition will then simply include a track offset which is the actual main memory of 64k. (With a 4k granule, the first 'track' of the MDISC is the seventeenth granule in the addressing.)

When you are defining a disc parameter block for 'floppies', there are various standards to which you must adhere. With the block for MDISC, you have complete freedom of choice. A datablock shold be kept to the minimum of 1k (unless your RAM is likely to exceed 256k). This also means that your number of file directories will be a minimum of 32 (32 x 32 = 1024, or 1k). Since there is no permanent storage in MDISC, you are unlikely ever to need more entries than that !

Examples of MDISC parameters for two widely different granule sizes are these -

Granule size	1k	16k
Sector size	128 bytes	128 bytes
Sector per track	8 sectors	128 sectors
Datablock	1k	1k
Sectors per		
datablock	8 sectors	8 sectors
Directory entries	32	32

The actual read and write with these examples is then a single transfer between the DMA (Direct Memory Access) address and the actual memory address, once the banked memory is switched in. The track - which is also the memory granule number - is selected, and the address is given by 128 times the sector number from the start of the granule.

The actual switching of the memory granules is hardware dependent. With some systems, the 128 byte record must first be copied into the BIOS 'common' area. Then the MDISC memory granule can be swopped with the lowest program memory granule. The record is then copied from the BIOS common area to the MDISC RAM. Reading would take place in reverse. The steps required to write a record to MDISC in a 16k memory banked system are these -

WRITE TO MDISC - the 'subroutine steps'.

Copy record into BIOS data area.
Switch first 16k to bank specified by track number.
Calculate memory address (sectnum x 128).
Copy record in BIOS into memory bank.
Switch back the first memory bank replacing the MDISC bank.
RETURN

This, as you can see, represents a fairly simple coding task - disc selection and initialisation are rather more substantial.

11.3.2 A use of MDISC.

Since it is possible (details later) to include routines so that a SUBMIT file is invoked at cold boot, you may, when you have installed MDISC, want to use such a facility to set up in MDISC the programs you most use, automatically.

A software programmer who regularly uses, say WordStar, RMAC and LINK would probably configure the system to load these into MDISC automatically at switch-on. You may have a different set of requirements.

Incidentally, if you have an option during linking to store the symbol table on disc - why not allocate it to MDISC ? And if your gymnastics in BIOS are up to it, why not call the thing drive M: - even if you have only two other drives ?

CHAPTER TWELVE

Hardware.

12.1 Fundamentals.

In this chapter we will include some comments about hardware, and how the complete hardware and software package influences what you can do and how you do it. We will concern ourselves largely with discs, but will mention other features. It is useful to know what is meant by some of the terms you will meet - like 'sector skewing'. Each of the topics we will cover - and there is no particular sequence to the topics, because they are not related other than their general 'hardware' bias - will have its own heading. You could regard this chapter as a group of short notes, all related to 'hardware' and implementations, rather than to the nature of CP/M itself.

12.2 Discs.

As we have said, there was originally an 8" disc, recorded on one side only, at a recording density and track separation which was decided by IBM when the product was first created. Now there is a smaller disc - usually called a 'diskette' - which is five and a quarter inches in diameter. Recently, smaller discs again have been announced - and there are at least two sizes vying for popularity. Disc drives have now been constructed with reading heads on both sides - so that 'double-sided' discs can be used, in either of the two common sizes. Hard sectoring - lots of holes in the disc to be detected as they pass the hole in the cover, and Soft sectoring (one 'start of track' hole in the disc) are available in a range of sizes and data capacities. Track separation has been reduced, and the actual recording density per track has been increased, so that there is a very wide range of drives and discs available. Some of the draft material for this book was originally written at the keyboard of a machine

213

with the standard 8'' single sided, single density discs - later drafts were produced on double sided, double density diskettes.

There is, with any disc system which uses either hard or soft sector read/write, a potential problem of speed of reading or writing. To put the problem at its simplest, one could say that having written one sector, there is not enough time for the CPU to note that the write has finished and to present a further 'sector full' of data to the drive *and to get that written on the next physical sector*. The disc is spinning continuously, and there is simply not time to write a file on contiguous sectors. If you actually wanted to do that, you would have to wait for the latency of the drive (the time for one revolution) plus a bit, before you could write the second sector. To get round that problem, the idea of 'sector skewing' was introduced.

At its simplest, this is a decision to allow one or more sectors to pass under the read/write head before writing the next logical sector. Skip over five sectors, so that file sectors one and two are on physical sectors one and seven, and that gives you the rough idea. Naturally, nothing is *that* simple.

All CP/M files are actually split into 'extents'. This is principally for addressing purposes. Also, there are maximum file sizes for the different versions of CP/M.

The maximum size of a file under version 1.4 is 4 M bytes (4 megabytes) That is rather more than 4 million bytes, because 1 K bytes is 1024, not 1000, so 1 M bytes is 1048576 bytes. Under version 2.2, the maximum size of a file is 8 M bytes, and under version 3.1 (CP/M Plus) the maximum file size is 32 M bytes.

In all cases, whatever the maximum file size, an 'extent' is 16 K bytes.

In the simplest case, a file with, say, three extents (numbered 0, 1 and 2) requires three entries in the directory, one for each extent. However - there is something called 'extent folding'.

We can best explain this - having introduced the terms and given a general idea of what is involved - by following through the effect of extents and extent folding in the different versions of CP/M.

Under 1.4, each extent requires a directory entry. The second and further extent entries are slightly modified versions of the original entry.

214

Normally, you would not know, or need to know, anything about extents - they are 'transparent'. DIR does not mention multiple extents, and such transients as PIP cope with them quite happily. However, the STAT command contains an 'extent' column - as we saw in chapter 3. If you have a low limit to your number of directory entries (STAT DSK: will show you the number), and several large files, you could run out of directory entries even though the DIR command indicates that you have fewer than the maximum number of files. Incidentally, the STAT command in both 1.4 and 2.2 shows 'extent' - but none of the replacement commands in 3.1 show it ! However - the DIR command under 3.1 shows the total number of directory extents used.

If you are a 'user' - you now have all the information about extents you are likely to need.

If you are a programmer, you may need a little more. If you use 1.4, and you want to use direct access, you have to set the extent number in the FCB. If you use 2.2, the FCB has a three byte record number, and you can use the random disc access functions 33 and 34 (see the following chapters). To use these, the 'ex' field of the FCB is simply set to zero.

If, in your program, you want to use functions 17 and 18 to scan the disc directory all through, you may find that there is more than one entry for a given filename. If the reason for the scan is to display a complete - or a partial - directory, that could be confusing. So you want to remove the duplicates before you display. Under CP/M 1.4, its easy - you look for only those entries with a zero in the 'ex' field in the directory FCB entry.

Under 2.2, it is not quite that easy. There may be no entries with zero, or there may be more than one ! If your file exceeds half a megabyte, you use more than 32 extents. But the extent number only runs from zero to 31. So the 33rd extent is numbered zero again - with an overflow bit set in 's2'. There are only 5 overflow bits in version 2.2 - so the maximum file size is 8 M bytes, as we said. There are 7 in version 3.1 - allowing a 32 M byte maximum file size.

If there is no zero 'ex' in the directory, this will have been caused by 'extent folding'. Now we need to introduce the idea of 'logical' and 'physical' extents.

If a program reads a file sequentially, it will be able to see the FCB changing each time a 16 K byte boundary is crossed. However, if the same program searches the directory tracks, it may not find a directory entry for each of

215

those 16 K extents. During a file access, the FCB which is pointed to by register pair DE in the BDOS call will be updated by the 'logical' FCB which satisfies the filename and extent number specified. If a file is opened directly (by an OPEN function call), or by implication when a 16 K boundary is crossed, the FCB will describe a logical extent of 16 K. In the FCB, the 'ex' will contain the extent number, and the 'rc' will specify the last 128 byte record in that extent.

A program which searches through the directory using the SEARCH FIRST/NEXT function, will of course scan the physical extents. The BDOS returns an offset (from 0 to 3 in CP/M 2.x) with which the program can extract the searched FCB from the copy of the 128 byte directory record (sector) held in the current Direct Memory Access (DMA) buffer.

Under 1.4, physical and logical extents are the same. The only differences between the FCB in the directory and the FCB returned to the program which is reading it is in the two bytes 'dr' and 'cr'. The program FCB uses the 'dr' byte for the drive number, but the directory FCB uses it to show if the FCB is empty (value 0E5H) or (under CP/M 2.2) to specify User Number. The 'cr' byte is not in the directory FCB.

Under 2.2, a physical extent may actually describe more than 16 K bytes. (16, 32, 64, 128 or 256 K may be specified.) The disc parameter block holds an Extent Mask byte (EXM). The disc parameter block (DPB) also holds related attributes such as the Block Shift Mask (BSM) and Disc Storage Maximum (DSM), as well as the physical characteristics of the drive. The EXM holds one of five values, dependent on how many logical extents (how many 16 K records) the physical extent contains. This is what is called 'extent folding'. The values of the EXM are these -

No of Folds	Size of Extent	Value of EXM	Disc Block Size -byte-	Disc Block Size -word-
1	16k	0	1024	2048
2	32k	1	2048	4096
4	64k	3	4096	8192
8	128k	7	8192	16384
16	256k	15	16384	n/a

A disc may actually be split into tracks and sectors, but as far as the FCB is concerned, it is partitioned into data blocks. On the standard IBM 8" disc, the data block size is 1024 bytes - in other words, eight consecutive 128 byte sectors (which may be part on one track and part on another). There are therefore, on that disc, 243 data blocks - two blocks are reserved. The data blocks are numbered from 0 to 242. Since there are less than 256, the data block number can be completely specified in one byte. With larger capacities, two bytes (a 'word' in the table above) are used to number the data blocks. The value of DSM (which is the number of the highest possible data block - 242 in our 8" example) also indicates whether a byte or word is needed.

As you can see, any physical extent must be at least 16 K bytes. So if the DSM is greater than 255, the smallest BLOCK is 2048 bytes. If 1024 bytes was allowed, and there are eight sectors in an extent, we said, so an extent would be 8 times 1024 - 8 K bytes. This is less than the minimum - so all blocks must be 2048 bytes (if the DSM is greater than 255). On the discs being used to record this text, the DSM is over 255, and the STAT command shows that any file has a minimum allocation of 2 K bytes, the smallest block - as you would now expect.

Obviously, too, the physical extent must be capable of being unpacked into a 16 K logical extent. So the block size cannot be greater than 16 K bytes.

Now we have the rules for a PHYSICAL EXTENT -

1. Maximum BLOCK size of 16k.
2. Extent folding must be 1 (no fold), 2, 4, 8 or 16 (max).
3. The minimum block size for data blocks with BYTE numbering is 1024 bytes - and for data blocks with WORD (two byte) numbering is 2048 bytes.

We could devote a whole chapter to further details of extent folding, and the exact differences between the PHYSICAL FCB (in the directory) and the LOGICAL FCB - extracted from the physical FCB and presented to the program which has opened the file. We will simply summarise with the following example.

Crossing an extent boundary with the 'random read' (say) causes the programs FCB (logical) to be updated by the BDOS from the directory FCB (physical) if extent folding is used.

There are few references to other publications in this book - for the simple reason that this is itself a fairly detailed reference book. However - this book cannot replace the absolutely up-to-the-minute information which is published by the CP/M Users Group (UK). There are all kinds of relevant, comprehensible 'goodies' in the Journal of CPMUGUK. And if you have bought this book, you may well wish to be kept as up-to-date as possible.

12.3 Screen Handling.

The screen handling on your particular machine will be specified for you in the hardware manual - but you will usually find that there is some kind of direct screen addressing.

What is not always clear is how you actually invoke that addressing. If you are in CIS COBOL, that is normally done by using the AT extension to the ACCEPT and DISPLAY verbs. AT is always followed by four numbers, the first two being 'line' (from 01 at the top of screen) and the second two being 'column' (from 01 at the left). So you could say -

DISPLAY "ENTER DATE (DDMMYY) <   > " AT 1220.
ACCEPT DATE-IN AT 1241.

In some implementations of MBASIC there are similar ROW/COLUMN facilities.

However, almost any VDU will move the cursor to a given position if you send a suitable character sequence to the display. That is the point of this brief note - the fact that when a cursor control sequence is specified, you use it by actually sending a character string to the display.

In the manual for the machine being used to enter this text, there is a 'grid' showing what character is required for each line, and what character for each column. There is also a little incantation along the lines of -

"To move the cursor to a desired position on the screen use the command ESC, Y, r, c where r and c are the characters indicated by the grid."

That may be just a little opaque to someone new to computers. If you look at the characters along the sides of the grid, you will probably find that they represent a sequence of ASCII decimal codes, starting somewhere after the 'non-printable' characters. On this machine, column 1 and row 1 are both indicated by the 'space' character - ASCII 32. So for row 14, you use the character ASCII (31 + 14). The ASCII character for ESCape is 27, so the function in MBASIC which allows you to specify cursor positioning on this machine could be -

50DEFFNC$(R%,C%) = CHR$(27) + "Y" + CHR$(31 + R%) + CHR$(31 + C%)

and you could move the cursor to row 12 column 40 with the instruction -

5010 PRINT FNC$(12,40);

(Note the semicolon which in MBASIC leaves the cursor in position. Without it, the cursor would automatically jump down to row 13 column 1.)

12.4 Non-functional and missing characters.

Many hardware implementations contain 'traps' or special interpretations of some keys - particularly 'Control and ..." keys. There is little or nothing that the programmer can do about them, except to make sure that they are not used in software which might be run on that hardware.

Two examples will suffice to illustrate this point.

The Apple II, with one of the CP/M boards, is fairly common, at the time of writing. However, an unmodified Apple II has no 'shift' key. To change from upper case to lower, and vice versa, you use ^ A. (Control and A.) (The IIe does have upper and lower case.)

Therefore - the ^ A editing command is simply not available. If you try to run WordStar, you will find that you cannot use the 'word right' facility. Editing in MBASIC, similarly, is inhibited.

On most SuperBrains, the ^ W has no effect. This is less important than ^ A, perhaps, but irritating at times. Since the 'configuration' programs with CP/M 2.2 for the SuperBrain allow the user to redefine the meanings of several of the keys, you can get round it by re-specifying one of the cursor control keys to perform this function.

Also, there is a problem with all CP/M machines, that you can 'lose' or appear to lose a single character, when typing ahead. This is only a problem if you do not know the reason.

219

In the BDOS there is a single character buffer, which is used to look ahead to any console input. This is provided so that you can use ∧ S to suspend console output - and ∧ C to abandon the current job and return to CP/M. Fine - but if the program which you are running ends, and re-boots, then as we have said before, the BDOS is re-loaded. Any character in the buffer is lost. Some programs (some commands) do not actually re-boot - they simply RET to the CCP. STAT, for instance, is small, does not overwrite the CCP, and so can RET directly. No character is lost. PIP will use all the memory it can get - and always ends with a 'warm boot'.

There may be a time when your ∧ S *seems* not to work, to suspend output. That is almost certainly because you have accidentally or deliberately pressed another key first. If you did, and the key is not a command, that character stays in the look ahead buffer, and blocks you from putting a ∧ S in there.

We have said previously that even a warm boot reloads the BDOS (though only a cold boot reloads the BIOS). This could be regarded as unnecessary, but is a safety device. Obviously a program could, by chance, corrupt the BDOS. There is a better reason. Sometimes, programs take the BDOS entry point as the top of the TPA. This is not strictly accurate, because the first 6 bytes of BDOS contain the CP/M serial number, which is checked occasionally by the CCP. If an invalid serial number is found, the system will halt. Naturally, you will only re-activate the CCP when you re-boot. If BDOS was not reloaded at the same time as the CCP, the system might crash. If you had overwritten the first 6 bytes with something totally unlike a serial number, and BDOS was not re-loaded, it *would* crash !

If you need more information about the oddities of your particular hardware - whatever it is - then there may be a magazine or users group letter devoted to your system - and the CPMUGUK Journal has a wealth of this kind of detail, often from members who have written in. (Beware - they may not understand CP/M as well as you do - so there might just be the odd mis-conception !)

CHAPTER THIRTEEN

Using the FDOS

13.1 Fundamentals.

Some programmers never progress beyond their high level language into 'assembler level' work, but even they will occasionally feel the need to carry out some particular task which is either very long-winded, or even impossible, in the particular language they use.

Also, there will often be occasions when a particular program would benefit from 'tuning' - improving the speed at which certain often repeated tasks are carried out.

Similarly, an application may demand something which can only be done as an assembler routine, called into the main language program.

Even if none of these apply, if a programmer wants to inspect some compiled code, either to identify a 'bug' or simply to find out exactly what a high level statement compiles into, the programmer will need to be able to read and understand the way in which the CP/M facilities are invoked.

And the assembler programmmer will certainly need to address CP/M directly.

In all these cases, it is only necessary to know where, and how, to transfer control to CP/M, to give the programmer full control of the way a program works. And that is simplicity itself.

To transfer control from your programme to CP/M, all you do is to JMP to location 0005H, having first put appropriate values in Register C, and sometimes also in the DE pair.

If, for some reason, the system parameter region, at the bottom of memory, has been moved up, then the address to jump to is the BOOT address (normally 0000H) plus 0005H. (BOOT + 0005.)

That address itself contains a JMP instruction, and the next two locations contain the FDOS entry point - which is the same for **all** transfers to FDOS.

You put into Register C a numeric code which is interrogated by FDOS, which is effectively an instruction to FDOS to perform some specific task. The codes are called 'functions'.

If the task requires an address, FDOS will look for that address in the Register pair DE. That is it. That is how you enter, and use the facilities of, FDOS.

Actually, you are entering BDOS - which, as we saw in Chapter 11, is the standard part of FDOS - the 'non-customised' part.

The remainder of this chapter will be concerned with the different functions and their meaning.

13.2 The Function Codes.

For quick reference, we include here the standard list of CP/M codes. It is always worth checking your own CP/M manuals to ensure that your version of CP/M does actually cover all these. The asterisk (*) against some of the codes indicates that the code has been added or altered since the issue of CP/M 1.4. If you have 1.4 - or even earlier versions, not all of the codes apply to your system. However the BOOT + 0005H certainly does !

Where we have put two asterisks (**), the function has been added or amended in version 3.1.

There are two sets of functions, the Basic Input/Output set - and the Disc Input/Output set. We have listed them separately. We have also included a note for each function, of the parameters needed to be input **to** FDOS and the parameters (if any) returned **by** FDOS after the completed function. The parameters are all passed through registers, lettered A to L. All these are explained in greater detail further on.

222

In the first set, the 'basic I/O fuctions', Console, Reader, Punch and List devices are referred to. These are the logical device names (CON:, RDR:, PUN: and LST:) which are allocated to physical devices by the IOBYTE (chapter 11). The read buffer contains a binary number in the first byte, which is the maximum length of the buffer - and if values are returned in the buffer, the second byte contains the actual length (the 'current buffer length'), and the data which is returned follows, up to the stated number of bytes. This first set of FDOS calls are actually carried out by BIOS - the part of FDOS tailored for your hardware - but the entry point is the same for BDOS or BIOS calls.

Basic I/O Functions

(* means added/altered in 2.x; ** means added/altered in 3.1; 'character' is abbreviated to 'char' throughout)

Function and Number	Input Parameters	Output Parameters
System Reset	0	None	None
Read Console	1	None	ASCII char in A
Write Console	2	ASCII char in E	None
Read Reader(Auxin)	3	None	ASCII char in A
Punch(Auxout)	4	ASCII char in E	None
Write List	5	ASCII char in E	None
Direct Con I/O	6 *	ASCII char in E	I/O status in A if reg E = 0FFH
Auxin status	7	None	A = 01H if ready or 00H if not
Auxout status	8	None	A = 01H if ready or 00H if not
Print buffer to console	9	Address in DE of the string which is terminated by $	None
Read to buffer from console	10 *	Address in DE of start of the read buffer	The Read buffer is filled
Console Status	11	None	The least sig bit of A is 1 if there is a character ready, 0 if not.

223

Basic Disc (and other) Functions.

Function and Number Input Parameters   *Output Parameters*

Function and	Number	Input Parameters	Output Parameters
Get version no.	12 *	None	H = 00 if CP/M, H = 01 if MP/M L = 00 if v1.x, L = 2x if v2.x (L value in Hex, up to 2F)
Init BDOS	13	None	None
Reset disc	13 **	None	All drives to r/w, def to A
Log-in Drive	14	Reg E = 0, drive A: = 1, drive B: = 2, C: etc	None
Open file	15 *	Address of FCB in DE	Offset mult'r to address of FCB if found, 0FFH if not. Mult'r values 0 to 3.
Close file	16	Address of FCB in DE	Offset mlt'r to add FCB if found, 0FFH if not.
Search for first	17 **	Address of FCB in DE	Offset mult'r to add of FCB if found, 0FFH if not.
Search for next	18 **	Address of FCB in DE	Offset mult'r for next FCB if found, 0FFH if not.
Delete file	19 **	Address of FBC in DE	Offset mult'r for FCB if found, 0FFH if not.
Read next record	20 **	Address of FCB in DE	A is 0 = successful read 1 = read past EOF higher values are errors.
Write next record	21 **	Address of FCB in DE	0 = successful write 1 = error in extending 2 = end of disc data 255 = no more dir space other error values in 3.1
Make file	22 **	Address of FCB in DE	Offset mult'r for FCB or 255 if no more dir space. Password creation under 3.1
Rename File	23 *	Address of FCB in DE	Offset mult'r for FCB or 255 if no match

Return Login Code	24	*	None	Login vector in HL
Read Drive No	25		None	Number of logged drive (0 = A:, 1 = B:, 2 = C: etc)
Set DMA address	26		Address of 128 byte buffer in DE	None
Get Alloc vector	27		None	Alloc vector address in HL
Write prot disc	28	*	None	None
Get R/O vector	29	*	None	HL = R/O vector value
Set file attrib	30	*	Pointer to FCB in DE	DIR code in A Physical or ext. error in H
Get disc params	31	*	None	HL = Disc Param Byte address
Set/Get USER code	32	*	for Get, E = 0FFH for Set, E = code	For Get, A = current code for Set, no value.
Read Random	33	*	Address of FCB in DE	A = return code, as follows - 1 = reading unwritten data 2 = (not used) 3 = cannot close curr extent 4 = seek to unwritten extent 5 = ** random record no out of range 6 = seek past end of disc 10 = media change occurred
Write Random	34	*	Address of FCB in DE	A = return code, as follows - 2 = no data block 3 = cannot close curr extent 5 = out of dir space 6 = random recno o/o/range 10 = media change occurred

225

Set Random Rec   36   *   Address of FCB in DE   Random Record Field is
                                                 set.

(NOTE - versions 1.4 - 2.x contained only those functions which are listed above. The following are MP/M and/or CP/M Plus (3.1) functions)

Reset Drive	37 **	16 bit drive vector in DE	None
Access Drive	38	MP/M only-not available under CP/M	
Free Drive	39	MP/M only	
Write Random with Zero fill	40 **	Address of FCB in DE	As fn 34 but prev unalloc data block is zero filled before writing
Test and Write	41 **	Add of FCB in DE	Test not used in CP/M but used in MP/M to check that original rec is unchanged
Lock Record	42 **	Add of FCB in DE	No action in CP/M, used in MP/M when more than one prog has r/w access to a file.
Unlock Record	43 **	Add of FCB in DE	As 42 above.
Set multi-sector Count	44 **	No of Sectors in E	Logical record blocking
Set BDOS err mode	45 **	Err mode in E	E = 0FFH means Return Error = 0FEH is Return and Display = other is normal default
Get disc free space	46 **	Drive in E	First 3 bytes of DMA buffer is binary count of free sectors (128 byte recs)
Chain to prog	47 **	Chain flag in E	None

Flush buffers	48 **	0FFH in E to purge	Forces write of pending recs in internal buffers - purge clears them to force read verify to read from disc not buffer.
Get/Set SCB	49 **	Add of SCB in DE	Access to System Control Block. Not supported in MP/M.
Direct BIOS call	50 **	BIOS PB Add in DE	Used for all BIOS functions except Console I/O and List, which can be called thru the BIOS jump vector.
Load RSX	59 **	FCB Add in DE	A contains err code if any
Call RSX	60 **	RSX PB Add in DE	A contains err code if any
Free Bocks	98 **	None	Temp allocated blocks are released. Close files before using and before warm boot, to avoid loss of data.
Truncate file	99 **	FCB Add in DE	Set last record of a file to the recno in the FCB. File must not be open.
Set dir label	100 **	FCB Add in DE	Label values determine use of password and time stamps. Note that in non-banked 3.1, the file DIRLB.RSX must be resident, or reg H will return error code 0FFH.
Return dir label	101 **	Drive in E	A contains dir label
Read stamps and password mode	102 **	fcb add in DE	The information on the directory is loaded into the FCB specified.
Write XFCB	103 **	FCB Add in DE	Dir code in A.
Set time/date	104 **	TOD Add in DE	Starts at Jan 1 1978. Two byte day counter. Hrs and Mins

227

			are one byte each.
Get time/date	105 **	TOD Add in DE	As stated, plus seconds in A
Set def passw'd	106 **	Passw'd add in DE	None
Return Serial No	107 **	S/No field add in DE	puts the CP/M Serial Number in the 6 bytes starting at address in DE.
Get/Set Prog Return Code	108 **	DE = FFFFH (Get) or = Return Code (Set)	Used to pass codes onto chained programs, or to CCP.
Get/Set Con mode	109 **	DE = FFFFH (Get) or = Console Mode (Set)	Sets or gets the mode parameter (enable/disable∧ C∧ S ∧ Q ∧ P etc)
Get/Set Output Delimiter	110 **	DE = FFFFH (Get) or = Character (Set)	Used to set or get the output delimiter. (default is $)
Print Block	111 **	Add of CCB in DE	Send char string at CCB to current CONOUT. Obeys Con Mode setting (∧ P etc).
List Block	112 **	Add of CCB in DE	As for 111, but to LST dev.
Parse Filename	152 **	Add of PFCB in DE	Looks for delimiters in filename to set up correct FCB, with password etc correctly identified.

Now we can investigate the details of each of the above, identifying any places in which a function code has altered from version 1.x to the functions listed above for 2.x and showing how 3.1 differs from the previous versions.

Function 0 - System Reset

This is exactly the same as a tranfer to location 0000H - the 'boot' instruction. Control is passed to the CCP which re- initializes the discs by selecting and then logging in drive A:. In version 3.1, this does not reset the discs - it does in earlier versions.

Function 1 - Console Input.

This reads a single character from the console - normally the keyboard. If the character is ^ S, this stops any scrolling output. If ^ S has been detected - the release character is looked for. Also, ^ P for echoing of the output to the LST: device is detected if present. Any character which has a 'graphic' - that is it can be displayed on the screen or printed on the console printer - is output to the CON:, as are such as the Carriage Return and Line Feed. If ^ I is detected, this is expanded to 'tab' along in 8 character columns. If *no* character is found,

then FDOS does not return control to the program in the TPA, and this stops execution of the system - until an input is received. Any character found is placed in register A. Note that ^ Q is required in CP/M 3.1 to restart after a ^ S.

Function 2 - Console Output.

This is the reverse of function 1, in that any character in register E is sent to the CON: output device. Again, the checks for ^ P and ^ I etc are made and acted on.

Function 3 - Reader Input.

This is exactly like function 1, except that the character is sought from the device allocated to RDR: by the IOBYTE (Chapter 11). When one is found, it is placed in register A. There is no 'echo to console output', of course. Version 3.1 refers to this as 'Auxiliary Input' - losing the 'old-fashioned' reader/punch image.

Function 4 - Punch Output.

A character in register E is sent to the device currently allocated to PUN: by the IOBYTE. Version 3.1 uses the term 'Auxiliary Output'.

Function 5 - List Output.

An ASCII character in register E is sent to the device currently allocated to LST: by the IOBYTE.

Function 6 - Direct Console I/O

If register E contains FFH, the function is to input a character from the console, into register E. If register E contains some other value, that value is output to the console.

There are no checks on ⌃ S or ⌃ P etc, there is no 'echoing' to the display of an input character, you are completely on your own. f you have any programs written under CP/M 1.x which dive straight into BIOS to perform this type of I/O, you are recommended to alter them to use this function - so that your programs will be compatible with current and future releases of CP/M and MP/M.

This is, as an example, the function used by INPUT$(n) in MBASIC to obtain keyboard input without screen echo.

Function 7 - Get IOBYTE (Versions up to 2.2)

The current state of the IOBYTE is copied to register A. We identified the IOBYTE as the fourth byte of the System Parameters at the bottom of memory (byte 03H), and the table of values and their meanings which is in chapter 11 is repeated here for convenience.

Bits	Ref to	Values 00		01	10		11	
6&7	CON:	=	TTY:	CRT:	BAT:		UC1:	
4&5	RDR:	=	TTY:	PTR:	UR1:		UR2:	
2&3	PUN:	=	TTY:	PTP:	UP1:		UP2:	
0&1	LST:	=	TTY:	CRT:	LPT:		UL1:	

Function 7 - Auxiliary Input Status. (Version 3.1 only)

This is, as you can see, a radical alteration. If a character is ready for input from the auxiliary input device (which used to be called 'reader') then the least significant bit of register A will be 1. If no character is ready, the bit will be zero. (A has value 00H.)

Function 8 - Set IOBYTE (Versions up to 2.x)

Whatever set of values (bit pattern) you have set up in register E is copied into the IOBYTE. The previous content is lost, unless you retrieved and stored it prior to the code 8 function.

Function 8 - Auxiliary Output Status. (Version 3.1 only)

As for function 7 above - A = 00H means the device is not ready to receive, A = 01H means it is ready. The device which used to be called 'punch' is now referred to as the 'auxiliary output device'.

Function 9 - Print String

This is an extended (and useful) form of function 2. The 'print' is to the **console**. Whatever is in register pair DE is taken as the start address of a string of characters to be output to the current CON: device. The system checks for ∧ P, ∧ S and ∧ I (tabs, extended as the output takes place) and looks for a dollar sign ($) which terminates the function and returns control to the user program in the TPA. The $ is not output. Note that in version 3.1, the delimiter, the $ sign, can be altered to some other character with function 110. Also, version 3.1 expects ∧ Q to release the 'suspend output' caused by ∧ S.

Function 10 - Read Buffer (the C register contains 0AH, for 10)

This is the extension to function 1, allowing a string of characters to be input. The buffer into which the string is input may be from 1 to 255 characters long, and the address for the input buffer to which register pair DE points actually contains the maximum buffer size allowed in that input. The next character will, when input is complete, contain the actual numbers of characters from DE + 1 (where the actual length is) to the end of the string. If no carriage return / line feed sequence is detected before 256 characters have been input, the 256th is ignored, and the function terminates with the buffer full, and 255 in both the first and second byte.

In versions 2.x +, all the line editing commands described at the end of chapter two are suported by this function - which was not the case for earlier versions. Also, in earlier versions, the line editing commands which did operate and which returned the cursor to the start of line, returned to the actual line start - column 0, whereas in version 2.x + , the cursor returns to the position under the first input character - after the position of the 'prompt'. If the buffer already contains the input values when the function 10 is called, it may end with a 'null' (binary zero), in which case further input charcters can be added. If it ends with a 'linefeed' or 'return' (∧ J or ∧ M), the string can be edited. Pressing 'return' accepts the string as it is at that point. In version 3.1, if you are using it unbanked, the edit is normal, but in banked versions, there are additional edit characters.

Function 11 - Get Console Status. (C = 0BH)

This allows a program to inspect the console input port to see if a character is there or not, before issuing a 'read'. If the content of Register A is FFH, then there is a character waiting. Normally, register A contains 00H if there is no character waiting. If you want your program to run until a character is typed - this is the command you use to keep checking the console status. If you used, say, function 1, the program would be suspended until an input took place. In version 3.1, the 'character waiting' signal is 01H (not FFH). Also, in 3.1, you

231

can set the console status to accept^ C only, and in that case, only the ^ C will return the 01H in A.

Function 12 - Return version number. (C = 0CH)

In CP/M 1.4, this was the 'lift head' function which actually did nothing except put 0000H into register pair HL. Now, in versions 2.x + , the registers H and L contain values to indicate which version of CP/M or MP/M you are using. If you find 00 and 00 in the registers, your program is running under version 1.4, and you cannot use the random file access functions of 2.x + . If you know in advance that your program may be required to run under 1.4, this check will enable you to switch to code which does not use any of the 2.x functions.

The actual values returned are 00 in H for CP/M and 01 in H for MP/M. Register L contains 00 (as we said) for versions before 2.x, and contains 2nH for later versions. If L contains 22H, you are running under version 2.2, and if it contains 31H, you are running under CP/M Plus (version 3.1).

Functions 13 ff.

These functions, under 2.x + , use a reserved area for directory operations, which does not affect the 'write buffers'. In 1.4 directory operations did affect the write buffers. (Functions 17 and 18 are an exception to retain compatibility upwards from 1.4)

The File Name Table was described under the directory entry section in chapter 11, and the entries in the File Control Block are exactly the same as the entries described for the disc directories except for the first byte, which contains a drive code in the FCB, not the Entry Type and User number. (If the user number was not current, there would be no FCB - because you cannot manipulate a file which is not in your curent user area, without skull-duggery.) The drive code in the first byte is slightly different from all other drive code entries in other places, in that 00H means the default drive, which is stored in the system parameter area in the fifth byte (04H). Values 01H up to 10H take the meaning A: to P:. Watch this one, because in byte 04H of the SPA and elsewhere, values 00H to 0FH take the meanings A: to P:. The one or three byte extensions to the directory entry (according to version) are as described in chapter 11.

A summary of the FCB contents is included here, for easy reference.

Decimal	Hex	Content
0	00	Drive code
1-8	01-08	Filename
9-11	09-0B	Filetype
12	0C	Extent number (used during I/O)
13	0D	not used
14	0E	n/u in 1.4 - part of ext count in 2.x +
15	0F	Record count (how many in this extent)
16-31	10-1F	disc map of block utilisation
32	20	current sequential read/write record number
33-35	21-23	Random record number (0-65535) with 21

containing the lower byte of the number, 22 the higher, and 23 acting as overflow.

Function 13 - Reset disc system.

This resets discs to Read/Write status, and is familiar to MBASIC programmers as RESET. It allows change of disc(s) and re-logging of new one(s) while a program is running, so that all discs will accept 'write', but without system re-booting. Under 3.1, if you are in CP/M, re-logging is automatic on disc access, but you still need this function within a program.

Function 14 - Select Disc.

This ought to be called 'Select Drive'. The value in register E when this function is encountered is placed in the SPA in byte 04H, and the directory of that drive (0 = A:, 1 = B: etc) is activated. If the disc medium is changed, with no subsequent reset, boot etc, then any access to that drive will perform function 28 (see below) and the drive will be set to Read Only. An attempted write operation will be blocked.

The value 00H in the first byte of an FCB tells FDOS to look in byte 04H for the drive code. Booting the system sets byte 04H to 00H - drive A:

Function 15 - Open File.

This is 'open an **existing** file'. (See function 22 for 'open a **new, previously unknown file**'.) The directory of the referenced disc is brought into the transient buffer in the SPA (bytes 0080H onwards), one 'record' (that is 128 bytes, or four directory entries) at a time, and the filename and type are compared with the filename and type in the FCB set up by the programmer (or in some cases CCP). "Wild card" characters (the '?' or 3FH) in the FCB match any character. If a match is found, the offset in units of 32 bytes is returned in register A. (If the third entry in the particular record in the SPA matches, then register A will contain 02H.) The offset is called 'directory code' in the CP/M manuals, and has to be used to get at the directory entry like this -

Address of directory entry = 0080H + 'dir code' * 32

If the disc directory does not contain a file match, the search is abandoned, and register A contains 255 (FFH).

When a match is found, the disc map is copied into the FCB in memory. If your program is going to start reading from the first record - sequential read - make sure that the 'current record' pointer is set to zero. (Byte 20H.)

Note that in version 3.1, if the file is password protected in read mode, the correct password must have been put into the first 8 bytes of the DMA or must have been set as the default password. Also, if the current user is not 0 (zero), and the file is not found in the current user number, user 0 is also searched. If you find the file under user 0, when you were in some other user, you can only read from the file, not write to it. Access time and date are recorded for the file (extent zero only) if those were required by the CP/M INITDIR command.

Function 16 - Close file.

This will close any file which exists - but is not strictly necessary for files from which you have only read. It is essential for any file to which you have written.

As for function 15, a failure to find the file results in FFH being returned in Register A, and a match both returns the offset multiplier (see fn 15) and copies the FCB from memory onto the disc.

In version 3.1, you can set one of the interface attributes (f5') to 1 instead of

234

zero (normal) and this will update the directory with the state at that time, but will leave the file open.

Function 17 - Search for First

This function will search for the first file in the directory of the specified or default logged drive (specified in the FCB) which matches the name and type in the FCB. Any '?' replacing a character matches any character in the directory.

If a match is found, the offset multiplier (see fn 15) is returned in register A but no other action is taken. The file is not opened.

If no match, then 255 is returned in A.

If the drive code in the FCB is a '?', then the search takes place on the default drive (indicated in SPA byte 04H) and matches any file of any user number. If the drive code is a '?', then the extent number (byte 0CH) is not zeroed - otherwise it is.

You must use function 17 before you use 18. This function 'initialises' the next one.

Function 18 - Search for Next

This is exactly like function 17, except that it carries on the search through the directory from the last match found. A function 18 is assumed to be preceded by a function 17.

Function 19 - Delete file.

This is a directory search, as the previous functions, and searches the records (each of four entries) which make up the directory of the specified drive ('?' not allowed for the drive) for any record which matches the FCB name and type. Any ocurrence of '?' in the FCB (not drive) is allowed to match any character. If no file is found, register A returns the value 255. For any file that is found, the first byte of the directory entry is set to E5H (an impossibly high user number, and the 'format' character) and the record is re-written to the disc. The delete file command returns the offset multiplier (see fn 15) of the last file found and deleted.

In version 3.1, if the attribute f5' is set to 1, the search will be only for XFCB's. Since non-banked CP/M 3.1 does not support XFCB's (or passwords), a call to function 19 in non-banked 3.1, with f5' set, has no effect.

Function 20 - Read Sequential.

Provided that the FCB addressed has been 'activated' - by a function 15 (open) or 22 (see below) - this command will look at the value in the 'next record' byte of the FCB (20H) and use that to read the record from the current extent at that position. Then the 'next record' byte is stepped on. If the 'next record' value overflows (exceeds one extent), then it is set to zero and the extent number is stepped. The 'next record' byte is then ready to read again if required.

Register A contains 00H if the read was successful, and a non-zero value if the read was not successful (eg read beyond end of file).

The record is read into memory at the current DMA address - either the transient file buffer in the SPA or some other location if you have modified the DMA.

Since version 3.1 can handle multi-sector reads - the function also looks at the count (see function 44) for the number of records to be read. (The count can be from 1 to 128.)

Function 21 - Write Sequential.

Provided that the FCB addressed in register pair DE has been activated by a function 15 (open) or 22 (see below) and the file is not R/O, the value in the 'next record' byte of the FCB (20H) will be used as the pointer to the next record position and the record of 128 bytes, starting at the current DMA address, is written. The 'next record' pointer is stepped on, and if it overflows (exceeds one extent), then the next extent is opened, the 'next record' pointer set to zero, and all is left ready for a subsequent write. At this level of operation, you are permitted to write to an existing file, and the previous contents of the record are overwritten. Register A contains 00H after a successful write operation, or is non-zero if the write failed because the disc was full.

If the directory calls for update time/date stamping, and if there has been no previous write (or 'make') for this file - the time/date stamp is updated.

Function 22 - Make File.

This is the operation to open a file which does not currently exist (or has been erased) on the specified (or default) disc. FDOS created the file and created a blank FCB and directory entry, except for the file name and type. You, the programmer, must ensure that the name is not duplicated. A 'delete filename' (see fn 19) will be sufficient to ensure this - and the prior existence or otherwise of the file will be indicated by the value in register A after the 'delete', if this is useful to you. The content of register A after the 'make file' will be the offset multiplier (see fn 15), if it succeeds, or will be 255 (FFH) if the directory is full, and the 'make file' fails. The FCB created is activated as though the 'open file' (fn 15) had been given, so it is not necessary to 'open' as well as 'make'.

If the drive has a directory label which requests Creation time/date stamping, then this is performed under version 3.1. Similarly if update stamping is called for.

Function 23 - Rename file.

You have to put into the FCB the existing filename in the first 16 bytes (as usual, including the drive and pointers) and the new filename into what would otherwise be the disc map - the second 16˙bytes. The function then changes the name of the file to the new name, and re-writes the directory record. If there is more than one occurrence of the filename, all are re-named and re-written. The value in register A will be the offset multiplier (see fn 15) of the last re-name, if successful, or will be 255 (FFH) if unsuccessful - name not found. Again, as with 'make file' (fn 22), you must take care that the new filename which you use is unique, not already on the directory.

Function 24 - Return log-in vector.

This enables you to test (with a mask) whether or not a drive is 'logged in'. The value returned in register pair HL is a binary pattern, where zero means

237

'not logged in' and 1 means 'logged in', with drive A indicated by the least significant bit of L, and drive P indicated by the most significant bit of H.

The appropriate mask with an AND operation will give you a non-zero result if the drive specified by the single 1 bit in the mask is logged in.

Function 25 - Return current disc.

This simply reads location 04H in the Sytem Parameter Area, and places the value in register A. Zero is drive A:, 1 is B: and so on up to FH (15) for drive P:.

Function 26 - Set DMA address.

The DMA (direct memory address) is taken to mean the location of the first byte of a 128 byte record which is to be written to, or has been read from, disc. The default location for this, and the location in which the offset multiplier (fn 15 ff) is used, is byte 0080H, in the System Parameter Area (SPA). If the BOOT jump instruction is located somewhere other than the very bottom of memory, the DMA will be BOOT + 0080H.

Using this function allows you to re-direct disc I/O to a different area of memory, and the new DMA set by this command will remain in operation until another fn 26, or a cold or warm boot, or a system reset (fn 0). The address for the new DMA is stacked into register pair DE before the function is invoked.

Function 27 - Get Allocation vector address.

The disc map which indicates where a file has records on the disc is a subset of the full disc allocation vector maintained in the memory for each disc currently logged. You can get the address of the vector for the currently logged drive with this function. However, although systems programs use it, be careful, because if the medium has been changed since the drive was logged on, although it will be marked 'read only', the disc allocation will not have been renewed to the new disc directory until a reset or boot has taken place. That, of course, is why the disc is marked 'read only'. The address of the allocation vector is found in register pair HL after the function is performed. Function 14 allows you to change the current default drive to a different one. To check for R/O, use function 29.

If you are using banked CP/M 3.1, the allocation vector could be placed in bank 0. If so, a transient program cannot access it. However, there is function 46 (see below) which returns the number of free 128 byte records on a disc. (DIR and SHOW both use fn 46.)

Function 28 - Write protect drive.

This is the command invoked by the STAT n:R/O command (versions up to 2.2) and by SET n:[RO] (version 3.1) and simply sets the drive to read only, until this is reset - or a boot takes place.

Function 29 - Get Read Only vector.

Two bytes are reserved for a bit map which indicates which - if any - drives are R/O. The sixteen bits are returned to the register pair HL, with drive A corresponding to the least significant bit of L, and drive P to the most significant bit of L. A 1 bit indicates that the drive is R/O, a zero that it is R/W.

These bits are set either by function 28, or by FDOS when you change medium, and are reset by booting or resetting the drives. You can, of course, reset a drive to R/O with the STAT (or SET) command.

Function 30 - Set file attributes

In CP/M 2.x, seven high order bits of the characters used for the filename/type are reserved as file attributes. The seven are the last four of the name, and the three of the type. We indicated the use of two of the seven bits earlier, in chapter 11, under 'File Name Table'. These were the h-o-b of the first letter of type - which is used as a Write Protect which is **not** reset at boot or system/drive rest, and the h-o-b of the second letter of type, which is used to hold the $SYS attribute. In version 3.1 the h-o-b of the third letter of 'type' (t3') is the Archive marker.

The other four high order bits are available for your use, if you want to make special use of them - as for example MBASIC does when you SAVE a program with the P option - protecting it from being listed or edited.

The register pair DE point to an FCB which contains the ufn which you wish to modify, with the appropriate h-o-b's set. The function searches for a matching drive/filename/type, and then replaces a found one with the one in the FCB. The register A returns either an offset multiplier (see fn 15) or 255 (FFH) if the filename is not found in the directory.

The five h-o-b's which are reserved but not used, are for versions of CP/M beyond 2.x. For example, in 3.1, f6' specifies whether or not the last record byte count is to be set by this function. (f6' = 0 do not set, f6' = 1, set the byte count.)

Function 31 - Get the address of the disc parameters in BIOS.

The disc parameters are held in a block in BIOS, and the address of the start of that block will be returned in register pair HL.

You may use the values for space calculations or (in 2.2, they are used in STAT DSK:) for display. You may also alter the values during a transient program, if perhaps you want to simulate a different disc environment. However, remember that the BIOS is only re-loaded when a **cold** boot takes place - so take care.

Function 32 - Set or Get User Code.

If register E contains FFH, the function will take the value currently in the record of 'current user' and stack it into register A. This is, as user numbers are, 0 to 31 (1FH).

If register E contains any other value then the current user is set to the value of the least significant five bits of E. (Mod 32 of E, or 'the remainder after dividing E by 32') Register A does not contain a value after the Set User function.

Reading and Writing Random Records.

This set of functions was introduced at CP/M 2.0 and allows you to specify a record number in a file and read from or write to it directly. The functions use the set of three bytes at the end (top) of the FCB. As you will have seen with the previous read and write functions - the actual disc access is a direct one anyway - but it looks like sequential access, because the mechanism is to set a record number within extent to zero, and then step it on as part of the read or write function. With the Random Record functions, you specify the record number within **file**, and the functions do **not** step the record number.

A file must be opened or made first, with the extent set to zero, so that the file has a correct FCB and the directory has a conventional entry - although you do not actually need to put anything into that (or any particular) extent.

This is how the record number is handled. The last three bytes in the FCB (21H-23H) are used to contain a number in the range 0 to 65535. Byte 21H contains the least significant bits, 22H the middle and 23H the most signigicant bits. However - if 23H is not zero, the file is full - because each byte can hold 256 values, and 256 x 256 = 65536.

In fact the third byte (23H) is always zero, but is used by function 35 (qv). As you can see, a record number up to 65535 as in version 2.2 gives you access (with 128 byte records) to an 8 Megabyte file.

One of the aspects of the STAT command, which we discussed in chapter 3 was the facility to add a 'size' column to the list of file statistics. That size, for a random file, is the size that a sequentially written file would have been, in order to reach the record number of the last record. However - if only high numbered records are written in Random mode - there will be large gaps - non-allocated block or extents, so the size column will appear unnaturally large. The space utilisation of a file which is only written in Random mode can be seen, very roughly, from the difference between the 'Size' and 'Recs' columns.

Every time you 'read randomly' or 'write randomly', the extent and record number within extent are re-calculated, and the values recorded. But these values are not stepped on by the 'random read' as they are by the sequential read.

You can change from random read to sequential read, if you wish, but notice that you will always re-read the last record read randomly - and you must do that, in order to step the counters correctly, taking charge of 'end of extent', for example. We will discuss what happens when you change from one mode to the other, after we have described the functions.

The functions themselves are these -

Function 33 - Read Random.

The value in the FCB 'last three bytes' is taken as the record number and the record from that place on the file is written to the DMA location (unless the file is R/O or the disc is full). The extent and record within extent are re-calculated.

If the read is successful, then register A will be zero. If not, there are six error codes. These apply to random read and write, except for code 5 - so we have tabulated them once only, here.

Error code	Meaning
01H	You have attempted to read from a block which has not been previously written.
02H	Used during 'write' attempts only. The system has tried to allocate a new data block, and there are none left.
03H	The FDOS cannot close the current extent. Try re-reading - or re-open extent zero. If the disc is 'write-protected', (with or without the 'notch' covered) then you cannot close any extent, but nor should the error occur.
04H	Seek to extent which has not been created. This is effectively the same as code 01 but refers to an extent, instead of a block.
05H	This cannot occur in a read, but after an attempted write, it tells you that the directory is full, and you cannot write to the new extent, because it cannot be created.
06H	Under version 2.x, this will occur when the third (highest) byte of the address is non-zero. By implication, you have attempted to write beyond the physical end of disc.
10H	Media change has occurred.
255H	Physical error - refer to reg H for BDOS error.

Function 34 - Write Random.

The content of the 128 bytes starting at the DMA are written into the file at the position indicated by the record number. If the extent is a previously unused one, it is allocated before the write takes place.

As for the 'random read', the extent and record within extent are calculated and recorded, but only of the record actually written - there is no automatic stepping to 'next'.

Error codes (or 00H for no error) are as above for the 'read'.

242

Function 35 - Compute file size.

This sets the three 'random address bytes' of an FCB to the value one greater than the highest numbered record previously written. The DE register pair contain the address of the FCB, as usual, and the ufn in the FCB is used for the directory scan. It is the 'three bytes' in that FCB which are set by this function.

If you have a sequential file, and you want to open it and add to the end of it, (eg COBOL 'OPEN EXTEND') then all you need do after opening it is to perform this function once, and then random write to the file - step the counter yourself - random write again - and so on.

Take care that you have not written to the file before using this function, because if you have, you may get a wrong file size. However, since a file does not have to be open when you use this function, a 'close' will ensure that you get the correct size.

Function 36 - Set random record number.

A file which is read or written randomly has the 'sequential' counters of extent and record calculated automatically each time a 33 or 34 is performed.

A file which is read or written **sequentially** does **not** have the random record count calculated automatically. So to change from sequential to random, at a particular point in the file, you need this function to calculate where you are.

Changing from Random to Sequential and vice versa.

From random to sequential, first. Since the sequential record number/extent is always kept in step with the last record read or written, changing from random read to sequential read inescapably repeats the last record read randomly as the first read sequentially. Changing from random write to sequential write is equally straightforward, but again the last randomly written record is re-written sequentially. There is no other way than performing a read or write sequential, of correctly and automatically stepping on the sequential counters.

From sequential to random, now. After sequential read, say, you perform fn 36, because (to retain compatibility with version 1.4, not because it is difficult) the random record number is not stepped on with the sequential ones. Then *you* can step the counter by one - and off you go - no duplications. Similarly after sequential write - perform a fn 36, step the counter and off you go.

Functions unique to Version 3.1 (CP/M Plus).

Function 37 - Reset Drive

Use this in your program to reset one or several drives to R/W.

Function 38 - Access Drive.

This is actually only available in MP/M - it is included here for completeness.

Function 39 - Free Drive.

As function 38.

Function 40 - Write Random with Zero Fill.

This is very like fn 34 above, except that a previously unallocated data block is filled with zeros before the new record is written. Creating a file with this function allows detection of unused (unwritten) random record numbers (all zeros). Use of the fn 34 leaves the blocks unchanged from what they were before-uninitialized.

Function 41 - Test and Write Record.

This is an MP/M function, in which a copy of the original record read is kept, and compared with the record currently on the disc. If they are the same, the write takes place. If not, another program has altered the record since the read took place, and the updating must be repeated on the new record content. Since only one program can be active at one time with CP/M 3.1, the test phase is not implemented.

Function 42 - Lock Record.

Again, this is an MP/M function, since only one program can be active under CP/M 3.1, but it is included in the CP/M set so that programs can be compatible between MP/M and CP/M environments.

Function 43 - Unlock Record.

As function 42.

Function 44 - Set Multi-sector Count.

This is the function which allows you to specify how many 128 byte physical records make up one logical record - to be read or written with a single operation.

Function 45 - Set BDOS Error Mode.

There are three modes in which BDOS errors can be handled. In the two 'Return' modes ('Return' and 'Return and Display'), a BDOS error is noted in register H, and control returns to the program, instead of the 'default' mode in which the program is terminated. The 'default' and 'Display' modes both display the error at the console.

Function 46 - Get Free Disc Space.

After this function, the first three bytes of the DMA buffer contain the count in binary of the free sectors on the drive specified in E.

Function 47 - Chain to Program.

Before giving this function call, a command line must be set in the default DMA buffer, and it must end with a 00H (null). This enables control to be passed directly to another program without re-booting.

Function 48 - Flush Buffers.

If you have any internal blocking or de/blocking buffers, this empties them onto the file. You can also 'Purge' the buffers to ensure that a file 'read after write' actually reads the file, not merely the buffer content.

Function 49 - Get/Set System Control Block.

This - unlike most other functions - is in CP/M 3.1 only - and is not in MP/M, for example.

245

The System Control Block (SCB) is 100 bytes in the BDOS containing flags and data used by the BDOS, the CCP and other parts of the system. You access it, with fn 49, through a parameter block which carries the necessary offset and whether a word or byte is being set, as well as the new value (set).

Your CP/M 3 Programmers Guide has the table of offsets and the meanings of the different values.

Function 50 - Direct BIOS Calls

This allows you, again with an offset in a parameter block, to call BIOS directly from your program.

Function 59 - Load Overlay or Resident System Extension.

Transient programs which have an RSX header in them can use the program load function. The RSX header forces the loader to remain resident after the load.

Function 60 - Call RSX.

This is a special function to be used when calling RSX's. RSX's filter all BDOS calls, and handle all they can. If they cannot - and there is no other RSX resident that can, the call is simply passed through to the BDOS.

Function 98 - Free Blocks.

If there are any blocks which have been allocated as a result of a write operation, but have not been recorded in the directory, this function returns them to free space. The CCP uses this call after a warm start so make sure that you close your files - particularly if you have written to one or more - before using fn 98 or before re-booting.

Function 99 - Truncate File.

If you have a file which you want to shorten for some reason, then make sure it is closed, that there is data in the region where you want to truncate to, and set the random record number of the record you want to be the last in the FCB. Then fn 99 will perform the truncation for you.

Function 100 - Set Directory Label.

Once you have used the CP/M 3.1 INITDIR command, an SFCB is written in as every fourth directory entry, ready for time/date stamping and password protection. Each disc has a label, which indicates what form the date/time stamp and password protection is to take. This function writes that label onto the disc.

Function 101 - Return Directory Label.

If you use this function, you get the value of the specified disc label in register A. (Provided there is such a label..)

Function 102 - Read File Stamps and Password Mode.

This refers to the files - not the disc. After the call, the FCB will have the password mode (read/write/delete) marked, and will have the time/date stamps from that file. Note that you cannot have passwords in a non-banked CP/M 3.1, so the password mode will always be zero. In a banked system, the password mode will be zero if you have not set the mode.

Function 103 - Write File XFCB.

This function writes a new XFCB or updates the old one. If you use the function in non-banked CP/M 3.1, it will always fail, because there is no password protection.

Function 104 - Set Date and Time.

After you have set up four bytes with the date and time in the correct format, you can use this function to set the system time and date to the values in the four bytes. These values will be used in all subsequent time/date stamping - the clock runs, of course, from the moment this function is complete, starting at zero seconds.

The first two bytes (0 and 1) contain a 16 bit binary number which is the number of days since January 1st 1978. The next byte is two BCD digits of Hours, and the fourth is two BCD digits of Minutes.

247

Function 105 - Get Date and Time.

This is the opposite of fn 104 - the date/time are put into the four bytes starting with the address you specify in DE.

Function 106 - Set Default Password.

Tell the system where the password is (address in DE) and whenever you subsequently try to manipulate a password protected file, both the DMA and the default password are checked. If either contains the correct password, access is permitted. So this function allows you to set up the default.

Function 107 - Return Serial Number.

The first 6 bytes of the BDOS - as we said in the last chapter -contain the serial number of the particular copy of CP/M you have. You can interrogate it with this command.

Function 108 - Get/Set Program Return Code.

If you are running a batch of jobs - or chaining programs - you can set or get a return code which contains an error code or value. The CCP will set the return code to zero, unless you chain programs, bypassing the CCP.

Function 109 - Get/Set Console Mode.

The Console mode is a 16 bit parameter which contains information about the way the console functions under certain conditions. This was mentioned before in Function 11. See your manuals for the values of the various bits and their effects.

Function 110 - Get/Set Output Delimiter.

Function 9 (print string) expects a $ sign as the string terminator, unless you change the expected delimiter with this function. You can see what the current delimiter is by using the 'get' facility of this function.

Function 111 - Print Block.

While function 9 prints a string to the console from a specified location, this prints a string identified by the Character Control Block specified. The difference is that the first two characters of the CCB are the address of the character string, and the second pair are the length of the string. No delimiter is assumed.

Function 112 - List Block.

This is exactly like fn 111, except that the string is directed to the LST device.

Function 152 - Parse Filename.

Since filenames under 3.1 can have drive, name, type and password, with a whole range of delimiter characters with special meanings, this function is used to 'unpack' the filename and initialise the FCB accordingly.

13.3 Summary.

You now have the full set of calls to FDOS - the ones which are performed by routines in BDOS - the standard CP/M ones - and the ones which may need some special routines in BIOS instead of - or in addition to - the ones provided in the skeleton BIOS. Each of the calls requires a numeric value in register C - the number of the function. Many also require a value in E or an address in DE, or return an address to HL, and most single byte replies are found in register A. It may be worth noting that for compatibilty between 1.4 and 2.0+, register A is always returned equal to register L, and similarly B = H. Version 1.4 and earlier only expected the responses to be in A and B or the BA pair.

The wide range of extra functions available under 3.1 is somewhat restricted if you use 3.1 in an unbanked memory. With the banked memory, you can have bigger programs, too, since a single program may have access to up to 60 K bytes of TPA.

CHAPTER FOURTEEN

Using the BIOS.

14.1 Fundamentals.

This is not a 'fundamental' chapter - since it is concerned with assembler programming access to the actual routines in the BIOS - the part of CP/M which is normally produced by the hardware manufacturer or supplier. The chapter starts with a discussion of the early problems which made programmer access to BIOS a useful feature, explains the standard approach to this, and gives detailed guidance as to the method and results of the approach. This applies, of course, to the early versions of CP/M up to 1.4. With later versions up to 2.2, the method needs to be modified, so a modified method is explained, using a BIOS jump table. With version 3.1 (CP/M Plus), there is a direct call to the BIOS contained in the functions which we discussed in the preceding chapter.

The remainder of the chapter is concerned with various facilities which you will find useful under versions up to 2.2, such as access to all the peripherals implemented in BIOS - not only the four apparently available. Access to, and the meaning of the disc parameter tables and the disc directories is explained, with the code needed.

14.2 How to call BIOS routines.

Since the BIOS is only included as a skeleton by Digital Research, for completion by the hardware manufacturer or supplier - or some sofware house with the need and the skills - it came as something of a surprise to Digital that programmers did actually want to access the BIOS routines directly from their programs, without being restricted to the functions available through FDOS calls. Therefore, there was no convention in the original 1.4 manuals. As a result, everyone used their own method - sometimes rather tortuous - and not everyones method worked if a MOVCPM or a different version of CP/M were used. Now, however, the routine which Digital themselves use - or one very close to it - is in common use. Here it is, called BIOS -

```
BIOS;ENTRY TO THIS SUBROUTINE HAS OFFSET IN DE
      LHLD      0001H  ;GET BASE ADDRESS FROM SPA

      PUSH      D
      DAD       D      ;ADDTHEOFFSETYOUPLACEDINDE
      POP       D
      PCHL             ;AND JUMP TO THAT ADDRESS
```

Note that this works well with - but only with - version 1.4.

It may be relevant to note **why** there was any confusion. First, as we said, the BIOS is unique in CP/M, and is one of the reasons why CP/M has been successfully implemented on so many machines. Digital Research have provided the 'skeleton' - but have written relatively few complete BIOS's. CP/M is an operating system for computers with any of the following processor 'chips' - 8080, 8085, 8086, 8088 or Z80. This degree of promiscuity makes it essential that all I/O to and from CP/M is channelled through the BIOS - leaving the BDOS, the CCP, in fact all the resident and transient parts of CP/M absolutely standard.

So that BDOS (FDOS if you like) and BIOS can communicate effectively there is a jump table sited in the base of BIOS - which is in the top of the memory, as we indicated in chapter 11. Access to BIOS is through a chosen element of this table - the 'jump vector'. The actual address of the table will vary according to the BIOS and the size of memory (or the size used by the version of CP/M then resident !).

Most programmer activity is handled quite adequately by standard FDOS calls with the set of functions we described in the previous chapter. However, there are occasions when this is not enough. For example, a programmer trying to implement a 'password' entry, without echoing the entry from the keyboard to the screen, could not do that with the functions in CP/M 1.4. Implementing a database program which bypasses the standard CP/M relative sector addressing - whether for speed or simplicity - needs direct BIOS entry. Some directory manipulations are just not possible without absolute sector addressing. It is even possible to use a different disc operating system which uses BIOs only, provided that BIOS is accessible.

The routine we spelt out on the last page is the one which is in, for instance, SYSGEN, which accesses BIOS directly. Now we have to list out for you the values which you should stack into register pair DE, in order to get at the routine you want. Notice that the offsets all relate to the address contained in the system parameters at location 0001H and 0002H. This, as you will know if you have been with us so far, is the address of 'warm boot'. Location 0000H contains a C3H (JUMP) instruction, and the two bytes following are the address to which the JUMP takes place. All we are doing in the routine, therefore, is taking the 'warm boot' address, adding an offset address to it - which takes us directly to the jump vector we want - and so to the actual routine we want in BIOS. Notice that whatever size each routine is, in BIOS, that 'jump vector' must be correct, because FDOS uses it and so do routines like SYSGEN. Incidentally, if you are going to access the BIOS - it is a convenient convention to use the actual names of the BIOS routines in your program - because this makes your program intelligible to others - communication !

14.2.1 Where the BIOS routine calls are.

The table of offsets, with the CP/M routine name and a description of the CP/M 2.x routine follows here -

Offset	Name	Routine
−3	BOOT	(Cold Boot) This routine is put in for completeness, though you must never access it. The cold start loader is the only routine to access BOOT. If implemented, it sets the IOBYTE in the TPA to its default value and prints the sign-on message. BOOT may also initialise the hardwade components of the system. In common with WBOOT, the jump table and the rest of the parameters in the TPA (page 0 of memory) are set, CCP, BDOS and BIOS are loaded, and the routine transfers control to the CCP, ready for a keyboard input. If you have set up your own automatic sign-on system, (see next chapter), this will be entered.

If your BIOS keeps the default drive/user number at the fifth byte (0004H) of the TPA as is normal - then by setting a value in there, you can dictate which drive and user is to become active when CP/M is loaded. (If the byte is 'null' - all zero bits, this is user 0, drive A, as we explained in previous chapters.)

0   WBOOT   (Warm Boot) This reads the CCP and the BDOS from the system track(s) of the disc. In CP/M 2.0 and following versions, the writer of the BIOS can specify the number of reserved tracks used for this purpose. Although the system is normally read off drive A the BIOS can be altered to warm boot off a different drive. The 'stack' is reconfigured in the TPA, and control passes to the CCP. The BIOS sets register C to the default drive/usr before jumping to the CCP. The CCP reads the content of register C on entry and sets the logged drive accordingly. In CP/M 2.0 +, the top four bits of register C hold the current user number after the 'set logged drive' routine.

3   CONST   (CONsole STatus) This is the function 11 routine exactly. If the currently defined console (CON:) device has a character waiting, CONST returns with -1 in the A register (0FFH) - otherwise it returns with 0 in the A register. Unless speed is absolutely essential, use function 11 rather than addressing this routine directly.

6   CONIN   (CONsole INput) This was a very useful routine to use in versions 1.4 and earlier, because it gave the only way of taking a character from the console input, without console output echo. In fact, it was for this reason more than any other that direct BIOS calls were used in application progams. The routine when entered, loops, polling the keyboard or console status until a character is detected, then puts it into the A register, and returns. The character does not appear on the console. Note

253

that the system is completely blocked until a character is entered, once you have invoked this routine.

9   CONOUT   (CONsole OUTput) The character in register C is output to the console. Some BIOS's may zero the parity bit as part of this function. FDOS function 2 is the same except that function 2 **will** sent the character to the printer as well, if ^ P is in operation, whereas this routine will **not** echo to the printer.

12   LIST   (Write character out to LST: device) This routine sends the character in A to the current LST: device - usually the printer. It assumes that the character is in ASCII, with the parity bit zeroed, but does not alter the character, thus allowing graphics or other special characters through unchanged. This is identical with function 5 - so use that instead.

15   PUNCH   (Write character out to current PUN: device) Since 'punches' are not common on today's micros, you may find that this function is not even implemented in your BIOS. If it is, it will usually access a specific port. In any case - it is identical with function 4

18   READER   (Read next character from RDR: device) As with the 'punch', this was more used when a paper tape reader was a common input method. The character is returned in A. The parity bit on the character in A is set to zero. If the end of file on the reader has been reached, ^ Z is returned in A. Just as PUNCH is function 4, this is function 3, in the list of FDOS calls. If the function is not implemented, the BIOS should return a ^ Z.

21   HOME   (Move the head to track 0) This was originally intended to be used to move the head physically to track zero, and calibrate the disc controller. Currently most BIOS's perform the calibration either

either through the disc select routine, or as part of the physical READ or WRITE.

HOME has an important function as part of the deblocking algorithm. It is called whenever the directory is scanned from the beginning. If deblocking is not used, the HOME may simply return. Some versions of SYSGEN may require a HOME call to be translated into a call to SETTRK with register BC set to zero.

24	SELDSK	(SELect DiSK drive) The contents of register C are used to set the currently selected drive. 0 = A, 1 = B etc up to 15 = P. The routine returns the address of the disc parameter header in HL, or returns zero in HL if the drive to be selected does not exist. This is accessed through FDOS call 14. The BIOS should validate the value in register C against the allowed range. In versions after 1.4, the SELDSK command also passes a bit in register E to indicate whether or not this is the first time the drive has been selected after a warm boot or a disc reset. If the least significant bit (bit 0) of E is a one, the drive in C has already been selected. If the bit is a zero, the drive has not been selected since a reset/boot. The SELDSK function may use this bit to carry out initialisation of the Disc Parameter Block or Disc Parameter Header. The bit is also used to initialise the deblock buffer for a 'first time' select.
27	SETTRK	(SET the stated TRacK number). This routine selects the track to be used for a subsequent read or write to disc. A valid track number must be in registers BC before you enter the routine. (0 - 76 on a standard 77 track IBM single sided 8″ disc.)
30	SETSEC	(SET the stated SECtor number) This is the only way, in CP/M, to set the sector number for the next read/write. The sector number must be in BC, and must be valid. (1 - 26 on the standard system.)

Naturally, you will use SETTRK, SECTRAN and SETSEC together before a read or write for which you do not intend to use the FDOS routines. No commun ication takes place with the disc drive controller when these routines are used - the heads are not positioned. The communication is made when the actual read or write is given. Ideally, if the Digital Research de-blocking algorithm is used, SETSEC should reduce the sector count by 1 (see SECTRAN below).

33   SETDMA   (SET the Direct Memory Access address) The register pair BC must be loaded with the base address of the 128 byte buffer which is to be used for all subsequent disc transfers. Until you change it again, the DMA will remain at the value set here. The default buffer in the TPA starts at 80H.

36   READ   (READ the sector selected by the last SETTRK and SETSEC into the 128 byte buffer starting at the address set by SETDMA) If the read works, the accumulator will be set to zero. If it went wrong, the accumulator will contain 1.

39   WRITE   (WRITE from the buffer starting at address set by last SETDMA to the track and sector set by SETTRK and SETSEC) If the write was good, the Accumulator will contain 0, if not it will contain 1. Under CP/M 2.x, the deblock information must be passed in register C when the WRITE function is called.

42   LISTST   (Return the LIST device STatus) This routine was not specified for BIOS routines before version 2.0 - but it is useful. It returns in A the value 0FFH if the assigned LST: device is ready to accept a character, and it returns zero if not. This is used by such routines as DESPOOL and WordStar, which can perform quasi 'background' printing. (You can be running a foreground program at the same time

as a print routine. For example in Wordstar you can fill the 'waiting' time while the keyboard is being used with LIST commands. This slows down the foreground program - since with two devices competing for disc access, there is often a great deal of lost time during head movement. It also makes the print rather 'spasmodic'.

45   SECTRAN   (TRANslate the logical disc address to the physical SECtor address). This routine is only specified and only necessary in CP/M versions 2.0 +, where the 'skew' table was moved from within BDOS to within BIOS. This made alteration to hard disc, or to 5 1/4" drives much easier. SECTRAN should be called before any SETSEC call. SECTRAN takes the logical sector number in DE and the address of the skew translation table in DE, and produces the physical sector in HL. If the skewing is contained on the disc, SECTRAN should return the physical sector = logical sector + 1. In practice, most BIOS's return physical sector = logical sector, as the deblocking algorithm supplied by Digital Research expects the sector numbering to start at 0 - whilst the normal disc controller begins with sector 1. This can cause problems, and the best way out is for the SETSEC to reduce the sector number by one for the deblocking algorithm. Then, after deblocking, the physical sector is incremented by one. However, because of the variations, any program making direct BIOS calls for READ or WRITE must use SECTRAN, if only to determine the base sector number for use with SETSEC.

48 + +

CP/M 3 has an extended BIOS table which is not of real use to the programmer. Some implementations of BIOS contain only the essential elements listed above. Others contain various enhancements unique to the particular machine or range of machines. These extra routines are not accessed directly by CP/M, and therefore **are** always addressed by the

257

always addressed by the programmer directly. The usual way of addressing them is simply to extend the BIOS jump table that we have been inspecting, so that they are accessed as though they were standard BIOS routines.

14.2.2 BIOS extensions.

Some of the common extensions to the BIOS are these -

Provide additional console I/O editing
Provide a clock
Insert a 'cold start' command
Provide I/O port control (eg baud rate/char size/parity)
Read n sectors with incrementing DMA
Write n sectors with incrementing DMA

The machine on which this chapter is being written, under WordStar, has the second, third and fourth of that list, but not the others.

14.2.3 BIOS enhancements.

Often, there is a trade-off between what might be desirable, and what is reasonable in view of the fact that the more BIOS you have, the less available TPA there is. In fact, every effort is made to write very 'dense' code - achieving the maximum in the fewest instructions - so that many systems have substantially extended the scope of the BIOS and implemented all kinds of tricks and devices to speed up a disc-bound machine - or to implement a device that was neither invented nor even envisaged when CP/M was written.

These are some of the common enhancements -

Implement the IOBYTE
Implement interrupt on peripheral I/O
Provide I/O handshaking for high speed data transfer
Implement a double density disc drive
Implement a double sided disc drive

Change the record size for a 5 1/4" disc drive
Implement a Winchester hard disc drive
Implement a pseudo-disc using memory banking (see MDISC, Chap 11)

14.2.4 Before and after CP/M 2.2.

In adapting the BIOS for so many different hardware contexts CP/M up to 2.0 began to lose some of its uniformity. This was obviously undesirable, so Digital Research were pressured by their own success into producing version 2.2. Before 2.2 two main techniques had evolved. Either the BIOS was so written that CP/M could believe that it was still handling the conventional peripherals, or CP/M itself was modified, either by direct patches, or by inserting a BIOS routine that performed the patch on booting.

When 2.2 came out, it was much easier to differentiate between the 'logical machine' of CP/M and the actual disc and other hardware. The range of possible enhancements and extensions was increased without loss of standardization, and even the 'basics' were simpler to implement, because of the increased clarity of the distinction between 'logical' and 'physical' machine.

However, having said that, it is not easy to make specific, universally applicable comments about the BIOS in the way that one can about, say, the FDOS calls. All responsible hardware manufacturers (which means that the Authors have come across exceptions) supply listings of their BIOS, so that the programmer can make use of the BIOS facilities. You can always get partial information about the BIOS with DDT, but that does not give you quite as much useful information as an assembler listing would. If you are going to make any use of the BIOS extensions, or the enhancements by accessing BIOS directly in your programs, study the listings.

14.2.5 BIOS calls.

There are several approaches which you can take to accessing BIOS routines directly. The important points are that your code must be comprehensible, and must not crash if the memory size is altered. (MOVCPM etc.) If you are only intending to access a few of the BIOS routines, then it is adequate to use the method we covered above. For instance, if you are going to use the

259

SETTRK routine in BIOS, write the following routine (also called SETTRK as we said earlier) into your code.

```
SETTRK:     LHLD        0001H
            LXI         D,001BH
            DAD         D
            PCHL
```

That subroutine will then access the BIOS SETTRK for you. (The value 001BH is 27 in decimal - the required offset - see table above.)

However, if you are intending to make extensive use of the BIOS routines, rather than coding up every access separately, you can construct a 'BIOS Jump Table' of your own. A simple block move will do what is necessary. For example - this routine sets up the base address and offsets, and moves the appropriate one into the required registers.

```
            JMP         GETTAB
            DS          42
WBOOT:      EQU         $
CONST:      EQU         WBOOT + 3
CONIN:      EQU         WBOOT + 6
CONOUT:     EQU         WBOOT + 9
LIST:       EQU         WBOOT + 12
PUNCH:      EQU         WBOOT + 15
READER:     EQU         WBOOT + 18
HOME:       EQU         WBOOT + 21
SELDSK:     EQU         WBOOT + 24
SETTRK:     EQU         WBOOT + 27
SETSEC:     EQU         WBOOT + 30
SETDMA:     EQU         WBOOT + 33
READ:       EQU         WBOOT + 36
WRITE:      EQU         WBOOT + 39
LISTST:     EQU         WBOOT + 42
SECTRAN:    EQU         WBOOT + 45

GETTAB:     LXI         D,WBOOT     ;LOAD THE ADDRESS OF
                                    ;THE TABLE BASE IN DE
            LHLD        0001H       ;LOAD THE ADDRESS OF BIOS
                                    ;BOOT IN HL
            MVI         B,48        ;LOAD BYTE COUNT INTO B
MOVEIT:     MOV         A,M
```

```
STAX    D
INX     H
INX     D
DCR     B       ;UNTIL ALL BYTES HAVE BEEN
                ;MOVED
JNZ     MOVEIT
```

With this table set up, the subroutines named can then be called just as if they were in your TPA.

14.3 Stack Requirements.

CP/M BDOS function calls consume one level of the stack - but direct BIOS calls vary in the amount of stack they require. Some of the more advanced BIOS's with deblocking and/or interrupts and/or direct screen memory mapping may require a large stack.

In general, the stack provided by the CCP cannot be guaranteed to be sufficient in all instances of direct BIOS calls. It is safest to provide at least 24 levels of stack in any portable software wherever a direct BIOS call is made.

14.4 Interlacing.

We have commented on skewing and extent folding earlier - but this is an appropriate point to re-introduce the topic of skewing. If you step through a program, checking the sector numbers as you do so, you'll find that the sequence appears jumbled. This is because in the early days of CP/M, which were also the early days of discs, the IBM standard was adopted. At that time, to attempt to read two sectors which were next to each other would have meant waiting for a full revolution of the disc, because the controller had not time to accept end of sector and re-initiate read in time for the next So the software device called interlacing was created which, for CP/M, means that there is a standard 'skew' of six sectors between two logically contiguous sectors in a file. Read sector 7, say, and the sector which contains the next data for that file might be 12.

This form or sector skewing is often called 'soft' skewing, because it is performed by the software. With sectors numbered 1, 2, 3, etc and the standard 6 sector skew, the translation from logical sector to physical is like this -

```
LOGICAL    0  1   2   3   4   5  6  ...
PHYSICAL   1  7  12  19  25   2  8  ..
```

More recently, hard skewing has been adopted on many discs - except th IBM standard. With hard skewing, the skew is written on the disc in the sector number held in the index for each sector. Adjacent sectors on the disc may be numbered 1, 7, 12, 19, 25 etc. The SECTRAN will then perform the logical to physical translation like this -

```
LOGICAL    0  1  2  3  4  5  6  ...
PHYSICAL   1  2  3  4  5  6  7  ...
```

In both the examples above, the sector is read from the same position on the disc.

The advantage of 'hard' sector skewing is that the skew can be altered without affecting the compatibility of the disc. A 'soft' sector skewed IBM disc must always have a skew of 6 if it is to be read by another CP/M system. In contrast, a 'hard' skewed disc can use any skew without causing compatibility problems. The skew can then be optimised for the hardware and the application - to give maximum speed of data transfer overall.

Now, with technology improvements, the speed advantage of 'soft' sector skewing seems minimal. The standard still exists, but it is there to solve a problem which has largely gone away - or at least altered significantly. In fact, one of the reasons for using direct calls to the BIOS may be to avoid the standard interlacing and test out different 'skew' factors until you find the one that works fastest. Which may be 'none at all'. If you are developing database software, this will be a near-essential.

CP/M 1.3 and 1.4 had the IBM 8" skew table built into BDOS, for converting logically 'next' to physically 'farther on'. In subsequent versions, the skew table was left out, so that the writer of the BIOS had to write the skew table. It is accessed by the SECTRAN routine, normally called by BDOS. However, this does mean that the skew on your system may need to be investigated before you assume any particular 'offset' between logically contiguous sectors.

14.5 The IOBYTE - Input/Output Device mapping.

The IOBYTE is an optional feature in CP/M - is not supported in MP/M or in CP/M 3.1 - and therefore must not be assumed in any portable software. However - if the IOBYTE is implemented in your system, and you are not writing portable software, the IOBYTE is simple but powerful.

The section on the IOBYTE in chapter 11 said this. There are four logical devices (CON: RDR: PUN: and LST:) understood by CPM. Each of these can be allocated to one of four values - as we saw in chapter 4 - the four physical devices available for each.

This byte is considered in four parts, with each pair of bytes in the part taking values 00 to 11 - four values. As you will see from the table, if bits 2 and 3 are set to 01, that means that the PUN: device (bits 2&3) is set to PTP: (the second possible value).

Bits	Ref to	Values 00	01	10	11
6&7	CON:	= TTY:	CRT:	BAT:	UC1:
4&5	RDR:	= TTY:	PTR:	UR1:	UR2:
2&3	PUN:	= TTY:	PTP:	UP1:	UP2:
0&1	LST:	= TTY:	CRT:	LPT:	UL1:

Clearly, although at any one moment only four physical devices can be accessed - the four selected by the values in the IOBYTE - the programmer can readily alter the IOBYTE during program execution, as many times as necessary.

This table could be used to access a total of 16 different ports - provided that TTY: on CON: is different from TTY: on RDR: and so on. If there is only one TTY:, you could access up to 12 devices. Also, in practice, the physical assignment actually used can vary from that suggested by the names. For example, a system might assume that TTY: is the default for the logical device. In that case, CON: TTY: is the console CRT, LST: TTY: is the serial printer. Alternatively, a system might use the IOBYTE to define the four physical ports denoted by the IOBYTE values 0, 1, 2 and 3. Since these variations exist, we can only illustrate, we cannot 'define'. Use the IOBYTE with caution, until you are sure of the way the system uses it.

The mnemonics for the logical and physical peripherals refer in some cases to obsolescent devices. It is most appropriate to think of a RDR (Reader) device as any device which can tramsmit data to the computer one byte at a time. Similarly a PUN (Punch) device is one which can accept data from the computer, one byte at a time in a serial stream.

Many BIOS's take advantage of the facilities in PIP.COM (see Chapter 4) by implementing the IOBYTE. This means that the BIOS contains many more than the four routines which a single IOBYTE can access. The kind of connections which are made in this way include plotters, digital tape recorders, card readers, paper tape punches, Analogue/Digital hardware, many kinds of data capture device, cash registers, 'floppy tapes', alternative printers, modems, acoustic couplers and other computers large or small. The connections can made made much more easily by use of the IOBYTE than any other way, and also, because the BIOS uses standard CP/M facilities in a standard way, the software is much more portable.

14.5.1 Altering the IOBYTE.

A simple way to change the IOBYTE would be to put the new values you want in a byte we'll call NEWBYTE, and do this -

```
MVI    A,NEWBYTE
STA    IOBYTE
```

However, that is more than a little clumsy for two reasons. First, you have to set up a complete byte, even to change one assignation. Second, the SYSTEM page should not be altered directly in that way. It should only be altered through a BDOS call. If you want independent assignments, then this is better -

```
LDA    IOBYTE
XRA    B         ;WHERE B CONTAINS THE FIELD
                 ;ASSIGNMENT IN THE CORRECT BIT
                 ;POSITION, THE OTHER BITS CAN BE
                 ;GARBAGE
ANI    MASK      ;WHERE THE TWO BITS OF THE DESIRED
                 ;FIELD ARE ZERO, THE OTHER ARE ONE
XRA    B
STA    IOBYTE
RET
```

An even better routine would use the stack and PUSH and POP from and to B, using function 5.

The mask for LST: would, for example be 00111111B or 03FH, and the mask for PUN: would be 0CFH and so on. This can be elaborated in the code, so as to make the whole thing completely automatic. Remember, as we said earlier, that if you access a BIOS routine or any standard element of CP/M, use the standard name in your routines which are used in CP/M, because this will make the logic comprehensible to you (later, when you have forgotten what you intended) and to anyone else.

14.6 Disc Parameter Block.

You may want to access the disc parameter tables within the BIOS, probably for the purpose of reading the DPB (Disc Parameter Block) for the current drive. In CP/M 2.2 (we said earlier that previous versions of CP/M handled this differently) and later versions, the information is held in a block of data for each drive. Any program which needs to compute file sizes, access the directory directly or otherwise discover the precise details of their drives and disc formats can do so by reading this block. The block is arranged like this - we have inserted some typical values for an IBM 8" SS/SD disc -

SPT:	DW	26	;Sectors per track
BSH:	DB	3	;Data Allocation Block Shift Factor
BLM:	DB	7	;Block Mask
EXM:	DB	0	;Extent Folding Mask
DSM:	DW	242	;Data Storage Max (no. of blocks-1)
DRM:	DW	63	;Directory Maximum - 1
AL0:	DB	0C0H	;Directory allocation bit map - Low
AL1:	DB	0	;Direct'y allocation bit map - High
CKS:	DW	16	;Directory Check Size
OFF:	DW	2	;Reserved Track Offset

The size of the unit of disc storage - a mandatory 1k in CP/M 1.4, is calculated by the expression -

$$128*(BLM+1) \text{ or by } 128*2*BSH$$

so your program can calculate the disc storage capacity, just as STAT DSK: does.

265

There are default values in program memory - so the most convenient approach is to move the entire table into memory from the BIOS, ove the top of the defaults. (In CP/M 1.4, do not use the subroutine, use the default values.)

Here is a dummy table, and the routine which writes the values from BIOS into the locations reserved

```
SPT:    DW    26
BSH:    DB    3
BLM:    DB    7
EXM:    DB    0
DSM:    DW    242
DRM:    DW    63
AL0:    DB    0C0H
AL1:    DB    0
CKS:    DW    16
OFF:    DW    2
SPD:    DW    16
```

;Call this routine immediately after a BDOS function call 31
;as HL will then point to the base of the current DPB

```
        MVI    C,31
        C ALL  5
        LXI    D ,STP    ;DE points to base of dummy table
        MVI    B,15      ;now we do a block move (17 in 3.1)
LOOP:   MOV    A,M       ; of the whole table
        S TAX  D         ; on top of our default table
        INX    D
        INX    H
        DCR    B
        JNZ    L OOP
```

And there are the actual values for the current drive in your table, ready for whatever manipulation you require.

14.7 A complete illustrative subroutine.

The code which follows is a routine which includes a BIOS call, because it needs to. The subroutine either reads the image of the entire directory into a buffer, or write the entire directory back into the directory track from a memory buffer. Although the routine itself is quite simple, it may not be immediately obvious. It uses the fact that BIOS should remember the last sector or track set. You should also be aware that the BDOS function which searches the directory alters the FCB given to it as a parameter, and you will see that the subroutine compensates for this. This subroutine only applies to versions 1.4 and 2.2 - in CP/M 3.1 you cannot rely on the BIOS remembering the last sector or track. If your software is portable, and you want to use this routine, you should put in some lines of code to test for version number, only allowing 14 and 22, and to call the BDOS labelled in the first line of this code, to set the DMA.

```
BDOS:    EQU    0005H
DBUF:    EQU    0080H      ;default CP/M directory buffer insert
                          ;version test here
PUTDIR:  XRA    A          ;enter here to replace directory from
                          ;buffer
         DCR    A          ;A register is true
         JMP    ON
GETDIR:                    ;enter here to read directory into buffer
         XRA    A          ;A register is false
ON:      STA    PUT        ;store A in flag describing operat'n
                          ;required
         MVI    A,"?"      ;make sure first byte of FCB is Ok
         STA    DUMMY      ;and is not altered by any previous call
         LXI    H,BUF
         SHLD   BUF.PTR    ;initialise buffer pointer
         MVIC   11H        ;search first function parameter
BACK:    LXI    D,DUMMY    ;specify our FCB
         CALL   BDOS       ;call to 0005H
         CPI    0FFH       ;was it the end of the directory ?
         JZ     END        ;if so, job done
         ANA    A          ;if it referenced first match of sector
         CZ     MVIT       ; then its time to act
         LDA    DBUF+1     ;are we somehow past end of the
                          ;directory ?
```

267

```
            CPI     0E5H
            JZ      END         ;then it's time to stop !
            MVI     C,12H       ;otherwise  search  again  BDOS
                                ;parameter
            JMP     BACK        ;and loop again


MVIT:       LHLD    BUF.PTR
            XCHG
            LXI     H,DBUF      ;Directory window pointed to by HL
                                ;(0080H)
            MVI     B,128       ;number of bytes to move
            LDA     PUT         ;are we reading or writing ?
            ANA     A           ;set flags
            JZ      MOVE        ;jump if reading ('getting')
            XCHG                ;if not swap p'ters so info goes other
                                ;way


MOVE:       MOV     A,M         ;do a block move
            STAX    D
            INX     H
            INX     D
            DCR     B
            JNZ     MOVE
            LHLD    BUF.PTR     ;bump buffer pointer by one sector
            LXI     D,128
            DAD     D
            SHLD    BUF.PTR
            LDA     PUT
            ANA     A
            RZ                  ;return if a read operation
            MVI     C,1         ;signal a directory write operation
            CALL    WRITE       ;do a directory sector write
            RET


END:        LXI     H,BUF
            SHLD    BUF.PTR     ;reset buffer pointer
            MVI     C,0DH       ;reset  CP/M  to  update  Directory
                                ;information
            JMP     BDOS        ;and return from subroutine
```

268

```
WRITE: LXI
D,39
          LHLD   0001H
          DAD    D
          PCHL

DUMMY:    DS     '???????????'  0,0,0

BUF.PTR:  DW     0000H
PUT:      DB     00H
BUF:      EQU    $              ;set this value to base of buffer as req'd
```

14.8 Summary.

In this chapter you have considered a mechanism for calling BIOS routines, using the jump vector in the base of BIOS. You have established what each BIOS routine in the minimal standard set does, and seen how this set might be enhanced, and extended. You have followed some useful mechanisms for IOBYTE manipulation, for accessing the disc parameter tables, and finally you have seen the use of calls to the BIOS in the case of a routine which has two entry points, and sets a flag (PUT) to true or false for use in the routine. The routine reads or writes the whole of a disc directory into the memory starting at a base specified by you in place of the $ sign in the BUF statement at the end of the routine.

You are now in a position to access the parts of BIOS which we have identified, and to inspect the listing of the BIOS which your manufacturer/supplier should have provided, to find out how the standard requirements have been met, and whether or not there are extensions to your BIOS, over and above the standard.

269

CHAPTER FIFTEEN

Configuration

15.1 Fundamentals.

This is a short chapter, giving general ideas rather than specific code.

At this level, when we talk about 'Configuring' your system, we refer to the facility that is usually provided with the Customised BIOS to select one of a choice of options. You will find a program called - almost always - CONFIGUR, on your system disc. You load it like any other transient, and it displays for you the current state of the BIOS, listing what the choices are, and which ones have been selected.

The kind of choice you may have - particularly in CP/M 2.2 and later versions - covers the items we mentioned in chapter 14, as well as a number of others.

For example, you may have the choice of having all 'write to disc' operations verified. This means that after a sector is written, the system waits until it comes round again, and reads it back, comparing what it reads with the original buffer from which it was written. Only if there is complete agreement is the 'write' considered successful - anything else will give a system error. Function 48 (Flush Buffers) in CP/M 3.1, used with the 'Purge' facility, makes this a very simple operation.

You may have a (battery powered) clock and calendar in your system - or you may not, but either way you may have the option of a clock display on the screen - usually top right corner of the screen.

The main configuration selections you do have to make are those concerned wih the 'ports' on your particular system. In CP/M 3.1, there are SET commands which allow you to alter these and other selections at any time -

useful if you have more than one printer, but only one printer port, for example.

In versions before 3.1, you use CONFIGUR for this. For example, you might have a port used for the printer, and it might be a 'serial' port. If so, you have to tell the BIOS how many start and stop bits are to be sent, how many bits make up a character, whether parity is odd, even or not used, and how fast the printer expects to recieve characters.

This last is the 'baud rate'. At one time, line speeds were quoted in 'bits per second'. The idea was that if you could send 100 characters of eight bits down the line, that would be an 800 'bit per second' connection. And if that was exactly what you were doing, that would also be an 800 baud connection. However, not all the characters sent down a line are 'information bits', there is always an overhead of some kind. For instance, there are the start/stop bits in an asynchronous line - and there are 'filler' characters to keep the two ends 'in step' in a synchronous line. Also - the way that information can be sent down a line using phase and/or amplitude modulation - means that the actual capacity of a line may be much higher that the apparent 'bits per second'. The term 'baud rate' was coined to remove the inconsistency and apparent inaccuracy of the 'bit per second' values. It means the number of 'changes of state' per second which are theoretically capable of being transmitted. This is a much truer measure of information carrying capacity. How it affects you is a matter of what system and peripherals you are using.

If you have a serial printer, say a 'daisy wheel', then you will be printing at, perhaps, 45 characters per second. That is 360 bits per second. However, there is probably much more information than just your printed characters being sent - so you would be wise to think in terms of at least 600 baud. And your daisy wheel printer probably has some 'memory' inside it. Fine - now you can send short bursts of characters, faster, to keep the printer memory filled up, and to allow the printer to run at full speed without pauses to interrogate the cpu. So most daisy wheel printers are interfaced with a 1200 baud line.

If you have a matrix printer which actually prints at, say, 130 cps, that is 1040 bits per second - and a 1200 baud line will probably not be supplying the printer fast enough to keep it running at full speed.

This is all very general - and there are parallel as well as serial connections, as well as a wide range of other facilities which you may be able to invoke

271

through your own CONFIGUR program. We cannot be more specific, because CONFIGUR is, like the BIOS, hardware dependent. How CONFIGUR works in practice is again hardware dependent, but a typical method of operation is like this.

You load CONFIGUR, and the program takes a copy of the BIOS and holds it in the transient program area. This will be the version which will be altered, not the one in high memory which is actually 'in use'. If your CONFIGUR also modifies the SPA (bottom page of memory), the CCP or the BDOS, these are also held in the TPA. When you invoke changes, the changes are made to that version in the TPA, not to the 'live' versions. When you have made all the changes you want to, you will indicate this to CONFIGUR, and the memory image you have created is written to the system tracks. Then the screen usually invites you to do a 'boot'. Since you have been changing the BIOS, principally, and since that is the one area which is not altered by a 'warm boot', you naturally have to perform a 'cold boot'. This is the 'reset' key - or a power off/power on sequence, depending on your system.

Now you are working with the 're-configured' version of CP/M.

15.2 CP/M Installation.

The previous paragraphs assume that you have a working version of CP/M - it may be at 60 hz instead of the UK standard of 50 hz (the modern name for 'cycles per second') - so the screen may present an unsteady picture - but at least you can run through the CONFIGUR options and very quickly have an appropriate, running system.

However - if your BIOS does not have appropriate routines for the peripherals you want to drive, then you have to 'patch' the BIOS with those routines. Even worse - you might be bringing up a new version of CP/M from scratch - in which case the problem covers a wider area.

The distribution version of CP/M that is supplied by Digital Research works as it stands with the INTEL MDS-800 micro development system. We will consider the two aspects of modification separately - patching the BIOS first, and then initial installation.

15.3 'Patching' the BIOS.

You will have the BIOS code for your system, as supplied (or at least it **should** be supplied) by the hardware provided or software house. If you have not - you will either have to work from the memory image that DDT will give you - or you will have to get the code.

At least you will have the CP/M system alteration guide. That includes two versions of BIOS - the MDS-800 version we mentioned above, and a 'skeletal' version.

If you have your BIOS, then it is no major task to write in the appropriate new code, and use SYSGEN and MOVCPM to construct the revised version on the system tracks. There are no 'generalisations' about this task - it is totally dependent on your current system, and what you want to do to it.

This is called by Digital Research 'second level regeneration' - where you have a working system, and can use the facilities of that working system to create a different (working) system using the same discs. However - when you do not have a working version - then you are into 'first level regeneration'.

15.4 First-time installation of CP/M.

If you are constructing CP/M on the same hardware as it will run - then you need to be able, at the very least, to develop and run assembler code on that hardware. If you do not even have that facility, then you have no choice but to generate a working system on some other - disc compatible - hardware.

Assuming that you can develop and run programs, there are two programs which you need to create first. These are GETSYS and PUTSYS. They fulfil the roles of MOVCPM and SYSGEN, in that the first will read the system tracks into memory - so that you can patch the system. The second (PUTSYS) writes from memory onto the system tracks, so that you have a 'cold start loader' at the beginning, which will then load the rest of the system. You will in fact need two versions of GETSYS - one to load the existing version of CP/M into memory, and the second to act as the 'cold start loader', which will be stored at the start of the system tracks, and which will then 'start' the new system automatically.

273

The System Alteration Guide (or in MP/M, the User's Guide) which is supplied by Digital Research will be your start point. In there you will find minimal versions of both GETSYS and PUTSYS, which will form the basis - or will at least give you the structure - of your new ones.

Normal practice is to call a new version of BIOS which you have created 'CBIOS' (Customised BIOS). You would - as we described in chapter 8 - create a HEX or PRL file which can be LOADed or Linked (L80) to give you the necessary COM file.

It should be obvious, of course, that any such program which you create will need careful testing !

CHAPTER SIXTEEN

Networking and Multi-User Systems

16.1 FUNDAMENTALS.

Now we are moving into the area of CP/M and its descendants which covers the sharing of facilities. CP/M, as we have seen so far, is an operating system which handles a single console, and one task at a time. There can be a number of 'users' (chapter two ff) but only one can be 'logged on' at once. CP/M itself, however, is only the first in a family of operating systems which have been, and are being developed by Digital.

The family is split into two areas - the operating systems for 8 bit machines, and the operating systems for 16 bit machines.

Within each of these, we can consider the following -

Single console, single task, 'local' storage. (eg CP/M)
Single console, multiple tasks, 'local' storage. (eg Concurrent CP/M)
Several consoles, each single or multiple task, with local and/or shared storage media. (eg CPNET)
Several consoles, one central processor and shared facilities. (eg MP/M)

We have been considering CP/M itself, so far, and this chapter is principally concerned with Networking and MP/M. However, we will include a brief description of each system here.

There is 'Concurrent CP/M', for example, which allows a single user at a singe console to initiate up to three tasks in addition to the one currently using the console. If the memory will contain sufficient programs, and there are peripherals to support them, four jobs can share the processor, with control passing from one to another according to the current demands. The user at the console can 'switch' the console to one or other of the running jobs, as appropriate to the task.

Then there is the area of 'networking', where several independent processors, each running under its own CP/M, can share a physical device, such as a Winchester disc. The processors cannot (unless the protocol has deliberately or accidentally permitted it) access files of other processors, but the speed and volume advantages of a Winchester can be made available to several users, without the need to provide each with an independent winchester. There are, as we'll see, other advantages of a network system.

And last there is the full multi-user system, with a central processor handling several consoles at the same time, and allowing various interactions between them.

Networking usually means the creation of a large file storage system - probably a Winchester disc, or several - which contains a processor for I/O scheduling and control. Two or more independent micro computers can then be connected to the processor/disc system, and can run quite independently, but share access to the disc. So you have several separate micros, each of which may have its own 'floppies', but which also has access to space on the 'big disc'. Each of the micros runs CP/M - in one version or another.

Multi-user systems are those which connect two or more terminals to a central computer, and the central computer does all the resource allocation and contains all the memory for the system. The terminals may be micros - but more often are simply consoles - a keyboard and screen, say. If a terminal is a micro - then it behaves like a 'dumb' terminal while it is logged onto the Multi-user system

16.2 NETWORKING.

As an illustration, we'll describe one specific set-up, in which a set of 12 micros share a 20M byte Winchester. What follows is a description of a typical system - and there are many variations.

The first thing that a CP/M user finds is that there is a program between him and CP/M. This is the networking program. It provides a standard 'protocol' for communication between the independent machines and the disc system.

CPNET is such a program. It has a range of functions, as we will see, but the noticeable element to the user is that you have first of all to identify yourself with a user name. This will be a name fed to the network program and stored with others in a file which is only accessible through the 'System Manager' - the interaction between one specialised user and the network program. The specialised user is the supervisor or controller of the system.

The user name may be echoed on the screen as you type it. Then you may be asked for your password. This will have been allocated, as with the 'user name', by the system manager. Normally the password is entered 'blind' and the user has to key the correct number of correct characters without any system response. There will often be a short pause after the correct number of characters have been keyed, to encourage the 'would-be intruder' to key more characters than the number required - which could be an error in itself.

Once over the 'user name and password' hurdle, you may be dropped straight into CP/M, or there may be an alternative system. Naturally, you choose CP/M. At this point you will have the SPA, the CCP, the BDOS and BIOS loaded into the memory of your local micro - and the CCP will display the A> prompt, waiting for your command.

Now you have a perfectly normal CP/M system, used in exactly the way we have been describing all through the book. The one difference is that you now have the Winchester disc.

On the system we are describing - there are many variations between systems - the supplier has chosen to call part of the Winchester 'drive A:', to keep all the 'system' software on that drive, and to make it 'Read Only' to all users except the 'system manager.' By 'system' software we mean CP/M itself, and all the transients like PIP and STAT, the editors (ED etc) the compilers and interpreters, (MBASIC COBOL RUNA etc) and the usual items like CONFIG, MOVCPM and so on. All of that software is on drive A:, and is accessible to any of the 12 micros (subject to delay if the disc is actually being read at the time of the request) but none of it can be written to, nor can that drive be written to.

Again, on this system, user drives have been allocated from D: upwards. Each user will have been allocated a 'volume' on one or more of the drives from D: up. These are normally R/W, of course, unless the user alters the attributes of his/her 'volume' on the specific drive using the STAT commands.

277

Since any of the attached micros can (in this case) have one or two 'floppy' drives on - any which does have them will be able to use them directly, as drives B: and C:. In the system, you may have micros which used to stand alone, but which are now attached to the network. If so, the drives may be actually marked A: and B:, but they are handled as B: and C:. (A has become B, and B has become C.) No other micro in the network can access the floppy disc files on the drives attached to your machine. Each user on a machine can READ from drive A, can READ and WRITE from/to drive D: or whichever has been allocated by user name, and both of these are the 'shared' facilities. Each user can access his/her own floppies which are physically attached to his machine - but cannot access floppies on other machines.

This has some interesting effects, when you come to use the system. For example, most software such as CIS-COBOL and WordStar has overlay segments which are called by the 'root' segments as required. The calling commands which are built into the software do not specify the drive - so CP/M automatically goes to the 'default' drive - the one onto which you are logged. For many purposes, it is more convenient to log onto drive D:, so that any file handling which you do automatically uses drive D - unless you specify otherwise. However, you cannot run software with overlays that way. If you have the D> on the screen, and you type in the following -

D> A:COBOL MFSETUP.CBL

then you will get the 'root' segment of COBOL correctly, and your file of source code will be sought from drive D correctly - but you will get a very rapid error response which says something to the effect that COBOL.IO1 is not found on the drive. It means, of course, that CP/M has looked for it on the default drive - which is D.

Therefore, obviously, you must be logged onto drive A, if you want to run any overlay software which does not (and most does not) specify the A drive in its 'overlay' commands. The command is then -

A> COBOL D:MFSETUP.CBL

and that command will automatically put the INT and LST files onto drive D, unless you use one or more of the directives - see chapter nine.

If you have been used to using a stand-alone micro, and you are moving onto a network system as we have been describing it, it makes good sense to avoid the 'default' drive as much as possible, and to get into the habit of defining the drive in every program or console command for file handling.

Note that this description is merely illustrative - other network systems vary from this in one way and another.

There are no 'extra' commands in CP/M when used as we have described for networking - the only extras are the user name and password which you need to key in to persuade the networking package to allow you in !

You could, of course, copy any of the drive A software into your volume of any drive that is accessible to you - but that would simply clutter up your space un-necessarily.

It is perhaps relevant to note here that you may hear people tell you that 'you must run XYZ package from drive A'. Well, that may be so - but more likely what they mean is that you must run the XYZ package from the drive on which you are logged when you invoke the package. This section of chapter 16 for example, is being typed using WordStar from drive B. The command was -

   B> WS A:CHAP16

and the whole of WordStar is on drive B, overlays and all.

There is also the point that you may want to use ED, with its temporary 'block move' file. (Commands X and R - see chapter ten.) This is written onto the default drive - so although you could use ED from drive A like this -

   A> ED D:MYSOURCE.PAS

you would not be allowed to use the X command. Better, in case you **do** want to use it, to enter ED from D like this -

   D> A:ED MYSOURCE.PAS

Get the idea ? In a network environment, **you** need to control what you would normally leave to the defaults in a stand-alone environment.

16.3 MULTI-USER SYSTEMS.

The MP/M prompt - the equivalent of A> etc in CP/M is this -

   0A>

where the 0 in front of the 'logged drive' is the current USER number. You use USER just as in CP/M, to change to another, so you might have your files recorded under user 3, say. You type in -

    0A> USER 3

and the system responds with

    3A>

To begin this section, we will cover, briefly, the three new commands that are in MP/M, but not in CP/M. The MP/M equivalent of SYSGEN will be described, and we will then go on to indicate how different versions of MP/M have been developed, to improve the facilities on offer.

16.4 MP/M Commands.

There are three special commands, all concerned with file conversion - or 'file transformation'. We will deal with these first. Page Relocatable files (which will be programs, probably written in a low-level language) have type '.PRL'. As we have seen, files which the CCP will accept as transient commands must be of type '.COM'. Original 'just translated' programs (files) will be of type '.HEX'. Since MP/M runs different programs from different consoles simultaneously (allocating resources and swopping control between programs as necessary) you can see that the assembler programmer needs the facility to generate a file of one type from a file of another type. These are the commands -

    GENMOD sourcefile.HEX destfile.PRL

or

    GENMOD sourcefile.HEX destfile.PRL $hhhh

or

    GENMOD sourcefile.HEX destfile.RSP (with or without $hhhh)

Sourcefile is a HEX file (drive name may be specified) which is treated as two concatenated hex files with the second offset from the first by one page (100H bytes). The destfile (again drive name may be specified) is a Page ReLocatatable version. The optional hexadecimal number ($hhhh) must be started with the $ sign, and indicates that the new program will require additional memory of the size indicated.

Files of type RSP are 'resident system processes'.

Note that the command does not require an ' = ' sign - which will serve to remind you that the 'direction' of the conversion is the opposite to that normally used in commands such as PIP and REN.

If you have a '.COM' file which needs to be converted to type '.PRL', then you must first convert it to HEX before you can use GENMOD. This requires the second command -

GENHEX filename.COM

or

GENHEX filename hhhh

This takes the COM file and produces a HEX version with the same filename (drive may be specified, and applied to the COM and HEX versions). The hhhh (no $) is an offset in hexadecimal. A two page offset (512 bytes) might be required when converting file D:SETUP.COM and would be specified like this -

0A> GENHEX D:SETUP.COM 200

assuming, of course, that GENHEX.COM or GENHEX.PRL is on drive A, and that both files are accessible to user 0. In fact, an offset of one page is much more commonly required.

Finally, you may have a '.PRL' file, which you want to locate absolutely in the TPA - in other words, you want a '.COM' file. To convert from PRL to COM - use the command PRLCOM (how do they think of the names ?!) - like this -

PRLCOM name1.PRL name2.COM

Name1 and name2 may be the same or different, and may or may not contain the drive letter. There is a small safety net in this command, in that if you convert a PRL file to a COM file with a name that is already used for a COM file, you will be asked whether you want to overwrite or to abandon the command.

Now some of the other MP/M commands.

First, it is always useful - sometimes essential - to know the status of the various processes within the system (running under MP/M). There is a

281

command which bears no relation at all to the STAT command we covered in chapter three, but which is, never-the-less, called MPMSTAT.

16.4.1 MPMSTAT

The display which results from this varies to some extent from system to system, but in outline it covers a complete list of all processes which are 'active', and groups them according to whether they are waiting for messages from queues, or waiting to send messages, whether they are waiting for CPU time or polling a terminal/device, and so on. It is fairly heavily coded, so check your system manual for a sample output.

16.4.2 ERAQ

This is regrettably not available under CP/M (up to and including 2.2) - it means ERA plus 'Query each deletion first'. We have seen that a comparable feature does exist in 3.1 - ERA afn [C].

You use it exactly like ERA (see chapter two). You would normally specify an ambiguous file reference, and the system would respond by listing each matching filename followed by a '?' and asking for a Y or N answer for each file. Y means 'Yes - erase it'.

16.4.3 CONSOLE

MP/M has a numeric code (0 upwards) for each console on the system. This is not the same as the USER number. Since the MPMSTAT command refers to console numbers, you need to know which console you are using. Type CONSOLE, and the reply

    CONSOLE = n

will tell you. (n runs from 0 upwards)

16.4.4 ABORT

This is vicious ! Any user, at any console, may terminate the run of any program, whether on the same or any other console.

The command is simple -

ABORT progname n

If n is omitted, the default is 'the program was initiated from this console'. If n is specified, it is the console number from which the program was initiated. You do not specify the COM or PRL file type - just the name.

16.4.5 ^D

This might not look like a command - but it is. 'Control D' will 'detach' a program running at your console. Provided that there is something which the program can get on with, it will contine to run. You, in the meantime, can initiate or re-attach (see below) some other process. If there is a program with only intermittent demands for input from the keyboard, it can usefully be detached while it is computing and filing or printing, releasing the console for other work.

16.4.6 ATTACH

This might be a normal 'ATTACH.PRL' file, or it could be a 'ATTACH.RSP' file (resident sytem process). Either way, provided it is accessible to you under the user number which is current at your console, this is the command -

ATTACH progname.PRL

- and the progname.PRL program will take over the console. However, progname. PRL must have been a '^ D' detached before you can re-attach it!

16.4.7 DSKRESET

With MP/M - all the facilities of the hardware are shared, and may be made available to an process from any console. Fine - but you want to change a disc, and it contains a file which may be being updated by another user at another console. At the moment you look at it - it may not be actually seeking, reading or writing, so you cant tell. What you do is to give the command to write all directory segments to all discs, to remove a disc. The command is DSKRESET. What happens is that a message appears at each console asking if the disc system can be reset.

Confirm reset disk system (Y/N) ?

appears on all consoles. If any one or more answers N then the disc reset is denied, directory segments are not reinstated to the up-to-date position, and you remove a disc at your peril! In fact, you do not do it.

16.4.8 SPOOL and STOPSPLR

The device currently addressed by the LST: functions - which may be one of several, re-directed either within a program by altering the IOBYTE (chapters eleven and fourteen) or at the console by using STAT (chapter three) - can, under MP/M, have a queue of files waiting to be LSTed. This is called a 'spool' or 'spool queue', and you attach a text file (in ASCII) to the spool queue with the command -

SPOOL filename.typ

and several filenames can be included in a single SPOOL command -

SPOOL file1.typ,file2.typ,

Notice that an extension must be specified if it exists. You may also specify the drive, of course.

To cancel the queue of waiting files, and to abandon the output to the LST: device you can use

STOPSPLR

If SPOOL.PRL is used to invoke a spool queue, then it can be stopped from a different console. If you were on console 2, say, and you invoked SPOOL from a PRL file, rather than a RSP file, then someone on another console could enter

STOPSPLR 2

and dump you off the LST: device! In fact, it can all get quite nasty if a proper protocol is not observed ...

16.4.9 TOD

Another MP/M command which needs co-operation between users is the TOD, or Time of Day command.

If you enter just -

TOD

the system will respond, perhaps,

Sat 2/18/83 09:05:55

which shows you the day, date (month/day/year) and time of day to the second **as it is currently understood by MP/M**. Fine - you can use that to schedule work to be run at some future time, with SCHED (see below). But an equally valid TOD command would be this -

TOD 2/19/83 22:10:00

and the system would respond with something like -

Strike a key to set time

The moment you touch a key, that date and time is/are stacked into the system, and that is the date and time understood by MP/M until someone changes it.

And any work SCHEDuled for the intervening 13 hours will not be run!

16.4.10 SCHED

This is the command which allows you - if you have confidence in your fellow users - to load the program called SCHED into the memory, and to give it a date and time and a program name. If you do, SCHED will sit in the memory, checking the TOD command for itself until it gets a match, and it then loads and runs the specified program. The command is -

SCHED mm/dd/yy hh:mm progname

where progname is a PRL or COM program - the type is not included in the command.

16.5 GENerate and LoaD an MP/M system.

There are two commands which are in MP/M but not in CP/M - their functions are loosely similar to SYSGEN and BOOT. The commands are GENSYS (generate an MP/M system with attributes as specified) and

MPMLDR (load the GENerated SYStem into memory). GENSYS enables the user to create a tailored version of the system in a file (MPM.SYS), which can then be loaded into memory with the MPMLDR command.

When you invoke GENSYS you are asked to complete a questionnaire related to your configuration and to the files on the system. Have you realised yet that in order to invoke GENSYS, you must have a CCP asking you for input ? In other words, there must be a CP/M or MP/M system loaded already, **before** you can invoke this command.

The questions are fairly straightforward - how much RAM have you got (answer zero, and MP/M will be given 'the lot') - how many consoles - where do you want the Breakpoint restart to be (you can not use 0) - do you intend to use CP/M '.COM' files as transient commands (if so, answer Y to the 'user stacks' question) - where do you want the user address banks to start (FF terminates the list of up to eight) - and which '.SRP' files do you want to hold in memory as resident commands. For this last, GENSYS will first ask if you want any (Y/N) and if Y it will list each System Resident Process (SRP) and ask if that one is to be resident. These are the basic set of GENSYS questions but it does depend on which release of MP/M you have, what the questions are. Use your MP/M User Guide to help.

Once you have a file MPM.SYS created by GENSYS, you can simply enter the command MPMLDR (for MP/M LoaDeR).

All this assumes that you have a complete MP/M, including the XIOS (the MP/M eXtended BIOS). Just as for CP/M, this is the interface which is produced for each hardware set-up. The standard CP/M BIOS for an MDS-800 is held as LDRBIOS.COM, and is used by MPMLDR to locate (and transfer control to) the new MP/M. You can use your CP/M SYSGEN command to save the new MPMLDR.COM with the new BIOS which you have created, after 'patching' it in the memory.

16.6 Priority within MP/M.

There are several ways in which MP/M can allocate priorities between tasks. If a task is running, it continues to run until one of a nmber of events occurs. If a resource is being used, say a record is being written to disc, then the task holds onto that resource until the transfer to disc is complete. Once the disc system is released, the 'dispatcher' of MP/M decides whether the same task should continue to run, or whether another should be allowed to take precedence. Each task has a 'descriptor', which not only contains a priority, and which is therefore what the dispatcher handles, but also contains various 'state' records which tell the dispatcher what the condition of the task was when it was last interrupted. Other ways in which a task can lose control of the processor are through interrupts, or when it issues a system call, or when the real-time clock moves on. If tasks are allocated different priorities, the dispatcher will inspect the descriptors and decide which of the competing tasks should be allowed to run. If the tasks are all given equal priority, a 'fifo' system is used - the one that has been waiting longest runs next. The tasks are 'queued' or 'spooled' - sequential additions can be made to the end of the queue or spool while items are removed sequentially from the start of the queue by being run.

There is also a way of using 'flags' which can be set by one task and examined by another, to synchronize the running of two or more processes, independently of any other interrupt mechanism. For example, one task could be carrying out a series of operations, and setting a flag when a fixed number have been performed, while the other, perhaps carrying out an 'averaging' or a display task, cannot run until the flag is set. Then, even if the dispatcher offers control to the second task, if the flag is not set, it wil be returned instantly to the dispatcher.

16.7 MP/M Version 1 versus Version 2.

All that we have said so far has been concerned with the 'basics' of MP/M. The concept of MP/M is by no means 'basic', of course - a full mulitiprogramming operating system on an 8-bit micro is a tremendous advance in itself. However, as with any new product, users are always looking for something better. Version 2 offers much that was thought to be restrictive in Version 1. The following descriptions identify the main areas in which Version 2 has advanced.

16.7.1 Record Locking in shared files.

Clearly, if two processes are allowed to update a single file, there can be problems. It would be possible, for instance, for two processes each to read a

287

record, and then each to update it, and write it back. This could result, if no precautions were taken to prevent it, in the update provided by the first to write being completely lost, because the second version would overwrite it without the process even knowing that it had happened. The obvious way out - though not the one adopted - would be to lock any record and prevent a second process from reading it until the first had released. This can lead to 'record lock' or 'deadly embrace' - where process A has record N and wants to read record M, but process B has already read record M (so it is locked) and wants record N. Both processes are suspended indefinitely. All kinds of devices are adopted to provide a 'soft' exit from such a situation, in database and other software systems, but MP/M version 2 has been able to capitalise on the way CP/M actually handles records to avoid the situation altogether.

A process reads a record, and keeps a copy of the original record and creates a second copy of the new updated version. Both are passed to MP/M when a write is issued, and there is a 'test and write' function which first tests to see if the record on the disc has altered since it was read. If it has not, the write takes place. If it has - the write is refused, the new state of the record is returned, and the process attempting to write can re-update (or do whatever is needed) and try again. In chapter 13 we identified the FDOS function which performs this. Incidentally, of course, the mechanism allows for logical records which are not exactly 128 bytes - the physical read/write unit.

16.7.2 New FCBs.

There are two new FCBs in Version 2. XFCB is the first. This is an optional FCB in addition to the standard one, and contains a password and two date markers. The two dates held can be selected from

> date created
> date last accessed
> date last altered (updated).

Adding password protection gives a substantial measure of security against deliberate intrusion, which 'user number' (which any user can select) did not. The dating of file creation/access is accessible to the programmer, and allows control of 'generations' and security or back-up copies without the confusion which can sometimes occur !

The second FCB is not optional, is also in addition to the standard FCB, and is normally completely transparent to the user. It is in effect a directory FCB which records whether or not the XFCB has been invoked, and other MP/M parameters.

16.7.3 File Structure enhancement.

In version 2, the maximum file size is now 32M bytes. This allows larger scale database types of application without the need for the complexities of multi-volume working.

Also, the new file structure allows for up to 16 'discs' each of which can have a maximum of 512M bytes. Eight thousand million bytes of on line storage - or eight 'gigabytes' if you like !

It might be worth commenting that you are actually unlikely to use this much, since it is quite possible for your ALLOC vector table to fill the whole of 64K bytes of RAM ! Actually, the 32M byte file size is likely to be of more immediate usefulness.

The design of BDOS for the new file structure makes the random access I/O very much more efficient than sequential I/O - even for sequential files. We therefore recommend that you use random access unless there is some valid reason for using sequential.

16.7.4 Special additional discs.

If you read the 'networking' section in the early pages of this chapter, you will have noted the use of a 'system' disc in the example we described - a disc which contains software (etc) accessible to all users, but in R/O form.

MP/M Version 2 allows you to specify a 'system' disc as part of your system generation. The only restriction is that all files on that disc must have the $SYS attribute.

The previous version of MP/M (and the USER facilities of CP/M) required you to hold all the software which you needed in an area accessible to you. So in a twelve user system, you would have twelve copies of PIP, twelve of

STAT, twelve of the compiler or interpreter, twelve of all the commonly used COM, SRP and PRL files. Nasty. Now, with version 2, you **may** have your own copy of any command file (etc) which you need, because MP/M will always search your area first, but if it does not find the file, it then looks on the special 'system' file.

This is a good point at which to mention, in passing, that if you have long directories - and larger 'discs' inevitably lead to larger directories - the time it take MP/M (or CP/M) to search the directories can become significant. Since directory search is always sequential from the 'top' - you will notice an improvement in performance if your most frequently used files are at the top of the directory. Since, from preceding chapters, you know that the directory is not a 'push-up stack' - so deleting and rewriting a file will not necessarily re-position it in the directory - you will need to ensure that you load the files into the directory in the most advantageous sequence for your operations. The next 'additional disc' will also have a bearing on this point.

If you do use the 'system' disc, you may be confused when MP/M reads from an unexpected disc - since this is reported on the screen as an extra line under your command line, containing the disc identity, the full ufn, and the date. This display can be suppressed, but is usually left active if the system disc is also invoked.

As well as the 'system' disc, you can now allocate a 'temporary' disc.

The principal reason for this is that the SUBMIT command always creates a temporary 'submit' file on drive A: In a system with Winchester or other mass storage (eg MDISC see chapter eleven) it can be very irritating to have the temporary SUB file created and used through the slowest (floppy) disc in the system. And often that is exactly what happens. So you can now specify a 'temporary' disc on any drive of your choice, and the SUBMIT command will use that designated disc as its location for the temporary SUB file.

If you have MDISC, of course, you will naturally designate that as the temporary disc - it is inherently 'temporary' - and is the fastest possible disc. You may also like to use that MDISC as the repository of all the current directories. Naturally, you will still have to write to the actual disc every time an entry changes - but think of the speed of directory search !

Small is beautiful (?).

MP/M has grown. Version 2 is bigger in total than Version 1.

However, the structure of MP/M Version 2 is now such that you can allocate it between resident and banked storage in 4k units, if you have a 4k bank system. So you can actually have less of MP/M fully resident.

How this is inmplemented will obviously depend on the supplier of the complete system, and it is assumed (not unreasonably) that anyone constructing MP/M will use memory switching to allow access to more than 64k of RAM or will opt for the 16 bit version MPM86.

In a memory bank system, a major objective is to cut down the amount of the operating system which has to be permanently resident to a minimum. Early memory bank systems used 16 banks, and it was quite difficult with MP/M version 1 to keep the resident portion down to 16k. And even 16k is a big chunk to loose. Many powerful programs which were required to run would not fit in the remaining 48k. Newer memory bank systems tend to use 4k banks, which give much greater flexibility.

For example, if you have a 128k byte system, you could apportion it into a 12k resident MP/M in half of the memory, leaving 52k transient program area, and a 12k system bank in the other half, leaving again 52k. So your 24k MP/M will be split between resident and banked portions in the same proportion as the rest of memory. Even the XIOS can be split, RESXIOS and BNKXIOS are the names used for the two portions. XDOS must be wholly resident - that cannot be split, but even so, it is not unreasonable to get the whole of the resident portion into the 12k suggested in the example above. That means that the user gets up to 52k of TPA, not much less than the 56k which is available under CP/M. Of course, the designer who finds that this is still too restricting has the option of going for the 16 bit version MPM86. This allows up to 1024k byte direct addressing, instant program re-location, and removes the need for bank switching, which is the major task in any implementation MPM80. There really is little comparison between MPM80 and MPM86 - the use of the 16 bit machine removes practically all the limitations of MPM80 - and in a sense MPM86 could have been named CPM86 - plus multi-tasking. It can be used as CPM86 is, as a single user system, and thus to some extent replaces CPM86.

An interesting advance which is becoming apparent is that when version 2 of MPM86 is implemented, it will not only incorporate all the improvements of MPM80 version 2 (as we have been describing above), but it will add many of the features previously unavailable under MPM80 - because of space limits - but which were available under UNIX. The author of this new MPM86 version 2 had not worked with micros before - he had been with Unix Systems.

16.8 Conversion from '80 to '86.

Intel supply a code convertor which will take a program written for the 8080 processor, and convert it to run on the 8086 processor. The resulting program will not normally run any faster - and it will usually be larger than the original. Digital Research have an improved version of this - called XLT86 - which works on the source code rather than the object, and which carries out extensive data flow analysis, and removes any redundant code. This also optimises the selection of 8086 counterparts of the 8080 code.

16.9 Summary.

In this chapter, we have looked at the different ways in which multi-user systems can be constructed, and have added the basic MP/M commands which are not available in CP/M. A discussion of the improvements available under MPM80 version 2, and comments on MPM86 completed the survey. Any product list is bound to be rather like an organisation chart - the story goes that if you have a printed organisation chart, the one thing you can guarantee is that it will be out-of-date! However, now or in the near future, this is the probable appearance of the full set of Digital Research operating systems for 8 and 16 bit use.

8 bit	16 bit	
cpm2.2	if you do not need more features.	
CPM Plus (3.1)	CPM86 v2	replacing v1
CPNET80 v2	CPNET86 v2	The network operating system
CPNOS80 v2	CPNOS86 v	Diskless slave network os
MPM80 v	MPM86 v2	as described above
MPMNET80 v2	MPMNET86 v2	Multiple master network
MPNOS80 v2	MPNOS86 v2	Diskless MPM slave network os

It seems that in future releases, '.REL' files will be made more use of, and SID RMAC and LINK will replace DDT and SAVE.

It also seems likely that the new manuals will be much improved from earlier ones - from MPM onwards. They will probable be in sets of three, a user manual, a programmers manual and a system manual, from which you can select according to the depth of the information you need.

CHAPTER SEVENTEEN

CP/M on the 8086

17.1 Fundamentals.

CP/M was initially produced for eight bit processors, such as the Intel 8080. We'll refer to all the 8 bit products as CP/M80 in this chapter. Now that an increasing number of sixteen bit processor based machines is becoming available, Digital Research have produced CP/M86 - the CP/M80 look-alike for the 8086 processor. The 8086 has an equivalent for every instruction on the 8080, and its considerably improved performance comes from the additional instructions which are available.

Although CP/M was produced for the 8080 - it was equally available for the eight bit Z80. However, CP/M86 is not available for the Zilog Z8000 16 bit processor.

CP/M86 has been designed to look and to perform like CP/M80, with an identical directory system. Software products for the 16 bit machines are, of course, in rather shorter supply than those for the 8 bit machine. Never-the-less, CIS-COBOL and Microsoft MBASIC are available - among others - so interest in the 16 bit systems is growing apace. There are 'prophets' who say that the 32 bit processors will be available so soon that it is hardly worth bothering with the 16 bit - time alone will tell !

This chapter tells the story of the implementation of CP/M86 on an existing machine with an 8 bit processor, to which a 16 bit processor was added. Many of the features and benefits of CP/M86 are introduced and explained. The speed of the 16 bit processor is, perhaps surprisingly, concealed by the fact that most programs are peripheral bound, even with CP/M80. But the vastly increased availability of TPA makes a tremendous difference to tasks which needed to be 'shoe-horned' into the TPA available under CP/M80.

17.2 The initial hardware.

There is nothing magical about the hardware described - it is simply that which was available when CP/M86 was to be implemented. What was done with this system could equally well have been done on others - though probably slightly differently.

The DSC4 is a Z80 based machine, and has a Zilog DMA chip. It has memory mapping up to 500k bytes in 4k banks, and the main memory is available on separate Multibus (An Intel trademark) boards addressable from 0 to 1024k.

The main advantage of this machine is its memory mapping. This is a technique to map the top four bits of an address into the top eight bits of the multibus address line. Each time a 16 bit address is output from the Z80, the top four bits are decoded by a set of high speed memory registers into the top 8 bits - making a 20 bit address. The time taken for this mapping is so small that it does not interfere with the normal timings. Memory mapping like this effectively partitions the absolute memory into 256 units each of 4k - like a bank of memory. This gives considerably greater flexibility over the more common memory bank switching, as we will see. In the DSC4 there is at the moment a restriction that the memory mapping can only address 128 units of 4k - a maximum of 512k bytes. Actually, when you have been used to 64K, 512k does not seem too restrictive.

One way of approaching the CP/M86 implementation would have been to replace the Z80 card with an 8086 card. However, the processor card with the Z80 also contains the floppy disc controller, the Winchester disc interface, the RS232 ports and the high speed RS422 port. There were obvious advantages to retaining the original processor board, and adding an additional 8086 processor, so producing a combined 8 and 16 bit computer.

17.3 The design decisions.

Initially, the prime purpose was to bring up CP/M86 as simply as possible. If all I/O was handled by the Z80, as it was before the change, this would represent a saving in complexity. There would have to be the minimum of hardware development on the 8086 board.

One of the main appeals of CP/M to users is the availability of a wide range of software. This was another factor in retaining the Z80.

Having decided to keep the actual I/O on the Z80, the outstanding question was at what point, and how, to effect the transfer from CP/M86. If the original processor had been an 8080, on which the powerful 'block move' instructions of the Z80 are not available, the decision might have been different.

In this case, because the clock speed of the Z80 and 8086 are not significantly different, and because Z80 disc transfers are performed partly using the DMA chip, and partly using the 'block move' instructions, it was decided that litle if any speed advantage would accrue from performing the I/O processing on the 8086. The specifications of the BIOS for 8 bit working (BIOS80) are practically identical to those for the 16 bit (BIOS86). This is not unexpected, since the disc structure is identical and all the BIOS80 calls could be translated into BIOS86 calls.

17.4 BOOT86

Once it was decided that the I/O processing and transfers would be handled by the Z80, all that was needed was a way to convert calls to BIOS86 to calls to BIOS80. The problem of implementing CP/M86 becomes principally one of designing the interface to a known and tested BIOS80, rather than the much larger problem of writing a BIOS86. This interface actually consists of a small amount of code in the BIOS86, and a program running on the 8 bit which we have called BOOT86.

To establish how the transfer between processors should be effected, each BIOS I/O call has to be considered.

It seemed that character I/O should be simple, requiring a common data area for access by both processors, in which register contents could be written and read as appropriate. In actual operation, when CP/M86 make an I/O BIOS call, the 8086 transfer the register contents to the common area, with the vector number of the BIOS80 call, and a flag. BOOT86 notes the setting of the flag, copies the register contents from the common data area to the Z80 registers, and makes a direct BIOS80 call. On completion of the BIOS80 operation, BOOT86 collects the return values and flags the 8086 to tell it that transfer is complete. BIOS86 takes the return values and copies them into the 8086 registers - and makes a normal return from the original BIOS86 call.

Disc I/O seemed less simple - since an equivalent idea would require a 128 byte common area, with a large time overhead in copying in and out character by character. However, the memory mapping on the Z80 processor board can be used to map a 16 byte address to the actual area of memory. The Z80 with its DMA chip can then transfer disc I/O to anywhere in the 8086 memory.

The BIOS disc table which describes each logical disc, and the uninitialised data area associated with it, need to be designed. They are, of course, already in the BIOS80 - but CP/M86 cannot use the 8 bit table directly - and even if it could, the high usage of the areas by CP/M86 makes it important to duplicate them in BIOS86. For full compatibility they should be identical. In the first implementation of CP/M 86, the disc tables are defined at assembly time - but the tables can be constructed dynamically from the CP/M80 tables.

Using the 16 address bits, the Z80 can only address 64k - but the memory mapping allows this to be mapped into any region of the 512k memory bus. The upper limit of 1024k is reduced because the top bit is used to select the RAM and ROM onboard memory or the bus. An important feature of the memory mapping is that each of the 16 blocks of 4k can be mapped anywhere - they could all address the same 4k, if that was wanted. This facility is used to compress the CP/M80 memory requirement down to 20k (from 64k), once CP/M86 is loaded.

The idea used in the memory mapping to enable CP/M80 to transfer I/O anywhere in the 512k CP/M86 memory is to create a 'window' at a fixed address in the 64k, and to map this 'window' to any location of the 512k. Thus CP/M80 can see through the 'window' into any part of the 'outside world' of CP/M86. To complete the disc transfer, the absolute address known by the BIOS86 is converted to an address which can be used by the window of the BIOS80.

17.5 Loading CP/M86

BOOT86 has a second function - in addition to the interfacing we have talked about. It has to load CP/M86 into memory, from a file. First problem, CP/M86 is designed to go where CP/M80 is. The interrupt vectors of

CP/M86 are in the first 256 byte of memory, and that is not something that can be changed. Therefore, CP/M80 must be moved away from the start of memory. The 64k it uses cannot start at 0000H. Memory mapping make it possible - and BOOT86 actualy moves the 64k - including itself - after creating the 'window' from 1000H to 4FFFH (16k).

From here, we will use four digit addresses to refer to the 16 bit address of the Z80, and five digit addresses to refer to the absolute address of the multibus and the 8086.

The top 20k of CP/M80 is copied to the top of memory in two steps. The diagram below shows this for a 256k bye total memory.

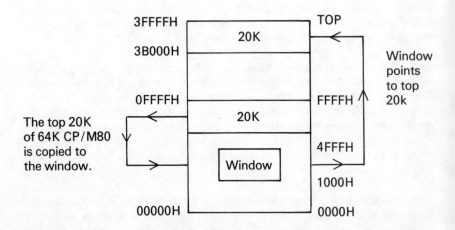

After the top 20k is copied, the bottom 4k bank is then copied - but again into the same area - at the bottom of the 20k. This keeps CP/M80 configured as a 64k system, but it only occupies 20k of actual memory.

The memory mapping of a system such as that above would be -

The * indicates the 4k bank pointing to the local 1k RAM which holds part of the BOOT86 program.

The Z80 relative 4k banks are set pointing to low memory, to help in debugging the CP/M86 system.

The 20k allowed for CP/M80 leaves space for BOOT86 and also for DDT. Without DDT, other utilities can be loaded and run inder CP/M80, even when CP/M86 has been booted.

For debugging, this configuration makes it feasible to boot CP/M86 from the CP/M80 debugger (DDT). With the help of the window to point to different areas of memory, one can monitor BOOT86, check that the CPM86.CMD file is loaded correctly, and then monitor the actual operation of CP/M86. If your imagination is up to it - you could then envisage loading DDT86 and using that to monitor the Z80....!

17.6 Processor conflict.

The multibus is designed to allow more than one master to share the bus, although the usual 8 bit configuration does not use the bus for memory access, because each master has its own local on-board memory. To access 512k, (theoretically 1024K) the 16 bit must use the bus. Now we have added a second processor - and both could be fighting for memory. If there was any conflict - this would result in delay, and would destroy at least some of the advantages of the whole exercise of having the two processors.

To avoid wasteful access to the bus, the design of the interface between the two BIOS's (the BOOT86) makes use of the local 1k of RAM on the Z80 processor board. When the 8086 processor is active, the Z80 loops within its own 1k on board memory, which does not require bus access. When the 8086 flags the Z80 to process a BIOS call, the 8086 performs a HALT and waits for the Z80 to interupt when it has completed the BIOS processing. The only time that both processors are active is during the I/O interrupts - an insignificant amount. For the whole of the rest of the time, only one of the two processors is active - so there should be no conflict, and no degradation.

That is all very well in the set-up we are describing, but there would need to be much closer study of the potential conflicts for the bus if you were looking at a multi-tasking environment. The problem may not be too severe, as a result of a feature of the 8086. The processor can fetch instructions in advance, from memory into its own FIFO buffer. This means that if there is a contention of the multibus, the 8086 can continue to run the instructions in the FIFO buffer, which would at least reduce the timing penalty of the conflict. Hardware must have priority over processing, and the Z80 is assigned the highest priority when requests for the bus are considered.

Provided we make sure in the design that any processor avoids using the multibus when it is idling, the contention should be minimal, even in a multi-tasking environment. It is likely that the majority of the Z80 active time will be waiting for hardware.

The BOOT86 program may sound complex, with its use of memory mapping, but once it has actually loaded CP/M86, it requires only a few instructions to read a requested BIOS call from the 8086, and create a call to BIOS80 at the required jump vector. For disc I/O, CP/M86 passes the number of the bank in absolute memory, with the byte offset to the start of the 128 byte block. BOOT86 points the window starting at 1000H to this bank, ready for a Z80 transfer into the relative bank starting at 1000H.

17.7 BIOS86

Once BOOT86 was designed and tested, BIOS86 was very much simpler. No deblocking was needed, because BIOS80 does that. Any BIOS86 call which does not involve I/O (such as SELDSK and WBOOT) is done within the BIOS86. The IOBYTE calls address the same byte as the BIOS80 IOBYTE calls.

On an I/O call, the necessary registers and the BIOS jump vector are written to the Z80 address starting at 0103H on the Z80. On completion, the BIOS86 reads the result from the same Z80 data area at 0103H. For some of the BIOS calls, there was also a need to convert addresses from the 8086 'SEGMENT and OFFSET' form (more about that in a moment) to 4 bit MEMORY BANK NUMBERS plus 16 bit ADDRESS for the Z80.

There is actually very litle processing required in the BIOS86 - but there is a new version of assembler to cope with. Although the 8086 has an equivalent for each 8080 instruction - the 8086 is naturally rather different from that of the 8080, and the instruction set is correspondingly different.

An address on the 8086 is in two parts - the SEGMENT and the OFFSET. The offset is easy, that is simply a value from 0 to 64k, and that provides the 8080 compatibility. If your program fits within 64k, then the segment does not change. In the BIOS86, you need to address the data area of the Z80 - which as we have shown it is at the top of memory - so you need the SEGMENT. In the early version of the assembler - using the SEG operator corrupted the symbol table, by incrementing all subsequent entries by 3 each time it appeared. Nasty ! Digital Research say that the new version does not have the problem.

Three major additions were made to the sample code of the BIOS as suplied with CP/M86. These were -

8259 Interrupt controller
Implementation of the IOBYTE
I/O performed through BIOS80

The 8086 supplies 256 vector interrupt locations as we said (in the very bottom of memory) which provide more than enought space for a fully vectored 8259 Interrupt controller.

The actual byte used to hold the 8086 IOBYTE is the same as that for CP/M80. That simplifies port mapping, since both processors use the same. There is just one problem - and you usually find some problem with a brand new product - which is that STAT86 does not address the correct byte in memory - so the IOBYTE, although implemented in the BIOS86, cannot be used.

Now we can see the full memory map of the way CP/M86 and CP/M80 were implemented. As before, the five digit addresses on the left are 8086 addresses, the four digit addresses are the Z80 ones. The CP/M80 allocation is shown within the | marks, and the total memory and CP/M86 is shown with | marks.

301

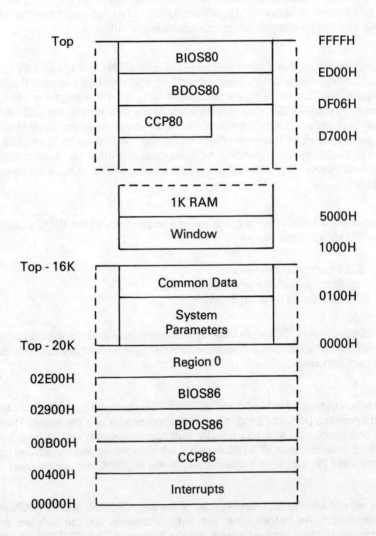

Top		FFFFH
	BIOS80	
		ED00H
	BDOS80	
		DF06H
	CCP80	
		D700H

	1K RAM	
		5000H
	Window	
		1000H

Top - 16K		
	Common Data	
		0100H
	System Parameters	
Top - 20K		0000H
	Region 0	
02E00H		
	BIOS86	
02900H		
	BDOS86	
00B00H		
	CCP86	
00400H		
	Interrupts	
00000H		

17.8 Using CP/M86

This is where, if everything has gone well, there is something of an air of anticlimax. CP/M86 cold boots quite normally - with a version of the CP/M80 sign-on message. The A> appears, and entering DIR or STAT give you a screen display exactly like the one you would get with CP/M80. After all the complexity of the memory mapping and the use of two different processors, it is difficult to believe that the CP/M86 is actually running at all. There is no speed improvement - the console and the disc speeds mask any change completely.

This is all very reassuring, of course. CP/M86 is, as we said at the start, a CP/M80 lok-alike - and it really does ! The user would quite likely be unaware of the fact that CP/M86 is there at all, unless the '.CMD' rather than the '.COM' filetypes are noticed.

The system programmer will notice the difference, once DDT86 is loaded. The same single character commands as in DDT80 are retained, but the very different processor begins to make its effects felt when you look closely at the responses. For instance - a 'D' request shows the SEGMENT and OFFSET of the address, instead of just 'the address'. Also, of course, the command which need an address have to handle both segment and offset - so you may find it safer to specify each separately, rather than using the simple 'G100' type of command.

'G0', if you are used to DDT80, can have unexpected results - because it does not exit from DDT86. The interrupt vectors are in the bottom of memory, if you remember. CP/M86 does not use 'CALL 0' as an entry to BIOS86 - instead there is (like in CP/M3) an extra BDOS call for direct BIOS calls. Entry to BDOS is not through the 'CALL 5' instruction - but instead a special reserved software interrupt is used. These changes are a necessary part of the move up to a larger address range, with the consequent split of the address into segment and offset. However, DDT86 does still respond to a ^ C to exit.

17.8.1 The Advantages of CP/M86.

Principally, unless you are doing some very substantial 'number- crunching', the advantage is more 'space' than 'speed'. If your programs are heavy users

303

of the console and peripherals you are unlikely to see much speed improvement, because the processor spends most of its time 'idling'.

There is a speed advantage, of course - and systems programmers are likely to notice it more than 'peripheral-bound users'. The actual BIOS86 program which was developed as we have described above, took two and a half minutes using the 8 bit Z80 cross- assembler, but only one and a half minutes on the 16 bit assembler. That was using a Winchester disc in both cases.

The newer versions of CP/M86 will certainly include many of the improvements which were incorporated into CP/M 3.1 - and provided that the 'pundits' who forecast that the 32 bit systems will supercede the 16 bit ones are wrong, there is clearly a great future for CP/M86. Many of the 16 bit systems now becoming available are - like the one we have described here - twin processor. That means that the range of 8 bit software will still be usable - until sufficient 16 bit is around to make a real impact.

CHAPTER EIGHTEEN

'Bug Fixes' from Digital Research

In this last chapter, we are including, with the permission of Digital Research, a set of Application Notes which allow you to perform various gymnastics with CP/M, to achieve things which the issued versions do not offer, or to correct errors. There are more available than we can include here - but these are the most likely to be helpful. If you want to get more, you could try Digital Research themselves, or, as we have mentioned before, the Journal of the CPMUGUK.

The following information is copyright 1982 by Digital Research, Inc., Pacific Grove, CA 993950 and is proprietary to Digital Research.

18.1 CCP AUTO-LOAD.

CP/M versions 1.4, 2.0, 2.1 and 2.2

Program to be amended - CCP.

Normally you interact with the CCP after the prompt. (A> etc.) If you use the CCP Auto-load feature, CP/M will execute an initial program immediately after loading the operating system.

Under normal operation, the CCP receives control from the BIOS after a cold or warm boot. The beginning of the CCP contains a two-element jump vector, and a command line which take the following form.

```
CCP:    JMP     CCPSTART        ;START THE CONSOLE
                                ;PROCESSOR
```

```
        JMP     CCPCLEAR        ;CLEAR THE INITIAL
                                ;COMMAND
        DB      127             ;MAXIMUM COMMAND
                                ;LENGTH
CL:     DB      0               ;COMMAND LENGTH
        DB      '       '       ;8 BLANK CHARACTERS
        DB      '       '       ;8 BLANK CHARACTERS
        DB      'COPYRIGHT...'  ;COPYRIGHT NOTICE
```

If control is transferred to location CCP (which is address 3400H in a 20k CP/M), the console processor examines the command length at location CL (3407H in a 20k CP/M). If that byte is zero, you receive the prompt and the CCP waits for input. If the byte is not zero, the CCP assumes that an initial command has been entered. It will execute the command on each cold or warm boot - if control is transferred to location CCP. However, if control is transferred to CCP + 3 (JMP CCPCLEAR), the initial command is cleared and the program enters CCP at command line level, displaying the default drive prompt as usual.

To put your initial command in, you specify the length of the command (not including the CL byte itself, or the terminating zero) in the CL byte. Then you specify the command in the folowing bytes. Although only 16 blank bytes are provided - a length of 15 (0FH) plus the zero - you can move the Digital Research Copyright notice for more spaces.

You can initialise the command line on the operating system track(s), or in the re-locatable image within the MOVCPM data area.

In MOVCPM.COM, or following SYSGEN and SAVE commands, the CP/M memory image is saved above the cold boot loader code starting at location 980H. If the system boot routines need more than 80H bytes, the CCP code may begin at location 0A00H. Modifying MOVCPM is similar to modifying the CCP. The difference is that the CCP starts at location 0980H (or 0A00H as above), after DDT reads the CCP into memory.

The procedure following uses DDT to modify the CCP to execute the initial command 'DIR' after each cold or warm boot. The screen displays from the system are in normal type, and the entries which you make are in **bold** type. The first display is to confirm that you have actually found the start of the CCP.

A> MOVCPM *.*

CONSTRUCTING 64K CP/M Vers 2.2
READY FOR "SYSGEN" OR
"SAVE 35 CPM64.COM"

A> **DDT CPM64.COM**
DDT VERS 2.2
NEXT PC
2400 0100
-**D980**
0980 C3 5C E7 C3 58 E7 7F 00 20 20 20 20 20 20 20 20 ..x...
0990 20 20 20 20 20 20 20 20 43 4F 50 59 52 49 47 48 COPYRIGH
09A0 54 20 28 43 29 20 31 39 37 39 2C 20 44 49 47 49 T (C0 1979,DIGI
09B0 54 41 4C 20 52 45 53 45 41 52 43 48 20 20 00 00 TAL RESEARCH

09C0 00 00 00 00 00 00 00 00 00 00 00 00 00 00 00 00 ....
-**S987**
0987   00 **3**
0988   20 **44**
0989   20 **49**
098A   20 **52**
098B   20 **0**
098C   20 **.**
-**D980**
0980 C3 5C E7 C3 58 E7 7F 03 44 49 52 00 20 20 20 20 ...x...DIR.
0990 20 20 20 20 20 20 20 20 43 4F 50 59 52 49 47 48 COPYRIGH
09A0 54 20 28 43 29 20 31 39 37 39 2C 20 44 49 47 49 T (C) 1979,DIGI
09B0 54 41 4C 20 52 45 53 45 41 52 43 48 20 00 00 TAL RESEARCH..
A> **S**
09C0 00 00 00 00 00 00 00 00 00 00 00 00 00 00 00 00 ....
-**G0**
A > **SYSGEN**
SYSGENVER2.0
SOURCE DRIVE NAME (OR RETURN TO SKIP)
DESTINATION DRIVE NAME (OR RETURN TO REBOOT)**B**
DESTINATION ON B, THEN TYPE RETURN

18.2 Reversing the functions of the Backspace and Rubout (Delete) keys

CP/M versions 2.1 and 2.2

Program to be amended - BDOS

In the code segment procedures which follow, the addessses given are hex offsets from the base of the CP/M system. The CCP (see previous section) is normally located at 980H but may be at A00H if a two sector boot is required.

You can assemble the patch for your size of memory. The CPMBASE will equal the BDOS entry point address at locations 6 and 7 in the base page of memory, **minus** 806H. Take care, because this entry point address is changed when DDT or SID is loaded. Under these programs, you must follow the jump at location 5 until an address is found with a significant digit of at least 6. In the example which follows, the CPMBASE would be E506H-806H or DD00H.

```
0005          JMP          CD00
CD00          JMP          D3A4
D3A4                       XTHL
D3A5          SHLD         E452
D3A8                       XTHL
D3A9          JMP          E506
```

To reverse the functions of Backspace and Rubout, patch into the SYSGEN or MOVCPM image exactly as you would patch in a new version of your BIOS using the DDT 'I' command followed by the 'R' command. Use the same offset as your customised BIOS and install the following code.

```
CPMBASE    EQU    ?                          ;SUBTRACT 806H FROM
                                             ;ADDRESS AT
                                             ;LOCATION 6H
           ORG    CPMBASE + 0A02H
           CPI    7FH                         ;WAS CPI 08H
           ORG    CPMBASE + 0A16H
           CPI    08H                         ;WAS CPI 7FH
```

308

Alternatively, you can install the above procedure directly into MOVCPM if you have MOVCPM.COM on your system disc. The patch will be applied automatically to any size system which you build using MOVCPM. Make sure that you have a back up copy of MOVCPM before you make the following changes.

A> DDT MOVCPM.COM
DDT VERS 2.2
NEXT PC
2700 0100
-L1402

```
   1402 CPI    08
   1404 JNZ    0A16
   1407 MOV    A,B
   1408 ORA    A
   1409 JZ     09EF
   140C DCR    B
   140D LDA    0B0C
   1410 STA    0B0A
   1413 JMP    0A70
   1416 CPI    7F
   1418 JNZ    0A26
```
S1403
1403 08 **7F**
1404 C2 .
-S1417
1417 7F **8**
1418 C2 .
-G0

A> SAVE 38 MOVCPM1.COM
A>

The new program MOVCPM1 is used instead of MOVCPM. The backspace and rubout keys will now have their functions reversed for any CP/M system generated with MOVCPM1.COM.

18.2.1 Make Rubout (Delete) identical to Backspace.

The early comments about the previous section also apply here.

Before you install this patch, the code at CPMBASE + 0A1BH should read -

```
MOV          A,B
ORA          A
JZ           CPMBASE+09EFH
MOV          A,M
DCR          B
DCX          H
JMP          CPMBASE+0AA9H
```

Patch into the SYSGEN or MOVCPM image exactly as before, using the DDT 'I' and then 'R' commands. Use the same offset as your customised BIOS, and install the following code.

```
CPMBASE EQU          ?
;
;
ORG          CPMBASE+0A1BH
;
MVI          A,8H
JMP          CPMBASE+0A07H
END
```

As an alternative, you can install the above procedure directly into MOVCPM if you have it as a COM file. The patch will then be installed automatically in any size system that you build with the new version. Make sure that you have a back up copy of MOVCPM.COM before using DDT as follows.

```
A> DDT MOVCPM.COM
DDT VERS 2.2
NEXT   PC
2700   0100
-L141B
141B MOV      A,B
141C ORA      A
141D JZ       09EF
1420 MOV      A,M
1421 DCR      B
```

```
     . . .
-A141B
141B MVI A,8
141D JMP A007
1420 .
-G0
```

A> SAVE 38 MOVCPM2.COM
A>

The new program MOVCPM2.COM is used instead of MOVCPM.COM. The generated system will have the Rubout and Backspace key function identical.

18.3 BIOS Error Return Code Options.

CP/M version 2.2

Program to be amended - BIOS

Normally, CP/M responds only to a zero or a non-zero value as the return code from the BIOS READ and WRITE entry points If the value in register A is zero, CP/M assumes that the disc operation was successfully completed. If the value in register A is non-zero, then the BDOS displays the message "BDOS ERR ON x: BAD SECTOR". You can then choose to press return - and ignore the error - or ^ C and re-boot.

This routine inserts three extra return codes, making a total of five.

0 - Successful READ or WRITE.
1 - Bad Sector, indicates permanent disc error.
2 - Select Error, indicates the drive is not ready.
3 - R/O, the disc is Read Only (used by the 'WRITE').
4 - File R/O (this is not normally used).

In the code segment which follows, addresses given are hex offsets from the base of the CP/M system. The CCP is normally located at 980H but may be at A00H if a two sector boot is needed - see earlier in this chapter.

You can assemble the patch for your size of memory system. The CPMBASE will be at BDOS entry point address minus 806H. See the note on this near the

311

start of the chapter, which includes an example of how to follow the jump vector to find the actual CPMBASE, and the use of DDT 'I' and 'R' commands.

Before installing this patch, the code at CPMBASE + BBDH should read -

```
LXI                     H,CPMBASE+809H
JMP                     CPMBASE+B4AH
```

The above code is replaced by the following code -

```
CPMBASE   EQU       ?
;
;
          ORG       CPMBASE+BBDH
;
          LXI       H,CPMBASE+807H
          JMP       CPMBASE+83AH
          END
```

Alternatively you can install the above procedure directly into MOVCPM if you have the file MOVCPM.COM. The patch will then be installed in any size of system you build with MOVCPM. Make sure you have a back up of MOVCPM before you use DDT to carry out the following -

```
A> DDT MOVCPM.COM
DDT VERS 2.2
NEXT PC
2700 0100
-L15BD
   15BD LXI              H,0809
   15C0 JMP              0B4A
   15C3 LHLD             15EA
   . . .
-A15BD
15BDLXI H,807
15C0JMP 83A
15C3.
-G0
```

A> SAVE 38 MOVCPM3.COM
A>

The new program MOVCPM3.COM is used in place of MOVCPM.COM. Additional error return codes for the BIOS READ and WRITE routines will be supported in any CP/M system generated with MOVCPM3.COM.

18.4 Error when using the optional block/deblock algorithms.

The modification following affects only those CP/M systems which use the optional blocking and deblocking algorithms listed in Appendix G of the System Alteration Guide. When updating a file under systems using the algorithms with no data added to the file, the last block of updated records is not written to that file. Contact Digital Research or your CP/M distibutor if you are not certain whether or not this patch applies to your system.

Patch Procedure.

Make sure that you have a back-up copy of MOVCPM.COM before using DDT to make the following changes. Use the Assemble command (A) and the Set command (S). After making the changes, return to the CCP using the G command and save the modified memory image on disc. Be certain to update the memory image on the system track(s) by executing the new MOVCPM and integrating your customised I/O system.

```
A> DDT MOVCPM.COM
DDT VERS 2.0
NEXT PC
2800 0100
-A1CD2
1CD2      NOP
1CD3      NOP
1CD4      LXI H,0
1CD7      .

-G0
SAVE 39 MOVCPM.COM
```

(The instructions were DCR C! DCR C! JNZ 12DF)

313

18.5 Phase error wrongly generated in ASM.

ASM occasionally generated an erroneous phase error when the identifier in a SET statement appears within an expression from another statement.

```
For example- X      SET   1
              Y      EQU   X
                     END
```

This patch applies to versions 1.4 through to 2.2.

Back-up ASM.COM before patching !

```
A> DDT ASM.COM
DDT VERS 2.2
NEXT PC
2100 0100
-L1DAD
  1DAD CALL 1352
  1DB0 CPI 05
  1DB2 CNZ 20DD
  . . .
-A1DAD
1DAD CALL 1B8D
1DB0 .
-L1B8D
  1B8D NOP
  1B8E NOP
  1B8F NOP
  . . .
-A1B8D
1B8D CALL 1352
1B90 ORA   A
1B91 JZ    1DB5
1B94 RET
1B95 .
-^C
A> SAVE 32 ASM.COM
```

18.6 Improving the ∧ S function.

CP/M version 2.2

Program to be amended - BDOS

We mentioned earlier that if you type a character before you enter ˜S, the earlier character blocks the look-ahead buffer and prevents ˜S from being effected. This is a way to avoid that problem.

In the following code segments procedures, addresses given are hex offsets from the base of CP/M. This is explained early in the chapter, as is the method of following jump vectors to arrive at the position of CPMBASE. Also as before, you should patch into the SYSGEN or MOVCPM image using DDT commands 'I' and 'R'. You use the same offset as your custom BIOS. The call at CPMBASE + 950H should be CPMBASE + 923H before installing the folowing code -

```
CPMBASE      EQU         ?
;
;

             ORG         CPMBASE+950H
;

             CALL        CPMBASE+92AH
             END
```

As an alternative, you may install the above procedure directly into MOVCPM if you have it as a file. Back-up MOVCPM before you change it, using DDT like this -

A> **DDT MOVCPM.COM**
DDT VERS 2.2
NEXT PC
2700 0100
-L1350
```
   1350 CALL  0923
   1353 POP   B
   1354 PUSH B
```

315

```
. . .
-A1350
1350 CALL 92A
1353 .
-G0
```

A> SAVE 38 MOVCPM4.COM
A>

18.7 Error in PIP when Start and Quit strings are the same ength.

To correct this error, use DDT as follows (back-up PIP first).

```
A> DDT PIP.COM
DDT VERS 2.2
NEXT PC
1E00 0100
-L1168
    1168 LDA     1F62
    116B STA     1DF7
    116E LXI     H,1F62
    1171 MVI     M,00
    1173 LDA     1DF9
    1176 INR     A
    1177 STA     1DF8
-A1168
1168 LXI       H,1F62
116B MOV       A,M
116C STA       1DF7
116F MVI       M,O
1171 LXI       H,1DF9
1174 MOV       A,M
1175 MVI       M,O
1177 INR       A
1178 DCX       H
1179 MOV       M,A
117A .
-G0
```

A> SAVE 29 PIP.COM
A>

18.8 Using XSUB and SUBMIT with PIP.

We identified in chapter 5 that you cannot include an exit from PIP in a SUBMIT file - because a SUBMIT file must not contain an empty line, (with just a carriage return) and the exit from PIP is just that. This patch modifies PIP to accept a period (.) as an exit instruction. Then you can put a single period in the last entry of a sequence of commands to PIP, and PIP will exit correctly.

Back-up PIP first, then use DDT like this -

```
A> DDT PIP.COM
DDT VERS 2.2
NEXT PC
1E00 0100
-L1168
  054F CPI    00
  0551 JNZ    055E
  0554 LHLD   1DFC

  . . .
-A54F
054F CPI  2
0551 JNC 55E
0554 .
-G0

A> SAVE 29 PIP.COM
A>
```


18.9 $$$.SUB file created on wrong drive.

If you run SUBMIT when A: is not the default drive, the $$$.SUB file will be created on the default drive, and will not be present on drive A: when required. Therefore, as it stands, you cannot run a SUBMIT job from any other drive than A:. If you make the following alterations (after backing up SUBMIT.COM) with DDT, the $$$.SUB file will always be created on drive A:.

317

```
A> DDT SUBMIT.COM
DDT VERS 2.2
NEXT PC
0600 0100
-D5BB
05BB 00 24 24 24 20 .$$$
05C0 20 20 20 20 53 55 42 00 00 00 1A 1A 1A 1A 1A 1A SUB...
05D0 1A 1A 1A 1A 1A 1A 1A 1A 1A 1A 1A 1A 1A 1A 1A 1A ......

-
-S5BB
05BB 00 1
05BC 24 .
-G0

A> SAVE 5 SUBMIT.COM
A>
```

18.10 PIP Object file transfer problem.

There is a problem which occurs when using PIP object file transfer options when copying file to file. Back up PIP before making the following changes with DDT.

```
A> DDT PIP.COM
DDT VERS 2.2
NEXT PC
1E00 0100
-L0713
  0713 LDA  1F5E
  0716 LXI  H,1E04
  0719 ORA  M
-A0713
0713 LDA  1E04
0716 LXI  H,1F5E
0719 .
-L1099
  1099 LDA 1E04
  109C RAR
  109D JNC 10B2
```

318

```
-A1099
1099 LDA 1F5E
109C .
-L1640
  1640 LDA 1E04
  1643 RAR
  1644 JNC 1652
-A1640
1640 LDA 1F5E
1643 .
-G0
```

A> SAVE 29 PIP.COM
A>

18.11 Using 'CTRL and n' characters in '.SUB' files.

SUBMIT does not accept control characters in submit files. It should accept the two characters 'up arrow' and 'Z' (ie ^ Z) as 'control Z'. Back up SUBMIT before making the following changes with DDT.

A> DDT SUBMIT.COM
DDT VERS 2.2
NEXT PC
0600 0100
-L0441

```
  0441 SUI  61
  0443 STA  0E7D
  0446 MOV  C,A
  0447 MVI  A,19
  0449 CMP  C
  . . .
-S442
0442 61 41
0443 32 .
-G0
```

A> SAVE 5 SUBMIT.COM
A>

319

18.12 Allowing PIP to copy to the PRN: device.

When PIP is used to copy to the logical device PRN:, the LPT: physical device is always selected. This patch disables the automatic selection of the LPT: and allows the PRN: logical device to be used without affecting the current IOBYTE setting. Back up PIP before altering it with DDT as follows.

```
A> DDT PIP.COM
DDT VERS 2.2
NEXT PC
1E00 0100
-LC66
  0C66 LXI   H,0003
  0C69 MVI   M,80
  0C6B JMP 0C71
  . . .
-AC69
0C69  NOP
0C6A  NOP
0C6B  .
-G0

A> SAVE 29 PIP.COM
A>
```

18.13 A Sample BIOS for a Serial Printer.

CP/M versions 1.4, 2.0, 2.1, 2.2

Program affected - BIOS

The code fragment which follows will drive Diablo serial interface printersor other serial devices which use the X-ON/X-OFF protocol for synchronisation. A device which uses this protocol receives data faster than it can print. The device tramsmits a ^ S to CP/M when its input buffer becomes full, and a ^ Q to receive more data after the buffer has been emptied. (Note the use of ^ S and ^ Q as implemented in version 3.1 - rather than the ^ S and any character which versions 2.2 and earlier accept.)

```
LIST$STAT   EQU 00H
LIST$DATA   EQU 01H
IN$MASK     EQU 02H
OUT$ MASK   EQU 01H
LIST:
                CALL LISTST !  JZ   LIST
                MOV A,C     !  OUT LIST$DATA
                RET
LISTST:
                ;return list status (0 not ready, FF if ready)
                LXI H,LST$FLAG
                IN LIST$STAT ! ANI IN$MASK ! JZ NO$INPUT
                IN LIST$DATA ! ANI 7FH ! CPI 'Q'-'@' ! JNZ S?
                MVI M,0FFH
S?:             CPI 'S'-'@' ! JNZ NO$INPUT
                MVI M,0
NO$I NPUT:      IN LIST$STAT ! ANI OUT$MASK ! ANA M ! RZ
                ORI 255
                RET
LST$ FLAG:      DB 255 ;must be 255 initially
```

18.14 Changing the 'P' (page) length in ED.

CP/M version 2.2 and v 2.2 4200H

Program to be amended - ED.COM

This modification alters the number of lines scrolled by the 'P' command in ED from the normal 23 to 14 - useful for short screens, or if you want the reduced scroll so that your most recent previous commands are not scrolled off the top of the screen. If you have a 4200H based system, add 4200H to each address shown below. Back up ED.COM for safety before using DDT as follows -

A> **DDT EDD.COM**
DDT VERS 2.2
NEXT PC
1B00 0100
-L17DA

321

```
17DA LXI    H,0017
17DD SHLD   1D1C
17E0 RET
. . .
-S17DB
17DB 17 E    (note - this is the line count of the scroll)
17DC 00 .
▲C
A> SAVE 26  ED.COM
A>
```

18.15 Nested SUBMIT Files.

CP/M versions 2.1 and 2.2

Program affected - SUBMIT.COM

The SUBMIT program allows a '.SUB' file to contain another SUBMIT command. However, control does not return to the original '.SUB' file after executing the nested SUBMIT command. (The exiting method of implementation is similar to a 'GO TO' rather than a 'PERFORM'.) To change this, use the following code. You should first create the program shown, with an editor, and call it SUBPATCH.ASM.

```
;
;
SUBFCB:    EQU        5BBH
BDOS:      EQU        5
OPEN:      EQU        211H
;
           ORG        22DH            ;submit erase
                                      ;subroutine
;
OPSL:      LDA        SUBFCB + 15     ;file open ok if ext not
                                      ;full
           RAL
           RNC
           LXI        H,SUBFCB + 12   ;try next extent
           INR        M
OPS:       LXI        D,SUBFCB        ;open extent
```

322

```
            JMP         CREATE

            ORG 25DH                    ;submit create
                                        ;subroutine
CREATE:     CALL        OPEN
            INR         A
            JNZ OPSL                    ;loop if open ok
            LXI         D,SUBFCB
            MVI         C,22
            CALL        BDOS
            ADI         1
            RET
;
;           the following code calls the routines above
;
            ORG         4FEH
;
            CALL        OPS             ;open the $$$.SUB file
            JC          517H            ;jump if not opened ok
            LDA         SUBFCB+15       ;set current record to
                                        ;end
            STA         SUBFCB+32
            JMP         51DH            ;jump if open ok
;
            ORG         SUBFCB
            DB          1               ;force $$$.SUB file to
                                        ;A:
;
            END
```

Assemble the above program SUBPATCH.ASM to create the fileSUBPATCH.HEX. Then use DDT to insert SUBPATCH.HEX into the SUBMIT.COM program as follows -

323

```
A> DDT SUBMIT.COM
DDT VERS 2.2
NEXT PC
0600 0100
-ISUBPATCH.HEX
-R
-G0

A> SAVE 5 SUBMIT.COM
A>
```

18.16 Configuring CP/M for Page boundaries.

CP/M Version 2.2

Program to be altered - MOVCPM.COM

Earlier, we discussed memory banked systems, and identified the improvement in memory usage which we could obtain if CP/M was configured to use memory in 256 byte pages, instead of the normal kilobyte boundaries. This is a patch from Digital Research which does exactly that.

The new version of MOVCPM will be called PGMOVCPM.COM, and the first argument to the new version (see chapter 6 for the normal arguments) is optional, but if it is used, it designates the size of the new system to be constructed *in pages.* It must lie between 64 and 255 pages (decimal).

Back-up MOVCPM.COM before making the following alterations using DDT.

```
A> DDT MOVCPM.COM
DDT VERS 2.2
NEXT PC
2700 0100
-L165
  0165 CPI     10
  0167 JC      0172
  016A MVI     L,00
  016C MOV     H,A
  016D DAD     H
```

324

```
-S116
0166 10 40
0167 DA .
-A16D
016D NOP
016E NOP
016F .
-L1A2
   01A2 ANI    FC
   01A4 MOV    H,A
   01A5 PUSH   H
   01A6 LHLD   0006
-A1A2
01A2 ANI FE
01A4 .
- G0
```

A> SAVE 38 PGMOVCPM.COM
A>

18.17 Summary.

In this chapter we have included some of the more commonly needed 'fixes' which are suplied by Digital Research for 2.2 and earlier versions. There are more than we have shown here, and there are also 'fixes' for CP/M 3.1 (CP/M Plus). In each of the cases we have shown, the DDT 'D' or 'L' commands have been used to display what the content of each location should hold before you make the alterations, to confirm to yourself that you have the correct address - particularly where this has to be calculated after following a series of 'jumps'. In is worth commenting, in conclusion, that the list of actual error corrections in all versions of CP/M is tiny, compared to the scope and power of the product. Most of what we have covered here is in the realms of 'if you want to, you can'. Perhaps, too, following each of the 'fixes' through - either in text or actually on your machine - will not only illustrate and give you practice in using DDT, but may give you more ideas for things that could be done, and how to do them. Tell the CP/MUGUK your ideas so that everyone can share them !

Appendix

Two useful addresses are:

Digital Research (UK) Limited,
Oxford House,
Oxford Street,
Newbury,
Berkshire,
RG13 1JB
telephone from UK numbers (0635) 35304

CP/M Users Group UK
11 Sun Street,
Finsbury Square
London
EC2 2QD
telephone (01) 247 0691

INDEX

329

330